D1614541

Deviant sexual behaviour

Deviant sexual behaviour

modification and assessment

BY

JOHN BANCROFT

DEPARTMENT OF PSYCHIATRY, UNIVERSITY OF OXFORD
FELLOW OF NUFFIELD COLLEGE

CLARENDON PRESS · OXFORD

1974

Oxford University Press, Ely House, London W. 1

GLASGOW NEW YORK TORONTO MELBOURNE WELLINGTON
CAPE TOWN IBADAN NAIROBI DAR ES SALAAM LUSAKA ADDIS ABABA
DELHI BOMBAY CALCUTTA MADRAS KARACHI LAHORE DACCA
KUALA LUMPUR SINGAPORE HONG KONG TOKYO

ISBN 0 19 857367 7

PRINTED IN GREAT BRITAIN
BY RICHARD CLAY (THE CHAUCER PRESS) LTD
BUNGAY, SUFFOLK

Acknowledgements

In the course of writing this book I have benefited greatly from many discussions with Andrew Mathews, and I am indebted to Michael Gelder, Rogers Elliott, William Parry-Jones, and Toni Whitehead for their careful reading of the manuscript and their constructive criticisms, most of which I have accepted. Sara Thomson and Lesley Coles willingly and patiently carried out the typing.

I am also grateful to Drs Rooth, James, Orwin, Turner, Mumford, Lodge Patch, and Andrews for allowing me to report their results before they are published.

Finally, I am grateful to my wife and children for having tolerated so much during this venture.

J.B.

Contents

Introduction

DEVIANT sexual behaviour is common and many people who behave in this way are distressed by their deviance or suffer in other ways the consequences of being stigmatized in society. Modification of such behaviour may therefore bring considerable benefits to such individuals.

Such an approach raises important ethical issues, however. These are issues which are both specific to sexual deviance and relevant to deviance in general. Should sexual deviance ever be treated? Is such treatment not only imposing society's standards on the nonconformist individual but also imposing a norm which is in conflict with that individual's nature? Should not the efforts of the helping professions be aimed at modifying society's attitudes in order to lessen the stigma rather than modifying the individual to help him to conform? If the individual is to be helped should not the goal be a greater ability to live with stigma rather than escape from it? These are questions which have been debated many times over the years. This book is about the treatment of sexual deviance and it is therefore desirable to place these ethical issues involved into some reasonable perspective before pursuing the subject further.

The attitude of the medical profession to the treatment of sexual deviance has presented a good example of the entanglement of moral and medical issues. Opinion has often been divided on questions which whilst purporting to be medical are, in fact, moral.

In the treatment of sexual deviance the goals fall into three main categories. In the first suppression of the deviant sexuality is the aim. Castration (Bremer 1959) or the use of hormones to suppress sexual desire (Golla and Hodge 1949; Tennent, Bancroft, and Cass 1974) are examples, and in the majority of cases represent the unequivocal imposition of society's standards on the sexual offender through the machinery of law. In this case the doctor is acting primarily on behalf of society, though the offender may be seen to benefit in some cases, if only to escape further sanctions.

In the second category, the goal of treatment is the better adjustment of the individual to his deviant role. In this the therapist will be acting unequivocally on behalf of the individual, supporting him against the stigmatizing influences of society.

In the third category, treatment aims at a lessening of the deviant pattern and a change towards a 'normal' conforming sexual role. Whereas there will be many who will reject the aims of the first or second category on clearly ethical grounds it is in this third category, which provides the subject matter of this book, that ethical and scientific issues are most likely to become confused.

The most relevant division of opinion in this respect is between those favouring 'evocative' methods and those favouring 'directive' methods of psychotherapy (Frank 1961). 'Evocative' methods, of which most forms of psychoanalysis are good examples, aim to create a situation that will evoke the full gamut of the patient's difficulties and capabilities, thereby enabling him not only to work out better solutions for his presenting problems but also to gain greater maturity, spontaneity, and inner freedom. He is thus better equipped to deal with future stresses as well as current ones. Such methods therefore aim to strengthen the patient's sense of autonomy and will seldom explicitly instigate change in the patient's behaviour.

'Directive' methods on the other hand aim to bring about change in the patient's behaviour which will overcome his symptoms or resolve his problems. They do so by employing advice, persuasion, and exhortation in addition to a variety of techniques aimed at directly modifying behaviour.

The evocative psychotherapist, by the nature of his method,

can more easily refute the accusation that he is imposing society's standards on his patients; if they change in the direction of conformity they do so, he would claim, as a result of their increased autonomy. The 'directive' therapist, however, is more open to such accusation; the fact that the patient asks for such help and direction and accepts it readily is merely a reflection of the pressures imposed on him by society. The therapist, according to such critics, is colluding with these pressures.

Over the past 30 years evocative methods of treatment have tended to become increasingly directive, often with a corresponding increase in their more tangible effectiveness, and in many cases the distinction between them has become blurred. The clearest examples of directive therapy have been hypnotherapy and the various forms of behaviour therapy. In both cases there are fundamental and important practical and theoretical differences from evocative psychotherapy. One of the main advantages of behaviour therapy has been the relative ease with which it can be subjected to experimental investigation. Some workers have gone so far as to define behaviour therapy on the basis of its inherent experimental design (Yates 1970). Although this is an extreme point of view there is no doubt that behaviour therapy has provided opportunities for the application of scientific method in the complex area of psychological treatments which have been much more difficult to attain with orthodox psychotherapy.

The main purpose of this book is to formulate what has been learnt from our experience in the behaviour therapy of sexual deviance, and to do so in a way which will be relevant not only to the treatment of these particular conditions but also to behaviour modification in general. Sexual behaviour has the additional merit of involving psychological and physiological responses and hence is a useful model of psychophysiological interaction. Furthermore, the ethical problems which will be considered will have both specific and general relevance; the modification of sexual deviance is a good paradigm for the modification of any deviant behaviour.

The book is in three parts. In the first the concept of sexual deviance and its historical development will be considered. Here the effect of social factors on medical attitudes will be examined. In addition the historical development of modern techniques of behaviour therapy as applied to such problems will be reviewed. In the second part the more systematic studies of behaviour therapy of sexual deviance will be assessed. It is not the aim of this book to provide an exhaustive review of the literature; a number of publications have already achieved this goal adequately. The aim is rather to evaluate, critically and constructively, progress in this field, illustrating from the literature as is necessary. Theoretical issues and the measurement of change will receive particular attention. The writer is aware that discussions of these theoretical issues have already appeared in the literature but it is his opinion, as a result of his own clinical and experimental experience in this field, that these previous accounts have often lacked balance and at times have been misleading. It should become clear that the results of research up to now are far from conclusive. This book has been written in the hope that future research may be slightly better directed than present trends would indicate.

The third and final part aims to provide an approach to the modification of sexual behaviour which can be applied in the clinical situation and which is based not only on the evidence provided by research but also on the author's clinical experience.

The reader will notice that throughout this book little attention is paid to deviant behaviour in females. This reflects the fact that such behaviour is seldom presented for treatment and hence there is little evidence to report. This is perhaps as it should be and it is to be hoped that in the future there will be less need for the modification of deviant sexual behaviour in the male also.

1 *The Concept of Sexual Deviance*

DEVIANCE in the sociological sense is behaviour that violates the norms of society. These norms result from the complex interaction of institutionalized norms or laws, shared and internalized norms or mores, and the pattern of behaviour that predominates in that society. For our purpose sexual deviance is most appropriately considered in this sociological sense. It may also be defined in two other ways; in terms of statistical abnormality or of psychopathology. The first of these is of limited usefulness; to recognize a pattern of behaviour as rare tells us nothing of its value or its need for modification. In the second case, as this chapter will show, the criteria used to define psychopathology may be considerably influenced by the social factors already referred to. In the absence of unequivocal scientific criteria of morbidity behaviour may be deemed pathological because it violates social norms.

Laws, mores, and behaviour, the three elements involved in the sociological concept of deviance, are usually highly correlated with one another, though not invariably so. Some behaviour may violate both laws and mores but be relatively common or even usual; premarital intercourse and oral–genital contact are examples. Masturbation violates mores but neither laws nor behavioural norms. These are examples of what Gagnon and Simon (1967) call 'normal' deviance. Most other forms of sexual deviance violate all three elements. They may be usefully divided according to whether or not they are associated with particular subcultures. This distinction between 'individual' deviance and 'subcultural' deviance cuts across behavioural categories. Some types of sexual deviance, such as paedophilia, incest, and exhibitionism, are invariably of the 'individual' type. Homosexuality and prostitution on the other hand are commonly but not invariably 'subcultural', i.e. homosexuals or prostitutes may or may not be part of a relevant subcultural group. Many homosexuals are isolated in their deviance except for the furtive and painfully anonymous forays into the homosexual underworld to make a sexual contact.† Homosexuals, by the weight of their numbers and the nature of their particular deviance, have organized themselves into groups to a considerable and varied extent (Hooker 1965), and have been doing so for some time. The existence of such subcultural organization is of crucial relevance to our subject. Identification with such a deviant subculture means that amongst the members of that group the individual is no longer deviant and consequently no longer stigmatized. His homosexuality becomes much more tolerable. The group, as with any other minority group, serves to protect its individual members against the stigmatizing influences of 'normal' society. The homosexual outside such groups either conforms (i.e. controls and conceals his homosexual tendencies) or 'goes it alone'. In either case he may suffer; in the first case the strain of self-control may be considerable, in the second, the full brunt of stigmatization may have to be faced. It is these isolated individuals who are most likely to seek treatment.

Other forms of sexual deviance are in the process of generating their own subculture. Transvestites, transexuals, and fetishists are beginning to organize themselves into groups and are no doubt finding their stigma easier to tolerate by doing so.

A further consequence of such subcultural organization is an increase in knowledge of the deviance involved. Much more is known and has been written about homosexuality than any other form of sexual deviation. This is probably not just a matter of numbers. The occurrence of 'individual' deviance will by its nature be underreported, often only coming to light as the result of a conviction or a request for help. Deviants

† The 'individual' deviance as here described is similar to the 'pathological' deviance described by Gagnon and Simon (1967). However, their use of the word pathological is open to criticism and appears to be a further example of the equation of social unacceptability and pathology.

relatively secure within their subculture are more likely to talk and write about their deviance.

If there are important social factors operating in the process of violating sexual norms what can be said about the factors determining these norms? Clearly they vary from culture to culture. The sexual laws and to a lesser extent mores vary even within the U.S.A. (Szasz 1965). When primitive cultures are also considered the variation is considerable (Ellis 1915; Ford and Beach 1952). Whereas most of these primitive societies have remained stable for some considerable time, societies such as ours have resulted from continual mixing of different social groups. Over the centuries marked changes in social attitudes to sexual morality have occurred (Taylor 1954).

HISTORICAL BACKGROUND†

In early biblical times homosexuality was apparently common in the societies of the Mediterranean (Genesis 19: 5; Judges 19: 22). Its most common form, anal intercourse, was generally considered a form of debauchery rather than anything particularly unnatural. Schrenck-Notzing (1895) has suggested that amongst societies with lax sexual morals, anal intercourse with women as a novel variation of normal intercourse preceded its use between men, and he cites the New Testament to support this (Romans 1: 26–7).

Some writers have suggested that the prevalence of homosexuality and the social attitude to it are closely related to the role of woman at the time (Schrenck-Notzing 1895; Taylor 1954). Taylor postulated that the crucial factor was the degree of matriarchy or patriarchy prevailing at the time (Taylor preferred the terms 'matrism' and 'patrism'). In matrist societies there is, he states, a permissive attitude to sex and women are accorded a higher status. Incest is the sexual behaviour most feared and most socially condemned; homosexuality is tolerated and considered unimportant. In patrist societies there is a more restrictive attitude to sex in general and women are considered inferior. Homosexuality is much feared and condemned, whereas incest causes less concern.

† This brief historical account has been based largely on the historical accounts of others rather than on the direct examination of source material. It does no more, therefore, than summarize the views of others.

Thus in early Judaism which was relatively matriarchal, homosexuality was tolerated, but later, with the Hebrews, patriarchal oppression was much in evidence. In Leviticus homosexuality was deemed an abomination (18: 22) and a capital offence (20: 13). It is, Taylor suggests, in the transitional stages between these extremes that homosexuality may become most prominent; when woman is losing esteem but the patrist system is not yet sufficiently repressive. The Greek empire does not fit easily into either matrist or patrist system, and may have represented such a transitional period. Here homosexuality between man and adolescent boy became not only widespread but idealized and romanticized. Taylor stresses the more idyllic aspects of these special relationships which served as a source of higher education for the boy, and in which the sensual elements were very much controlled. Other authors (Licht 1932; Fisher 1965) maintain that the sensual motives were usually uppermost and that abstemious paedophiles such as Socrates were the exception.

In pre-Christian Britain there was considerable sexual licence with widespread adultery and incest, though homosexuality was not apparently marked (Taylor 1954). With the coming of religious taboos in the later Middle Ages, homosexuality figured more strongly and became a particular concern of the Church, possibly because of the vulnerability of its own members. There was apparently a marked increase in England, in the twelfth century, which is sometimes attributed to the Norman invasion.

Although there is a lag between the Church's taboos and the conformity of the people, the social prejudice against anal intercourse may have been accelerated by the association of sodomy with witchcraft. Sodomy applied to both homosexual and heterosexual anal intercourse and was considered to be one way in which the witches had communion with the devil, who with his forked penis committed sodomy and fornication at the same time. The failure to discriminate between sodomy and homosexuality persists in the English law to this day.

With some lessening of the Church's control during the Renaissance concern with incest again became more marked, homosexuality being tolerated or at worst mocked. By the late seventeenth and eighteenth centuries homosexuality was apparently increasing in England and on the Continent. The role of woman was changing and, in Taylor's view, the relationship between man and woman was becoming increasingly one of emnity. Any clear-cut patriarchal or matriarchal tendencies were not apparent. By the end of the eighteenth century, however, puritanical condemnation of sexuality in general and female sexuality in particular was reappearing and reached its height in the Victorian era, which, in spite of the female monarch, was predominantly patriarchal. At the present time it is assumed that the pendulum is swinging back again, with greater tolerance of sexual expression including homosexuality and greater acceptance of female sexuality. It is impossible to assess the extent to which these changes in social expression and attitudes reflect real changes in the prevalence of sexually deviant behaviour.

Although, previously, medical writings had often tended to perpetuate religio-cultural conventions, from the mid-nineteenth century social and medical attitudes to sexual deviation, and in particular homosexuality, became obviously entangled and have remained so until this day. Previously, sexual deviance was considered a sin, and the subject was the province of moral theologians rather than medical men (Sprenger and Institoris 1928; Ellenberger 1970). Presumably these theologians had special licence as in legal terms homosexuality was referred to as '*pectatum illud horribile inter Christianos non nominandum*' (a sin so horrible that it should not be put into words by Christians).

Some attention to the subject had been given by ancient medical writers but they were mainly concerned with the males who persistently took the passive role in anal intercourse. The active participant was presumably not considered to be abnormal but rather getting sensual pleasure in an alternative way; a debauchee possibly who might be accused of depravity but not of disease. The passive homosexual was more obviously abnormal in that he showed effeminate characteristics and mannerisms, and his behaviour was more likely to be excused on the grounds of disease (Schrenck-Notzing 1895).† The disposition to this role was considered to be either hereditary

† It is of interest that the passive partner in pederasty was termed a 'pathicus' or 'pathic', a term which also means 'one who suffers' or, as a root, implies morbidity.

or acquired by force of habit. Parmenides considered the underlying condition to be a mental one, whereas Aristotle considered the hereditary form to be a disease of the rectum in which, owing to anatomical abnormality, the anus was the main erotic zone, a view which has since been emphasized by Mantegazza (1935).

It is not until the nineteenth century that medical references to the subject again become noticeable. Morison, consultant to the Bethlem Hospital, described cases of homosexuality in his book *The physiognomy of mental diseases*, published in 1838 (Hunter and McAlpine 1963). He used the term 'monomania with unnatural propensity' and made the following revealing statement: 'Being of so detestable a character it is a consolation to know that it is sometimes a consequence of insanity.' Morison's consolation apparently stemmed from his awareness that homosexuality was sometimes committed by people of high repute. The illogicality of deeming men of otherwise exemplary character as morally depraved or degenerate was apparent to him.

In the early nineteenth century psychiatry was in the grip of two conflicting forces. The one was predominantly humanitarian and striving to afford compassion for the poor and to avoid moral judgement of abnormal behaviour; men such as Pinel characterized this movement. The other was a school of thought associated especially with Heinroth which emphasized that mental disorder was a consequence of sin and should be treated as such (Lewis 1967).† Out of this essentially moralistic dialectic the medical profession synthesized a compromise with a medical flavour. The discovery of organic pathology underlying some mental disorder gave impetus to the somatic approach whereby mental illness was seen as a manifestation of organic disease. The moralistic overtones of earlier times remained, slightly obscured by such concepts as familial degeneration but tempered by the idea that such individuals were not fully responsible for their state.

Homosexuality reflected this process by being deemed first

† Heinroth defined sin as equivalent to selfishness. Alexander and Selesnick (1967) comment 'when Heinroth defined mental illness as the result of sin, he did not mean that all neurotics and psychotics perpetrated actual sinful acts. He referred to the sin of thoughts that offended our moral sense.'

the consequency of insanity and later, by men such as Westphal and Lombroso, a congenital anomaly.

Between 1880 and 1900 a considerable amount of attention was paid to sexual psychology and psychopathology (Ellenberger 1970). Medical opinion became polarized into two camps. First, there were those considering sexual deviance to be either an innate anomaly or the manifestation of a degenerative process and, second, those who considered it to be acquired as a result of learning and early experiences. Meynert, Dessoir, Moll, Féré, Binet, and Schrenck-Notzing all came into this latter category. Some, such as Kraft-Ebbing, wavered rather uncertainly between these two poles (Ellenberger 1970). The social implications of these two views are clear. On the one hand it was not justified or humane to persecute the victim of a congenital anomaly as he could not be held responsible, and in any case it was usually presumed, on rather dubious grounds, that a congenital condition was *ipso facto* irreversible. Neither treatment nor punishment could hope to correct the anomaly. On the other hand, if sexual deviance was acquired or learnt it was potentially reversible or treatable or, depending on how one viewed such things, it should be seen as an acquired vice which was not the problem of the physician and should not be exempt from legal sanction (Norman 1892).

It is easy to understand therefore that at a time when humane forces were attempting to counter oppressive attitudes to sexual deviance, and the deviants themselves were beginning to defend their position, any suggestion that such deviance was innate and immutable would be seen to aid the humanitarian cause whereas any suggestion that deviance was treatable would be seen to hinder it.

Not surprisingly those who on the basis of their 'acquired' theory of sexual deviance attempted to treat it (e.g. Schrenck-Notzing 1895) came in for bitter criticism from those who were concerned to protect the interests of the deviant minority. Thus of Schrenck-Notzing's attempts with hypnosis, Havelock Ellis (1915) had the following to say

> . . . in some cases this course of treatment was attended by a certain sort of success to which an unlimited goodwill on the part of the patient, it is needless to say, largely contributed. The treatment was,

however, usually interrupted by continual backsliding into homosexual practices and sometimes, naturally, the cure involved a venereal disorder . . . it is a method which found few imitators. This we need not regret . . . such treatment is a training in vice . . . the invert is simply perverted and brought down to the vicious level which necessarily accompanies perversity;

. . . a curiously emotive assessment. According to Hirschfeld (Ellis 1915) inverts 'cured' by hypnosis were either not cured or not inverted. Havelock Ellis, normally an erudite man, floundered hopelessly in his approach to the 'congenital–acquired' controversy. It seems likely that his wish to avoid the opprobrium that the 'acquired' explanation engendered contributed to his confusion. He was aware that people could pass through a homosexual phase and finally become heterosexual. He also rightly pointed out that both innate predisposition and the appropriate learning experiences are necessary for homosexuality to develop, rendering the distinction between the innate and acquired 'an unimportant, if not a merely verbal distinction'. And yet, throughout his writing, he used the term 'invert', by which he meant the innate, organically determined homosexual who could not be altered in his nature, as distinct from other less radical and deep-rooted examples of homosexuality which might be modified by experience or even treatment. At no time, however, did he indicate how one would distinguish between the 'invert' and the 'non-invert' homosexual. It would seem that the only way to tell, when faced with a homosexual, would be to attempt to change his sexual orientation, and if this succeeded then the condition was not true inversion. As Hirschfeld (1958) put it 'that the homosexual urge is not acquired but inborn is apparent from the phenomenon of its tenacity'. The circularity of such reasoning is obvious.

For the first 40 years of the twentieth century those who considered sexual deviance to be treatable were very much in the minority. The two schools of 'congenital' and 'acquired' continued; the first maintained vigorously by men such as Hirschfeld, the second by the psychoanalysts. Freud (1920) and, with a few exceptions, other early psychoanalysts (Wiedeman 1962) were pessimistic about the efficacy of psychoanalysis in helping homosexuals to become heterosexual, though they did not deny that it was possible. In brief they considered that homosexuality, which was initially part of the bisexual potential of a child, became established as a result of damage to personality developments stemming from anxiety-promoting factors in the oedipal situation. Thus the implication was that the condition was irreversible but, in contrast to the 'congenital' view, the factors operated postnatally rather than prenatally. This rather static view and its accompanying therapeutic pessimism gave way to a change of emphasis in psychoanalytic thought. Following the lead of Rado (1940), who challenged the Freudian concept of bisexuality, homosexuality and other sexual deviations were seen less as psychological scars resulting from early traumatic experiences and more as on-going defences or reparative processes to cope with the threat of heterosexuality (Rosen 1968). This more dynamic formulation, together with an increased tendency for psychoanalysts to take a directive rather than a strictly evocative role in psychotherapy, has been associated with an increased therapeutic optimism and reports of success (Ellis 1956; Bieber, Dain, Dince, Drellich, Grand, Gundlach, Kremer, Rifkin, Wilbur, and Bieber 1962; Mayerson and Lief 1965).

At the same time the development of behavioural techniques such as aversion therapy led to further therapeutic successes in a variety of sexual deviations (Freund 1960; MacCulloch and Feldman 1967*a*; Bancroft and Marks 1968). In the past twenty years, therefore, further doubt has been thrown on the concept of sexual deviance as an untreatable, immutable condition.

Hirschfeld and his associates, who were the main champions of the 'congenital' view, saw the innate nature of homosexuality as a form of intersex; some inherent biological abnormality that resulted in a mixture of male and female characteristics. Lang (1940) postulated that homosexuals are genetic females with completely masculinized bodies. He supported his theory with the finding that in a group of male homosexuals the male/female ratio amongst their siblings was 124:100. Thus there was an excess of boys which could be accounted for by the genetically 'female' male homosexuals. This theory was laid to rest by Pare who showed that homosexual males were genetically male (Pare 1956). Wiel, an associate of Hirschfeld, claimed that male homosexuals had physical constitutions that were different to those of heterosexuals (Hirschfeld 1958); several workers reported results consistent with this, but these findings were put into a better if still puzzling perspective by Coppen (1959), who showed that, although homosexual patients differed in their androgeny score from normals, they did not differ from heterosexual patients, any abnormality presumably being related to their patient rather than their homosexual status.

A genetic basis to homosexuality was suggested by Kallmann's twin study showing 100 per cent concordance for homosexual monozygotic pairs compared with 12 per cent concordance in dizygotic pairs (Kallmann 1952). Kallmann later modified his views, and more recent evidence suggests a much lower concordance rate (Heston and Shields 1968). This rate is still sufficiently high, however, to suggest some genetic factor, but as Pare (1965) points out it need not be the homosexual orientation *per se* that is inherited but some other contributory or predisposing factor which may sensitize the individual to environmental influences. Hirschfeld had predicted that hormonal imbalance would be demonstrable with a preponderance of female hormones in the male homosexual. Although early hormone studies produced conflicting results, it was eventually considered to be an untenable hypothesis (West 1960; Perloff 1965). Following a spate of studies on androgens and estrogens in the 1940s (Heller and Maddocks 1947), work in this field abated mainly owing to the serious limitations of the assay methods used. With new and better assay methods interest has been revived and the controversy reopened. Two studies (Loraine, Ismail, Adamopoulos, and Dove 1970; Kolodny, Masters, Hendryx, and Toro 1971), which claim abnormally low testosterone levels in exclusively homosexual males, are open to methodological criticism, however, and cannot be accepted as adequate evidence at the present time. Clearly more work needs to be done in this area.

A more sophisticated endocrine theory has stemmed from the animal work of Pfeiffer (1936) and later Harris, Goy, and others (Harris and Levine 1965; Goy 1968). This work has shown that the central nervous system of mammals, including primates, is masculinized *in utero* by the presence of circulating androgens at critical periods of foetal development. Interference with this mechanism can lead either to masculinization of the genetic female or failure of masculinization of the genetic male. These important and exciting findings have inevitably been used to explain human homosexuality (e.g. Feldman and MacCulloch 1971), but as yet such ideas are entirely speculative. More pertinent has been the effect these findings have had on the controversy concerning the concept of bisexuality and the development of gender identity and role (Bancroft 1972*a*).

The bisexuality of man as a concept had its origins in folklore and mythology (Rado 1940). It gained scientific credibility with the discovery in the mid-nineteenth century of the anatomical ambisexuality of the embryonic gonads. Later not only Freud but also Kraft-Ebbing, Herman, and Weininger postulated that man was behaviourally bisexual at birth, the final pattern of sexual behaviour depending on later environmental influences (Ellenberger 1970). Rado (1940) effectively criticized the bisexual concept and emphasized the role of anxiety in blocking the development of the normal or heterosexual pattern. Hampson and Hampson (1961) convincingly demonstrated the importance of early environmental experiences in the establishment of gender identity and role. They postulated a state of sexual neutrality at birth. The series of animal studies started by Pfeiffer have countered this view, however, and the present position has been fully reviewed by Diamond (1965), who showed the futility of trying to separate 'nurture' from 'nature' in sexual development. Havelock Ellis (1915) in one of his clearer moments had made the same points many years before but still this almost neurotic need to demonstrate the greater importance of either nature or nurture continues. Feldman and MacCulloch (1971), who have reported the best results in treating homosexuality with behaviour therapy, have continued the tradition of deeming the treatable homosexual aetiologically distinct from the untreatable. They had found that the homosexuals who most consistently failed to respond to treatment were those who denied any previous heterosexual interest at any time. On this basis they postulated two aetiological types, the 'primary' homosexual, who presumably would have been in Havelock Ellis's group of inverts, and the 'secondary' homosexual, in whom the homosexuality has been the result of faulty learning. Their argument will be discussed further when their results are scrutinized.

Twentieth-century social attitudes

Although attitudes to sexual deviance are probably more tolerant now than they were in the nineteenth century it would be wrong to assume that the medical profession has pioneered such change. In the 1920s and 1930s the mental hygiene movement again succeeded in confusing mental health with morality (Davis 1938). The tenets of this movement no doubt influenced the writers of a most extraordinary document on homosexuality and prostitution, published by the British Medical Association (1955) as their evidence to the Wolfenden Committee. The following is a characteristic extract:

> The attempt to suppress homosexual activity by law can only be one factor in diminishing this problem. The public opinion against homosexual practice is a greater safeguard, and this can be achieved by promoting in the minds, motives and wills of the people a desire for clean and unselfish living . . . people who are mainly concerned with themselves and their sensations associate together and obtain from each other the physical and emotional experiences they desire. Personal discipline and unselfishness have little place in their thoughts. If this behaviour is multiplied on a national scale the problem to society is apparent for widespread irresponsibility and selfishness can only demoralise and weaken the nation. What is needed is responsible citizenship where concern for the nation's welfare and the needs of others takes priority over selfish interests and self-indulgence.

The view that sexual deviance posed a threat to the health and security of the nation was frequently expressed in medical writing. Johnson and Robinson (1957), for example, write as follows:

> The outlook for eradication or even significant curtailment of the incidence of sexual deviation is as gloomy to the psychiatrist operating unaided as is the prospect of treating individual patients with small-pox in the absence of prophylactic vaccination to a family physician . . . the sexual deviants constitute a social problem of a magnitude beyond the reach of a limited number of highly trained psychiatrists . . . the family physician and paediatrician working in concert can 'vaccinate' large segments of the population against the virus of sexual deviation.

Correcting influences in the home, it was suggested, should include 'an uncompromising counsel of prohibition'.

The split, both of the medical profession and of society in general, into those who regard sexual deviance as a social menace which must be contained, and those who are moved to tolerate it, continues. There were sufficient medical and lay voices in high places to draw attention to the unsatisfactory state of the law relating to homosexual offences, leading in 1957 to the report of the Wolfenden Committee on homosexuality and prostitution. In their report they showed awareness of the implications of the disease concept of sexual deviance; that it is thereby deemed a medical problem and also implies diminished responsibility. But rather than treating these implications as social phenomena they considered them to be valid providing that homosexuality is, in fact, a disease. They therefore embarked on a naïve discussion of whether or not homosexuality is a disease and concluded in the negative (see Scott 1958). They rightly stated that a more important question is whether doctors should carry out treatment for this problem. An equally important question which they did not discuss is the effect the disease concept has on social attitudes.

Shortly after the Wolfenden Report in 1957 a *News Chronicle* Gallup survey showed nearly 25 per cent in favour of the reform proposed in the report. By 1965, following a period of continuing public debate and press coverage, the *Daily Mail* national opinion poll showed 63 per cent in favour of reform. However, 93 per cent saw homosexuality as a form of illness requiring medical treatment (Homosexual Law Reform Society Report 1963–6). Thus, for most people to accept or tolerate homosexuality as a variant of sexual behaviour the choice was still between regarding it as a vice or an illness. The increase in the latter view was a good example of what Wootton (1966) described as the 'concept of illness expanding continually at the expense of the concept of moral failure', a process which had presumably been continuing since the mid-nineteenth century. Once again, therefore, any evidence of the treatability of sexual deviance might be seen as a threat to the sexually deviant group, resulting in legal and social pressures to impose 'treatment' on deviant individuals.

The physician tends to get caught in these processes, partly because he is a member of society and follows the same social trends as its other members and also because he finds it easier to justify his involvement in a problem if it can be defined as illness. Consistent with this is the fact that most advocates of orthodox psychotherapy for sexual deviations see them as pathological conditions, usually involving neurotic fear of normal heterosexual relationships (e.g. Ellis 1956; Bieber *et al.* 1962; Rosen 1968). By contrast those advocating a behavioural approach are less likely to use the illness concept or the medical model. Their theoretical model conceptualizes the behaviour as maladaptive and due to inappropriate learning and therefore suitably dealt with by appropriate relearning (Bandura 1970). This is a view of sexually deviant behaviour which was not only widely held by educationalists in the nineteenth century before the increase in medical interest in the subject but was also clearly spelt out by Schrenck-Notzing (1895) in the rationale of his hypnotherapy. In addition behaviourists have been more ready than their psychotherapist colleagues to recognize the part that society plays in labelling behaviour as either deviant or symptomatic (Ullman and Krasner 1965).

What is also of interest is that, whereas the psychotherapeutic approach and the illness concept are advocated mainly by medically trained therapists, the behavioural approach has been the province of psychologists in particular. Not only do they have no need to justify their function in terms of treating illness but as a professional group they have a need to establish their role alongside and distinct from that of their medical colleagues. This may in part explain the extreme rejection of the medical model by behaviourists, such as Yates (1970), who are keen to demonstrate that what they do is quite different from what psychiatrists do. Here then are additional social factors, those generated by the separation and establishment of professional groups, which may influence to some extent attitudes to the treatment of sexual deviance.

In the face of this increase in therapeutic optimism in both psychotherapeutic and behavioural camps that has occurred in the past 25 years, what has been the reaction of those whose main concern is to protect the rights of the sexual deviant and in particular the homosexual? In most cases emphasis has shifted from regarding homosexuality as an innate condition that thereby absolves the individual from responsibility. Causation is accepted as being uncertain (e.g. Albany Trust 1965).

Emphasis is now placed on the importance of social factors in producing the homosexual's problem, only making the homosexual a problem to society in return (Hoffman 1968; Magee 1968).

This view was clearly stated by Schofield (1965).

> Homosexuality is a condition which in itself has only minor effects upon the development of the personality. But the attitudes, not of the homosexual, but of other people towards this condition, create a stress situation which can have a profound effect upon personality development and lead to character deterioration of a kind which prohibits effective integration with the community.
>
> A proportion of homosexuals are unable to withstand the pressures from outside and become social casualties. These are the homosexuals most often found in prisons and clinics. Their difficulties may take a form not directly connected with a homosexual condition, although originally caused by the social hostility shown towards homosexuality. On the other hand the homosexuals who have learnt to contend with these social prejudices can become adjusted to their condition and integrated with the community. These men are hardly ever found in prisons and clinics.

Attempts at modifying the homosexual's sexual orientation are regarded by such commentators with scepticism. When the homosexual is considered to be 'sick', as by the psychoanalysts, then it is pointed out that the psychiatrist only sees 'sick' homosexuals and cannot comment on 'healthy' homosexuals (Hoffman 1968). When sickness is not a necessary prerequisite for treatment, as in behaviour therapy, then the therapist is accused of imposing the wishes and norms of society on the individual (e.g. Whitlock 1964; Kalcev 1967). When aversion therapy is involved charges of 'brain-washing' may be made (Schofield 1965; Pringle 1971).

It seems an inescapable conclusion, therefore, that whilst certain forms of sexual behaviour continue to be labelled as deviant, and whilst people carrying out such behaviour organize themselves into groups and obtain support from certain sections of the community, then there will be opposition to any attempt to remove people from those groups by treatment or by any other means. The stigmatized minority group tries to maintain, and if possible increase, its membership. When the deviant behaviour is of the individual type, such as paedophilia or exhibitionism, there will be no such opposition.

It is because of factors such as these that discussion and evaluation of attempts to modify deviant sexual behaviour have been so often confused. In spite of these factors, however, there will continue to be individuals who are severely distressed by the consequences of their deviance whether of 'individual' or 'subcultural' type. It is of little help to such individuals to point out that social attitudes are gradually changing, however desirable change may be. They will continue to seek help in becoming less deviant from 'experts' such as doctors or clinical psychologists, and there will be some who for impeccable reasons will want to respond to their appeal for help. It is for them that this book is intended. The purpose of this chapter has been to put these confusing but important social and moral factors into a more reasonable perspective so that our undivided attention can hereafter be given to the problem of modifying sexually deviant behaviour.

2 *The Modification of Sexually Deviant Behaviour: Its Historical Development*

DIRECT modification of deviant sexual behaviour as a method of treatment is often considered under the heading 'behaviour therapy'. This term has certain connotations which are not intended in this book. 'Behaviour therapy' has been defined by most of its proponents as a method of treatment based on learning theory (Eysenck 1964; Ullman and Krasner 1965). However, very similar techniques may be carried out without any knowledge of learning theory. Although such knowledge has been used in recent years to devise precise methodologies, there is so far no unequivocal evidence that it has led to more successful results. It is the writer's opinion, as he will hope to demonstrate in the course of this book, that the 'basis in learning theory' has been emphasized in order to impart scientific respectability to the behaviour therapy approach. This emphasis becomes more understandable when the development of behaviour therapy is seen as a reaction to the manifestly antiscientific basis of psychoanalysis and more traditional psychotherapies. However, the learning theory basis has become, particularly in the United Kingdom, almost as much a form of doctrinaire dogma as the psychoanalytic theories that have provoked this reaction. Recently a more valid claim to scientific respectability has been made by Yates (1970), who has defined behaviour therapy not in terms of its theoretical basis but in terms of its use of the scientific method. In fact scientific method has only recently entered the behaviour therapy field but there is no doubt that it is more possible to apply such methods with a behavioural approach than it is with other psychotherapeutic approaches, particularly of evocative type. It is also easier to formulate and hence both evaluate and teach such an approach. It is for these reasons and not because of doctrinaire beliefs in their greater efficacy that behaviour modification techniques are the subject of this book.

A further reason for concentrating on the behavioural approach is that it allows one to escape from the medical model. The importance of being able to do this, it is hoped, has been explained in the previous chapter. Thus certain behaviour is deemed maladaptive and an attempt is made to modify it to a more adaptive form. Nevertheless there is a risk, in reacting against the medical model, that one goes too far in the opposite direction. The antithesis of the medical model is the 'training model' in which 'treatment' becomes simply a form of training or education like any other. This, of course, has been reinforced by the previously mentioned 'basis in learning theory' but has earlier origins in nineteenth-century pedagogic thought which also had its say in the management of sexual behaviour. It remains possible, however, that there are important differences between mechanisms of change operating in a typical 'educational' setting and those in a typical 'therapeutic' setting. Whilst we should learn what we can from any similarities that might exist we should not allow ourselves to become blind to the possible differences by applying the same model to both. It is also a mistake to assume that by avoiding the 'medical model' one avoids removing responsibility or autonomy from the patient or subject. Behaviour modification, if allowed, can be as controlling and as repressive as the most reactionary forms of care. No one would deny that orthodox educational methods can be abused in this manner also.†

Although the application of scientific method has only recently been in evidence in this field, direct attempts to modify sexual behaviour have a much longer history. Medical men and educationalists before them, with their misguided belief in the aetiological importance of masturbation made strong attempts to inhibit such behaviour. Although the claims that masturbation led to insanity seem frankly ridiculous today, the belief that masturbating with deviant fantasies might lead to

† These theoretical issues are discussed further in Chapter 7.

the establishment of deviant propensities (e.g. Norman 1892) if rephrased in modern behaviourist terminology is virtually indistinguishable from some very recent and apparently plausible suggestions (McGuire, Carlisle, and Young 1965; Evans 1968).

The most widely used form of behaviour modification before the advent of modern behaviour therapy was undoubtedly hypnotherapy, which had a particular vogue in the late nineteenth century. Just about every conceivable condition was treated in this way, sexual deviations included. Kraft-Ebbing and Schrenck-Notzing were the main proponents in treating the latter and their collective results and methods were described in a monograph by Schrenck-Notzing (1895). The rationale of this approach and the technique used had a strikingly modern flavour and are worth describing in some detail.

Schrenck-Notzing derived the principles of this treatment from the more general ones of education. The aim of education, as he saw it, was to 'create a series of habits by means of direct persuasion, acts, imitation and admiration'. Using suggestion in its widest sense he regarded all education as 'a combination of co-ordinated and well considered suggestions'. The effect of suggestion, he also states, is to convince an individual that things are or could be different from what they actually are or appear to be.

The main place of education as far as sexual behaviour was concerned was to prevent the development of 'faulty habits'—to counter a 'predisposition to perverse action'. In the clinical situation such habits may have been already established, but it was Schrenck-Notzing's view that if they could have been prevented by correct education then they should be to some extent reversable by re-education. In treating sexual deviations, therefore, 'the patient should be made to school his will, that he may be able to control his impulses'. To do this he considered it necessary to counter the beliefs that homosexuality is an innate and immutable condition. 'The conviction that one is perverse as a result of original cerebral constitution undermines all resistance to sexual impulses.'

The patient was urged to think of women in the sexual act and in any sexual excitement to attempt to substitute women for men in his thoughts. 'Many patients are finally able, in the struggle with themselves, to experience pleasant feelings and erection in the thought of heterosexual relationships. When this is attained the victory of the abnormal instinct is practically won.'

Because of the aetiological importance that was attached to it, masturbation was strongly discouraged. Instead the patient was advised to undertake 'regulated sexual intercourse' with a selected prostitute. In spite of failure this was to be repeated, if necessary with the help of alcohol and maximum co-operation from the prostitute. Eventually, it was claimed, there would be a development of pleasure and an increased ability and inclination to perform in this way. In general the regime aimed at producing a state of bisexuality which Schrenck-Notzing considered to be a natural step towards the development of a predominantly heterosexual state.

Except for the ban on masturbation and the insistence on repeated intercourse regardless of the consequences many behaviourists today would not argue with this regime. The social and moral milieu of the time made the co-operation of helpful prostitutes a more feasible exercise than it would be today, though nowadays the use of surrogate partners who are not prostitutes may, in turn, be more feasible than it would have been then (Masters and Johnson 1970).

This regime alone apparently sufficed in a number of cases, but in the majority is was not enough. In those it was found necessary to use hypnotic suggestion. When the rudiments of heterosexual feeling were present they were strengthened by such suggestion; when they were absent they were artificially created by it. Many of the cases were apparently difficult to hypnotize and in some cases narcotics were used to aid induction. Suggestions would stress the undesirability of men and the desirability of women, with direct suggestions of pleasure and potency in impending encounters and suggestions that masturbation was harmful and would be stopped. The detailed case histories showed that by repeated reinforcement under hypnosis these suggestions would start to have an effect, the most important being the increasing awareness of an ability to respond and perform heterosexually.

It is very clear that this approach is an extreme example of 'directive' therapy. The patient was persuaded by exhortation, and in particular, hypnotic suggestion, to indulge in heterosexual behaviour, and was encouraged to think that he was basically capable of enjoying such behaviour, which in the successful cases he actually was. The aims of such treatment were well circumscribed, the methods of persuasion were repetitive and insistent, maximal participation by the patient was required, and the patient could clearly assess his progress.

Schrenck-Notzing reported twenty-seven cases of homosexuality treated in this way, six by the author, eleven by Kraft-Ebbing, the remainder by various workers. He did not consider that total elimination of all homosexual thought or interest was either necessary or possible, but by 'cured' he meant actively and satisfactorily heterosexual, with homosexual thoughts being no more than occasional or transient and not giving rise to overt homosexual behaviour. Of the twenty-seven cases, eleven were deemed cured (41 per cent) nine of them remaining so at follow-up, the other two not being contacted again. A further ten (37 per cent) cases were greatly improved. Several of the cases, according to the full and detailed reports, showed strikingly successful outcome. Although the success he reported in many of his cases would be considered an achievement by modern behaviour therapists, his results, as mentioned in the previous chapter, were much criticized at the time (Ellis 1915).

Other attempts to modify deviant sexual behaviour by direct behavioural approaches were reported by Moll (1911) and Charcot and Magnan (1882). Moll suggested that in all perverse individuals there is a bridge with normal sexual interest. He therefore encouraged the development of these bridges with normality. Thus a man who is attracted to boys may be brought to love a boyish woman. This approach Moll called association therapy. Charcot and Magnan (1882) reported the treatment of a man who when he was six, had watched soldiers masturbating and since then had only been sexually stimulated by the sight of men, showing no interest in women. The treatment consisted of substituting the picture of a naked woman instead of a man, presumably during masturbation. After some months the man was having satisfactory heterosexual relations. Magnan (1913) reported a satisfactory 20-year follow-up, the man having successfully married.

Up to that time such direct approaches had been based on

the assumption that sexual deviance stems from inappropriate learning, usually at an early age. The rationale for such approaches, as clearly stated by Schrenck-Notzing, was to encourage relearning. In the early part of the twentieth century the experimental psychology of learning became well established with the work of Pavlov and Bekhterev and before long various workers were applying principles of conditioning, both 'classical' and 'instrumental' to the understanding of abnormal behaviour, including sexual behaviour (Bekhterev 1923; Kostyleff 1927). By 1930 the first report of aversion therapy appeared in the literature, though this involved the treatment of alcoholism. The stimulus of the sight and smell of alcohol was presented to the patient immediately followed by an electric shock, (Kantorovich 1930). In 1935 Max reported the treatment of a homosexual by what he described as the 'conditioned reaction technique'. The homosexual interest was partly fetishistic and

> an attempt was made to disconnect the emotional aura from this stimulus by means of electric shock, applied in conjunction with the presentation of the stimulus under laboratory conditions.
>
> Low shock intensities had little effect but intensities considerably higher than those usually employed on human subjects in other studies definitely diminished the emotional value of the stimulus for days after each experimental period.

This effect was gradually cumulative and 4 months after 'cessation of the experiment' the patient considered himself 95 per cent cured of his 'neurosis'. This report was extremely brief, most of it being quoted above, but the implication was that the author had been applying a method based on laboratory learning experiments. This report, being an abstract of a paper read at a meeting, passed apparently unnoticed in the literature until recently.

Little further attention was paid to the direct modification of sexual behaviour for some time. In the 1930s various attempts to treat alcoholism by aversion therapy were reported. The main effort came in the 1940s, in particular with the work of Voegtlin and Lemere (Lemere and Voegtlin 1950), who treated over 4000 patients with aversion therapy, in which the ingestion of alcohol was associated with chemically induced nausea and vomiting. Certainly these workers attempted to rationalize their procedure as a form of classical or Pavlovian conditioning of nausea to the conditioned stimulus of alcohol. Many proponents of behaviour therapy have in fact pointed to their method as a good example of correct classical conditioning procedure (Franks 1963; Eysenck and Rachman 1965; Yates 1970). If the reader is persistent enough to gather from divers journals these workers' various reports so that a complete picture of their technique can be obtained he will discover that what they claim to do in their 'theoretical' paper is not borne out by what they appear to do in their methodological papers (Bancroft 1966).

In 1956 Raymond used a form of aversion therapy similar to that used for alcoholism to treat a case of fetishism. This report was followed by several others involving chemical aversion techniques in the treatment of homosexuals, fetishists, and transvestites (Freund 1960; Lavin, Thorpe, Barker, Blakemore, and Conway 1961; Glynn and Harper 1961; James 1962; Oswald 1962; Cooper 1963). In most of these reports little more than lip service was paid to any basis in conditioning theory. Of these workers Lavin *et al.* (1961) were most thoughtful in this respect. They rightly concluded that as their treatment involved pairing of conditioned stimulus and unconditioned stimulus which was not only varied but quite unsuited for classical conditioning to take place, factors other than classical conditioning must have been involved to produce the effects that they reported. Such flaws in conditioning methodology were present in all these reported methods, as they were in the treatment of alcoholism by Voegtlin and Lemere (1942).

With the exception of Freund's method (1960) there was another factor which these early methods had in common and which bore no obvious relevance to experimental learning theory. In addition to using noxious (i.e. emetic) stimuli, treatment was continued intensively without a break, the patient often being kept awake by means of amphetamines. In some cases tape-recordings of derisive comments about the patient were played during treatment. Raymond (1956) remarked that 'modification of attitudes and psychological conversion are more easily obtained in states of exhaustion and hunger'. Cooper (1963) suggested that the desired changes were 'more easily obtained in fatigued and debilitated subjects'. Oswald (1962) attempted to produce a maximal emotional crisis in order to facilitate 'conversion'.

These views had apparently stemmed from Sargant (1957) who used Pavlov's concepts of paradoxical and ultra-paradoxical inhibition to explain a startling variety of phenomena in human behaviour, including 'brain-washing' and religious conversion. Pavlov (1928) found in his animals that following states of stress such as the Leningrad flood, or experimental tasks of impossible or stressful discrimination, a disturbed state would result which would show the following characteristics. In its most severe form, 'the ultra-paradoxical phase', only stimuli which were previously inhibitory would have positive or excitatory effects. A less severe state, the 'paradoxical phase', would show greater response to weak stimuli than to strong ones. A third phase of 'equalization' would show equal responses to all stimuli regardless of their strength. Pavlov's explanation of these interesting phenomena, rooted as it was in his mechanistic adherence to the interplay of 'inhibition' and 'excitation', is open to doubt. But in any case it is difficult to see how this concept can be used to account for the therapeutic outcome of the cases referred to above. There is no doubt that these patients were subjected to extreme stress, but the effects of treatment were more or less selective, which is not the case with Pavlov's animals which showed a general 'inhibitory' effect on all or most conditioned reflexes. Furthermore, these animal effects were transitory, though lasting a few days. It is quite possible that to produce any significant and lasting change in a person's attitudes and behaviour some form of emotional 'state' or condition must be provoked first; this could apply to any form of treatment including psychotherapy. But the nature of this 'state', how it is best produced or how it might have its effects are all unknown. Certainly the concept of ultra-paradoxical inhibition, as it stands, does not contribute much to our understanding of the effects of this treatment, and does not justify on theoretical grounds the intensely traumatic methods described above.

It is not surprising that these methods provoked criticism and charges that they were a regression to medieval methods or a form of 'brain-washing', a technique which was of topical interest at that time following the Chinese efforts with Korean prisoners of war. Because such charges are still being made (Pringle 1971), a comparison with 'brain-washing' or thought reform techniques is worth while.† As it happens the available information is sparse. Brown (1963) has written a useful though brief review of the literature. Attempts at psychiatric assessment have been mostly doctrinaire and devoid of even anecdotal evidence (Hinkle and Wolff 1956; Meerloo 1961). One serious and worthwhile attempt was made by Lifton (1961) who studied in depth a number of individuals who had just returned to Hong Kong from a period of 'thought reform' in China. The main features of these methods were total control of the victim's environment every minute of the day, with extremely unpleasant conditions involving severe mental and physical hardship. This resulted in inability and exhaustion plus the ever-present fear of death or long imprisonment. By this stage the victim would be to a considerable extent preoccupied with his lack of bodily comfort and at a suitable time in the disintegration process, 'positive reinforcement' in the way of improved mental and physical conditions would be offered and given in return for a confession. These 'confessions' could not be adopted lightly as they usually involved other innocent people or the denouncing of institutions or beliefs of considerable importance to the victim (e.g. the Church to a priest). The overpowering need to escape in this way from these intolerable conditions would often result in such guilt that considerable rationalization and attitude changes might result, and in successful cases a victim would be justifying his captors' actions and principles by the end of his 'treatment'. Lifton (1961) showed how the reactions and the final outcome would depend on the personality of the individual, and the exploitation by this method of the guilts and vulnerabilities present at the start.

There are similarities with the aversion therapy described above. The patient is subjected to intense unpleasantness and denigration and is offered a means of escape which up until then has not been part of his nature. There are on the other hand

† Eysenck (1964) considered it necessary to define behaviour therapy in such a way as to avoid confusion with such techniques the aims of which are not consistent with the 'victim's' wishes.

important differences; the 'brain-washed' prisoner is treated for 2–3 years, the patient for a few days. The prisoner cannot leave the environment, the patient can, although the extent to which he is 'trapped' in the situation may depend to a large extent on his motivation for treatment. In neither the 'thought reform' nor the aversion therapy as described can learning theory principles be applied with any confidence, except in the more general sense of controlling positive and negative reinforcements. Similarities to several psychological techniques of persuasion and attitude change are more striking (see Chapter 7).

In 1963 Blakemore, *et al.* treated a transvestite with a form of aversion therapy in which the noxious stimulus was electric shock. Since that time electric aversion has more or less taken over from chemical aversion and has enabled a wide variety of ingenious techniques to be employed. The greater control of stimuli that electric shock permits and the use of electric shock in many laboratory experiments has enabled a much greater degree of sophistication in applying principles of learning to treatment.

Not surprisingly, however, aversive procedures have been disliked by many therapists who have looked for non-aversive procedures as aesthetically more acceptable alternatives. This has led to the recent use of systematic desensitization for sexual disorders (Kraft 1967; Bancroft 1970*d*). At the same time a weakening of the noncognitive behaviourist tradition has been followed by more attention to cognitive processes. Thus, covert sensitization or 'symbolic aversion' was introduced (Cautela 1966).

Apart from this particular line of development, another very important approach to behaviour modification had been developing which only recently had much impact on the treatment of sexual disorders. This is the so-called 'operant approach'. The most important general principle of this approach is that a careful analysis of the relevant behaviour is carried out with a particular emphasis on recognizing how elements of the behaviour are normally reinforced. Reinforcement is then to be applied systematically and although this usually means positive reinforcement, negative reinforcers play an important part. The most important influence in the operant field has been B. F. Skinner. He and his followers have built up a very precise laboratory-derived methodology, with its own technical language, which has been applied to the modification of human behaviour. As yet such an approach has been used infrequently in the field of sexual behaviour (Quinn, Harbison, and McAllister 1970). As Krasner (1971) has pointed out, however, the basic principles can be applied in a much more general sense and this is now becoming increasingly prominent in the sexual field (e.g. Barlow 1973).†

This book has been written at a time when there is a great deal of reappraisal of behaviour modification techniques (e.g. Franks 1969). It aims to contribute to this reappraisal process in the particular field of sexual behaviour. However, the principal message of this book is one that applies to the field of behaviour modification in general. The traditional method of applying standardized techniques to particular 'conditions' is no longer acceptable; instead we should design each programme of treatment to meet the needs of the individual. As the book proceeds, and evidence of the efficacy of specific techniques is examined, this message, it is hoped, will become increasingly clear. In the final chapter some principles for designing such individual programmes of treatment are presented.

† The theoretical and clinical implications of the 'operant approach' are discussed at greater length in Chapter 7.

3 *Techniques of Modification*

A WIDE variety of techniques, ranging considerably in ingenuity and technical sophistication, have been applied to the treatment of sexual deviance. The variations in method have either depended on differing theoretical models of the conditioning or learning process or on the varying demands of the particular deviant behaviour being modified. In this chapter these various techniques will be described in practical terms.

In only one case (Solyom and Miller 1965) has a particular technique been reported as producing consistently negative results. In the others, improvement rates have varied widely. The 67 per cent improvement in a group of twelve transvestites and fetishists reported by Marks, Gelder, and Bancroft (1970) and the 58 per cent improvement in a group of forty-three homosexuals reported by MacCulloch and Feldman (1967*a*) are the best results. Other workers have reported improvement in as few as 25 per cent of cases treated (Freund 1960; Bancroft 1969). Further details of such uncontrolled studies will be presented in Chapter 6. Unfortunately, no useful comparison can be made between these various series. Not only have selection criteria varied or been unspecified but criteria of improvement and duration of follow-up have also varied considerably. Those studies in which different treatment methods have been directly compared will be considered in more detail in Chapter 4. The theoretical basis to these various methods and the specific effects that they produce will be discussed at length in Chapter 5.

AVERSION THERAPY

In aversion therapy the noxious stimulus has been used in a variety of ways. It has been associated with:

(1) an external deviant stimulus (e.g. picture, tape-recording or reading material);
(2) an overt deviant act (e.g. cross-dressing of the transvestite);
(3) deviant mental imagery or fantasies;
(4) a physiological response to a deviant stimulus (e.g. erection).

In the last three categories it will be seen that the noxious stimulus is associated with a response rather than a stimulus; in the first case a motor response, the second a 'thinking' response and the third an autonomic response.

Types of noxious stimuli used

Although a variety of noxious stimuli have been involved in aversion therapy (Rachman and Teasdale 1969) only two have been used with any frequency in the treatment of sexual deviance. These are chemical emetics and electric shock. Noxious stimuli of a cognitive or visual kind have been suggested (Mandel 1970). The use of imaginary noxious stimuli will be discussed in a later section.

Chemical aversion

The use of emetics to produce nausea and vomiting is for most people an extremely noxious procedure. However, control over the timing and severity of the noxious effect is very poor and does not permit any precise temporal pairings of noxious stimuli with deviant stimuli or responses. Two types of procedures using chemical aversion have been reported; the association of nausea either with external deviant stimuli or with overt deviant behaviour.

An example of the first type is reported by McConaghy (1969):

> For the first treatment 1·5 mg of apomorphine were administered by sub-cutaneous injection, and after five minutes a slide of a nude or semi-nude male was projected on the wall of the room within the

patient's vision. If the nausea produced by the apomorphine was not sufficiently unpleasant, the dose was increased with subsequent injections up to 6 mg. Severe nausea lasting about ten minutes without vomiting was considered a satisfactory response and continual modification of the dose was necessary throughout treatment (to produce the effect).

The patient was requested to attempt to respond to the slide with a feeling of sexual arousal and, to facilitate this, was left alone after receiving the injection . . .

Timing of the onset of nausea was carried out so that on subsequent trials the slide (i.e. the conditioned stimulus) could precede the nausea (unconditioned response) by approximately one minute. The patient turned off the projector shortly before the nausea was at its height in order to avoid associating the deviant stimulus with a reduction in nausea. Each patient received treatment on 5 consecutive days as an inpatient, receiving 4–6 injections a day at 2-hourly intervals, amounting to a total of 28 injections.

An example of chemical aversion in which the noxious stimulus is associated with deviant behaviour was reported by Pearce (1963) in the treatment of transvestites. Three treatment sessions a day were given for 5 days a week for approximately 40 sessions. At the beginning of each session an injection of apomorphine was given and the patient told to cross-dress in his usual manner. He was urged to continue the ritual and look at himself in a mirror whilst vomiting and nausea continued. As soon as the nausea began to subside he took off his clothes as quickly as possible. In between sessions the patient joined in normal ward activities.

Problems with chemical aversion. Two emetics have been used in chemical aversion; apomorphine and emetine. Both of them have their disadvantages. Apomorphine is a semisynthetic opiate produced by treating the morphine molecule with strong mineral acid. Its analgesic properties are minimal. As with morphine there is an initial stimulation of the chemoreceptor trigger zones in the medulla leading to nausea and vomiting, but this is followed by suppression of the vomiting centre. Therefore if the first dose does not produce emesis, subsequent doses are even less likely to do so (Goodman and

Gillman 1970). The usual vomiting dose is 5 mg to 10 mg subcutaneously, vomiting occurring within 10–15 minutes, preceded by nausea and salivation. In practice the emetic effect is unreliable. Furthermore, the drug may have central depressant effects leading to sedation and occasionally its effect may be quite pleasant. Fatal idiosyncrasy to the drug has been reported (Barker 1965).

Emetine is an alkaloid obtained from ipecac, which is mainly used for the treatment of amoebiasis. It is probably a more reliable emetic with a longer-lasting effect than apomorphine (Voegtlin, Lemere, and Broz 1940), though tolerance also develops. A 30–60-mg deep subcutaneous or intramuscular dose may be required. The main disadvantage of this drug is its potential toxicity, the most important being myocardial damage (Goodman and Gillman 1970). Severe cardio-vascular collapse from this cause has been reported during chemical aversion by Cooper (1963).

Several workers have used a combination of either apomorphine or emetine with pilocarpine and ephedrine or amphetamine (Voegtlin *et al.* 1940) presumably to increase the unpleasant salivation and sweating and to counteract any sedative effects of the emetic. Obviously chemical aversion which leads to repeated vomiting would be contra-indicated in any person with a debilitated physical state or with any gastro-intestinal lesions such as peptic ulcer or hiatus hernia.

Electrical aversion

The use of unpleasant electric shocks as noxious stimuli does permit much greater control over the timing, duration and possibly the severity of a noxious stimulus, than in the case of chemical aversion. Certainly since the early 1960s the majority of reports of aversion therapy have involved electric shock and all the types of association listed above have been used.

Association of shock with external deviant stimulus. Three models of treatment come into this category:

1. 'classical conditioning';
2. avoidance learning;
3. 'aversion–relief'.

Classical conditioning procedure. The deviant stimulus (e.g. slide of the deviant sexual object) is presented to the subject and immediately followed by an unpleasant shock. This procedure is repeated many times. This is best exemplified in one of the methods of treatment of homosexuality reported by Feldman and MacCulloch (1971). The patient watched a screen and at intervals a slide of an attractive male was displayed. In the last half second of the two-second period the subject received a shock. The slide and shock were terminated simultaneously. Approximately 24 such trials were involved in each session which lasted about 20 minutes.

Mandel (1970) has used a form of classical conditioning procedure in which the noxious stimulus is more easily related to the deviant stimulus. Slides of an attractive homosexual partner were shown and, as soon as the subject indicated sexual interest a second slide, showing 'nauseous running sores', was superimposed on the first. This procedure was contrasted with the projection of slides of attractive women unassociated with any unpleasant stimuli.

The relevance of the noxious stimulus in this case can be likened to the relevance of chemical aversion in the treatment of alcoholism, where nausea and vomiting are of special significance to the drinking pattern (see p. 97). Mandel suggested his technique as a way of gaining greater control of imaginary aversive stimuli as used in covert sensitization.

Avoidance learning procedure. The deviant stimulus is followed by the shock but the subject can learn to escape from and subsequently avoid the shock by responding in a certain way. This response is the 'avoidance response', the deviant stimulus in this case becoming the 'discriminative stimulus' leading to that response.

The most extensively used 'avoidance' technique is the 'anticipatory avoidance' procedure also used in treating homosexuals by Feldman and MacCulloch (1971). In this case the subject again watched a screen on which periodically a slide of an attractive male was displayed. The subject was given a switch and instructed to watch the slide for as long as he found it sexually interesting. Then by operating the switch he could switch off the slide. If after eight seconds he was still watching the slide he received a shock. He could terminate the shock (and the slide) by operating the switch (this is an 'escape response'). He could however avoid the shock altogether by switching off the slide before the eight seconds had passed (this is an 'avoidance' response).

This procedure was further complicated by the avoidance response being made ineffective in a proportion of trials (i.e. 'switching off' did not remove the slide or prevent the shock) and by delaying the avoidance in a proportion of trials (the 'switching off' was followed by a variable delay before the slide was removed). These complexities were incorporated on theoretical grounds which will not be discussed further at this point. As with the classical conditioning procedure each session lasted about 20 minutes and involved approximately 24 trials.

A further type of 'avoidance procedure' has been described by Abel, Lewis, and Clancy (1970). In this case the patient was asked to listen to a tape-recording of his own account of deviant sexual activities that he normally found stimulating. In the first 3 trials of each session a classical conditioning procedure was used in which an electric shock followed immediately after the tape-recording. In the remaining 7 trials of each session the subject was told that he could avoid shock if, whenever the 'deviant' tape-recording was started, he fantasized and verbalized an alternative non-deviant sexual behaviour. As soon as his verbalization started the tape was stopped. If he did not verbalize he received a shock as in the classical trials.

This procedure which has only been tried in a few cases, has an important difference to the MacCulloch and Feldman anticipatory avoidance procedure. The avoidance response, the verbalization of the normal fantasies, is relevant to the situation outside treatment. In the 'anticipatory avoidance' procedure the avoidance response, switching off the slide, does not have this relevance. This point will be discussed further in Chapter 7.

Aversion relief. Thorpe, Schmidt, Brown, and Castell (1964) described a method in which the relief following the termination of an aversive procedure was used to reinforce a desirable or normal stimulus. The patient sat in front of a box with a small window in it. A series of words appeared in the window presented by a revolving disc behind. All the words except the last one were connected with the undesirable behaviour (e.g. 'homosexual', 'sodomy', and 'in bed with a male'). As each word was presented the patient was instructed to read it aloud, whereupon he received an electric shock to the feet. If he failed to read the word he received an even stronger shock. The last word of the series was called the 'relief word' and concerned the desired behaviour, ('heterosexual' or 'sex with a woman'). When the patient read the 'relief word' the machine stopped and a light went on indicating that the aversive trial was over. One session a day was usually given consisting of 5 trials (each involving six shocks and one relief word).

The exploitation of this type of relief was also used in the classical conditioning and avoidance conditioning methods of Feldman and MacCulloch (1971). In the first case the shock was immediately followed by the presentation of a heterosexual slide in every trial. In the second the 'switching off' of the deviant slide by the patient was followed by the presentation of a female slide in a proportion of the trials in which shock was successfully avoided.

Association of shock with overt behaviour. For either practical or ethical reasons there are few sexually deviant behaviours which can be carried out in the treatment situation. The main exception is the cross-dressing behaviour of the fetishistic transvestite or the handling or wearing of other types of fetish objects.

A good example of such a procedure was described by Blakemore *et al.* (1963) in treating a transvestite. Each trial consisted of the patient standing naked on a wired mat through which a shock could be delivered to the soles of the feet. At the beginning of each trial he was told to start cross-dressing in his usual clothes. After a certain time he was given a shock through the mat which acted as a signal to start undressing. He would then continue to receive shocks at 5-, 10- or 15-second intervals until he was completely undressed. Thus the quicker he undressed the fewer shocks he received. After one minute's rest the next trial would begin. In order to spread the effect throughout the cross-dressing procedure, the time from onset to first shock was randomly varied. A similar technique was used in treating transvestites by Marks and Gelder (1967) and Marks *et al.* (1970).

Association of shock with fantasy. The use of deviant fantasy as a response to be punished was first described by McGuire and Vallance (1964). Obviously this is an extremely flexible approach as any type of deviant behaviour may be involved in the fantasy. This technique has been more extensively investigated by Marks and Gelder (1967), and Marks *et al.* (1970). The procedure is as follows. A relevant fantasy is first chosen, usually involving a scene described in reasonable detail. The patient is asked to conjure up the mental image of this fantasy in his mind's eye. He is told to signal to the therapist, either by pressing a button or tapping, as soon as he has the image reasonably clear in his mind. The patient's signal is followed immediately by an electric shock (e.g. to the arm or leg). After a pause the procedure is repeated. The patient is encouraged to use the same fantasy for the series of trials rather than move from fantasy to fantasy or to modify the details of the fantasy.

Association of shock with erectile response to a deviant stimulus. The rationale of this method, as described by Bancroft (1969, 1971), is that the shock is only delivered when the patient makes a sexual response to a deviant stimulus. The procedure is as follows. The patient is shown a slide or picture of deviant sexual interest (e.g. an attractive man in the case of a homosexual), and is asked, while looking at the picture, to imagine himself in a sexually exciting situation with the person in the picture. Erectile changes are measured by means of a penis plethysmograph (Bancroft, Jones, and Pullan, 1966) and when an erectile change reaches a predetermined level a shock is given. The level of erection used as a criterion of response is arbitrary. Bancroft has usually used an increase in diameter of the penis of 0·3 mm, a change of which the subject is only just aware.† The use of a higher level as a criterion of response may conceivably lead to different results (see Chapter 5). In Bancroft's

† A recent study (Bancroft and Staples 1974) has shown that a proportion of erectile responses to non-sexual stimuli (i.e. 'spontaneous change') exceed 0·3 mm. A change of 0·4 mm would have been preferable. See Appendix,.

procedure, following the first shock a further burst of three shocks was given if after 15 seconds the erectile response was not actually falling and was still above the criterion level.

Combination of techniques. One of the advantages of using electric shock is that different techniques can be combined in the same treatment procedure or used to treat different aspects of the problem. In the case of transvestites (Marks *et al.* 1970) shock can be used in association with both cross-dressing behaviour and deviant fantasy. This allows a wider range of the deviant problem to be involved in treatment. Bancroft (1970*d*) in treating homosexuals, used the punishment of erection procedure for the first 15 sessions of treatment and punishment of fantasy for the remaining 15 sessions.

Problems with the use of electric shock. Although it has been widely stated (Barker 1965; Rachman 1961) that the use of electric shock permits a precisely controlled noxious stimulus of known intensity and duration, such control is far from easy to obtain in practice. Workers who have depended on such control for experimental investigation of stimulus thresholds and the evaluation of analgesics have encountered considerable methodological problems. These have been fully reviewed by Green (1962), Tursky and Watson (1964), and Campbell and Masterson (1969).

Obviously one of the most important variables is the local skin resistance at the shock electrode site. Although the use of noxious stimuli is likely to produce a sympathetically mediated bilateral reduction in palmar skin resistance (GSR) many workers have not used electrode sites in these areas. Outside these areas, e.g. forearm or calf, skin resistance change is localized to the electrode site (Greenblatt and Tursky 1969). Tursky, Watson, O'Connell (1965) have described a shock electrode and method of application that with a constant voltage can effectively avoid this problem.

However, few if any aversion therapists have dealt with this aspect and though this is probably not important clinically, it does remove some of the theoretical advantages of using electric shock. Certainly with the average shock-box reported in the aversion therapy literature (e.g. McGuire and Vallance

1964; Marks and Gelder 1967) there is considerable variation in subjective intensity of shock. This is partly due to variations in the choice of electrode site, and the accompanying variations in cutaneous nerve supply. Not only the intensity but also the quality of sensation will vary, some shocks predominantly producing skin-burning, others marked muscle spasm. These variations can be avoided with proper electrode site selection and preparation.

Individuals also vary enormously in the amount of shock they can tolerate. It is a common experience to find that one patient will be exceedingly sensitive even at the lowest setting of the shock-box, whereas the next will find the maximum shock hardly painful. It is not technically easy to produce a safe shock-box which will be predictably strong enough for all subjects, particularly in view of the considerable tolerance to shock that can develop during the course of treatment. Some of this variation may be due to the changes in pain threshold brought about by changes in the level of anxiety (e.g. Haslam 1966).

The electric mat that Blakemore *et al.* (1963) used in treating a transvestite has obvious advantages in that particular treatment paradigm as the patient is free to dress and move about during treatment trials. However it is an unreliable method in terms of delivering effective shocks, and was given up by Marks and Gelder (1967) in favour of arm electrodes. By careful attachment of the flex to the patient it is still possible for the shocks to be delivered during cross-dressing.

Duration and spacing of treatment

None of the recent reports of aversion therapy have involved the intense nonstop treatment procedures described by some of the earlier workers. Few workers in the field nowadays consider the unpleasantness of the earlier methods to be justified. However there has been considerable variation in the duration of treatment and spacing of treatment sessions. The main determinant of this has been whether the treatment has been given on an inpatient or outpatient basis. Short periods of inpatient treatment with 2 or more sessions a day have been used, particularly in the treatment of transvestism. Marks *et al.* (1970) used an average of 19 sessions in a 2–3-week period, each session lasting 30–45 minutes. Pearce (1963), using chemical aversion, gave 40 sessions in 14 days, each session lasting 30–40 minutes. Freund (1960) treated homosexuals with daily sessions although it is not clear whether they were inpatients at the time. Feldman and MacCulloch (1971) used sessions lasting about 20 minutes each. Inpatients received 2 such sessions a day, with outpatients the interval between sessions varied according to convenience. The number of sessions given ranged from 5 to 38 with an average of 20. Bancroft (1969; 1970*d*) has used predominantly outpatient treatment with sessions twice a week on average, with a total of 30–40 sessions, the course of treatment usually lasting 3–4 months.

No systematic work has been done on the relative merits of inpatient and outpatient regimes, nor on the different degrees of intensity of treatment. Nor is it clear what the optimum length of treatment is likely to be, but the results suggest that from 15–24 sessions should be sufficient in most cases. From first principles it seems possible that treatment aimed predominantly at suppressing a deviant pattern (e.g. transvestism or fetishism) will be more effective with intensive courses (e.g. Marks *et al.* 1970). On the other hand treatment which also aims to encourage the establishment of new patterns of behaviour (e.g. increased heterosexuality) may be more effective if more widely spaced, to permit some behavioural change to occur between sessions. This point remains to be demonstrated, however, and until relevant research is carried out the duration and spacing of treatment can be chosen on an arbitrary or simply practical basis (i.e. what is convenient for the patient and the therapist).

OTHER TECHNIQUES OF MODIFICATION

For obvious reasons aversion therapy has never been readily accepted by the medical profession. In the face of its apparent efficacy, however, attempts have been made to develop other behavioural techniques which might be as effective if not more so, whilst avoiding the unpleasantness of aversion. A variety of methods have been reported with claims of therapeutic success although as yet each report has only involved a few cases. The majority of these techniques have involved direct attempts to modify sexual fantasies either rendering deviant fantasies less rewarding or normal sexual fantasies more attractive. Recently attempts have also been made to directly modify physiological responses (i.e. erections).

The modification of sexual fantasies

The use of imaginary noxious stimuli. The most direct development from aversion therapy is the treatment described by Cautela (1967) and called 'covert sensitization'. Instead of electric shocks or chemically induced nausea, unpleasant mental images are used as noxious stimuli. A patient is first taught to relax in a manner similar to that used in the systematic desensitization of phobias (Wolpe 1958). Once relaxed the subject is asked to visualize the deviant object (e.g. homosexual partner). He is then told to imagine a deviant sexual act with that object or partner with the imagined accompaniment of progressively severe nausea and vomiting on his part which can only be relieved by turning away from his partner. This fantasy procedure is repeated in each session. Clearly the method is not only dependent on the efficacy and clarity of the subject's imagery, but is also out of the therapist's control. The therapist must rely entirely on the patient's account. Obviously the nature of the aversive imagery is arbitrary and one advantage of this method is that the image can be chosen not only to be effectively unpleasant in each individual case but also to be relevant to the deviant behaviour involved. A comparable technique was reported by Kolvin (1967).

The modification of masturbation fantasies. McGuire, Carlisle, and Young (1965) hypothesized that sexual deviance may become established by means of the reinforcing effect that orgasm has on deviant fantasies preceding it during masturbation. Whereas such men as Schrenck-Notzing (1895) in the nineteenth century considered masturbation to be harmful for reasons comparable to the above postulated mechanisms, and urged his patients to avoid it altogether, McGuire *et al.* suggested that this reinforcing property of masturbatory orgasm should be exploited by encouraging patients to substitute normal for deviant sexual fantasies shortly before orgasm occurred.

Thorpe, Schmidt, and Castell (1964) had tried a comparable approach in treating a homosexual. The patient was asked to masturbate in the treatment room in response to homosexual stimuli and was presented with a heterosexual stimulus (slide) just as he was about to reach orgasm. This procedure, which differed from that suggested by McGuire *et al.* as external stimuli rather than fantasies were used, had little effect until it was combined with an electrical aversive procedure.

Davison (1968) reported a modification of the above method in the treatment of sadistic fantasies. The patient was asked to produce an erection by means of a deviant fantasy, and then to start masturbating whilst concentrating on an erotic picture from *Playboy* magazine. Whenever the erection waned the deviant fantasy was used to bring it back. The patient was instructed to focus on the normal stimulus as orgasm approached. After a week of this procedure the original *Playboy* picture was then used as the 'recall stimulus' to 'back up' other normal stimuli, the sadistic fantasy being kept in reserve. The patient's ability to respond to normal stimuli gradually increased. The remaining responsiveness to the original sadistic fantasy was dispelled by using aversive imagery as in 'covert sensitization' (Cautela 1967). Jackson (1969) reported a similar approach in treating a case of voyeurism.

Bancroft (1966; 1969) whilst using aversive and other modification techniques has routinely advised and encouraged his patients to masturbate privately with heterosexual fantasies. Many of his patients have reported how difficult it is to switch from deviant to normal fantasies once masturbation is under way. He has therefore encouraged them to start with normal fantasies and to strive to fight off deviant fantasies that might otherwise intrude. The success and ease in doing this that the patient reports is often an important indicator of progress during treatment. Frequently fantasies of normal sexual intercourse have a phobic quality which renders them anti-erotic. In such cases the subject is encouraged to find a fantasy, however remotely heterosexual, which is compatible with sexual arousal and to gradually modify this to make it closer to normal heterosexual coitus. Often, for example, a homosexual can masturbate with the voyeuristic fantasy of watching a man and woman having sexual intercourse. His difficulty is in seeing himself as the man taking part rather than watching. Gradual approximation of the two (i.e. making the active man more and more like the subject) can sometimes overcome this. In the author's experience, however, it is unusual for this approach alone to suffice although it can be a valuable adjunct to other methods. A more systematic use of this principle has been used by the author as a method of treatment and is described below.

'*Shaping of fantasies*'.† Various attempts to gradually modify deviant fantasies during treatment have been reported. Bancroft (1971) has made use of the erectile response to deviant fantasies to act both as a reinforcer of the preceding fantasy and as an indicator of its erotic effect. In this way a deviant fantasy can be changed in the direction of normality by steps sufficiently small to avoid impairing the erectile response. A 28-year-old masochist was treated in this way. Investigation of erectile responses to his fantasies showed that he produced consistently full erections to a specific fantasy of himself being beaten by a man dressed only in a loin-cloth (see Fig. 3.1). Slight modification of this fantasy (e.g. by dressing the man fully or exposing his genitalia) resulted in less erection. Imagining himself being beaten by a woman was even less effective. It was indicated to the patient, who had never considered himself to be homosexual, that the investigation of his fantasies revealed a homosexual component which he had presumably hidden from himself. He was therefore asked if he would prefer treatment to help him accept his homosexual tendencies or to increase his heterosexual ones. He was distressed at the thought of being homosexual and found it quite unacceptable, and therefore chose the second course. This decision was sufficient to produce a change in his response to fantasies and he began to get full erections to the fantasy of being beaten by a naked woman, rather than a naked man. This fantasy was then systematically modified. The imaginary whip used to beat him was made very gradually shorter until it gave way to a simple slap of the woman's hand. This slap gave way to a direct manual sexual stimulation, though at this stage it was essential that he should imagine himself as tied up and totally at the mercy of the woman. Retaining this completely passive role in the fantasy he

† The use of the term 'shaping' in this context has the disadvantage that confusion with the operant term may result. Marks (Personal communication) has suggested 'fading' as a more suitable term, to make the procedure comparable to that described by Barlow and Agras (1971).

was progressively released from this bondage, freeing at first one leg and finally all four limbs. Then in fantasy he became gradually more active until eventually he was taking the dominant role in sexual intercourse.

Each change in fantasy was monitored by his erectile response. Providing the erection continued, a further slight change

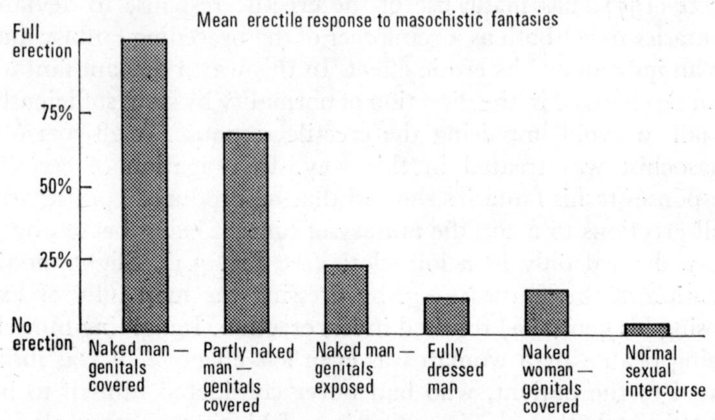

FIG. 3.1. The usual masochistic fantasy of being beaten by a man naked except for a loin-cloth consistently produced a full erection in this patient. When the fantasy was modified the erectile response diminished. It was apparently important that the person in the fantasy should be male, that his genitals should be covered but that the rest of the body should be naked.

would be made. Occasionally the erection diminished and he was then asked to return to an earlier fantasy and subsequent changes made more gradually. In each session an attempt was made to establish some significant change of this kind. After 18 sessions he was responding consistently to normal heterosexual fantasies. This method can be employed in cases where specific fantasies are consistently used during masturbation and lead to erection in the treatment situation.

A somewhat different approach to shaping fantasies was reported by Gold and Neufeld (1965). The homosexual patient was asked to imagine a potentially sexual situation which had absolutely no appeal to him (i.e. standing in a toilet beside a most unprepossessing old man). It was agreed that he would not under any circumstances solicit such a person. He was then asked to modify the image so that this man became slightly more attractive but was associated with some prohibitive factor (e.g. policeman standing by). Providing that the patient signalled that he had no desire to approach the man in such circumstances he was asked to modify the image further so that the man involved became progressively more sexually attractive, together with gradually less prohibitions present in the fantasy. Eventually with this procedure he was able to imagine rejecting an attractive young man with no prohibitions operating. This procedure was used effectively in the treatment of a homosexual adolescent male. In this case the shaping was aimed at rendering a deviant fantasy less attractive rather than the normal fantasy more attractive.

Systematic desensitization

Since Rado's (1940) paper, an increasing number of psychoanalysts have considered homosexuality to be a reparative response to anxiety about heterosexuality (Bieber *et al.* 1962; Rubinstein 1958). Certainly in some cases there is marked anxiety in relation to heterosexual behaviour or genitalia of the opposite sex. Not surprisingly, therefore, attempts have been made to treat homosexuality as a phobia of heterosexuality, using systematic desensitization, a technique used extensively for treating other types of phobia (Wolpe 1958). Kraft (1967) was the first to report a case of homosexuality treated in this way. The only systematic study of such treatment to be reported is that of Bancroft (1970*c*,*d*, 1971), whose technique was as follows.

The first 3 or 4 sessions were used for establishing hierarchies and training the patient to relax. The principles of hierarchy formation as applied to treatment of phobias in general were employed, except that in the second half of the hierarchy involving physical contact from kissing to coitus, a standard hierarchy was used. The first part of the hierarchy, involving social aspects of forming heterosexual relationships, was chosen to be relevant to the particular subject. A typical example of this first part is as follows:

1. Standing in a dance-hall looking at a girl who attracts you.

2. Walking across to her with the intention of asking her to dance.
3. Saying 'hello' to her.
4. Asking her to dance.
5. Asking her for a second dance.
6. Inviting her to have a drink.
7. Offering to take her home after the dance.
8. Taking her home.
9. Asking for another date.
10. One week to go before meeting her again.
11. One day to go before meeting her again—and so on.

Once kissing had begun the standardized hierarchy was as follows:

1. Kissing her lightly on the lips.
2. Taking her into your arms and kissing her more passionately.
3. Caressing her breasts through her clothing.
4. Undoing some of her clothes and caressing her naked breasts.
5. Caressing the outside of her thighs.
6. Caressing the inside of her thighs.
7. Gently touching the outside of her vagina.
8. (The girl) starts to caress your penis through your trousers.
9. Taking the girl's clothes off so that she is quite naked.
10. Taking your own clothes off.
11. Lying on top of her naked body and kissing and caressing her.
12. Feeling your erect penis touching the outside of her vagina.
13. Feeling the tip of your penis just inside her vagina for a brief moment.
14. Partly inserting your penis into her vagina and then withdrawing.
15. Starting sexual intercourse with her.
16. Feeling yourself approaching orgasm.
17. Ejaculating inside her vagina.

A simple relaxation technique was used to induce a state of

calm and low arousal. Once the subject was able to feel relaxed the desensitization was started. He would be asked to imagine the first item of the hierarchy. When he had this image clearly in his mind he was asked to signal by raising a finger slightly if he was calm and by raising his whole hand if there was any evidence of anxiety, the slightest degree of tension or uneasiness. If he signalled 'calm', then the next item in the hierarchy was presented to him. If he signalled 'anxiety', he would be relaxed again and the item repeated. This was done three or four times if necessary to eliminate any anxiety response, but if this was still present the therapist returned to an item lower in the hierarchy and proceeded again from there. In this study, which compared desensitization with aversion, a set number of 30 sessions was involved. Because of this, progress through the hierarchy was paced in such a way as to spread the treatment as far as possible over the full 30 sessions.

Positive conditioning of sexual responses, fading, and exposure

The most specifically sexual response in the male is penile erection (Bancroft and Mathews 1971; Bancroft 1971). Erection is an autonomic response and there is now substantial evidence that such responses can be conditioned by positive reinforcement (Miller 1969). Quinn *et al.* (1970) reported a technique in which operant reinforcement of erection was used to treat homosexuals. The reinforcer used was a pleasant drink. The subject was deprived of fluid for 18 hours, as well as receiving sodium chloride and frusemide, a potent oral diruetic, before each session. During the session he was presented with a female slide, with instructions that if he produced the slightest erection in response to the slide he would be rewarded with a drink. Impending reinforcement was signalled to him by a small cue light. Each session lasted for 45 minutes or until 30 reinforcements had been earned. Initially a very small phallic response was used as the criterion for reinforcement; this was gradually increased as treatment continued. After 20 such sessions the subject showed increased erections to heterosexual stimuli and an increase in heterosexual interest as measured by the sexual orientation method (Feldman, MacCulloch, Mellor, and Pinschof 1966).

These same workers (Quinn, McAllister, Graham, and

Harbison 1973) as well as Herman, Barlow, and Agras (1973) have also experimented with a classical conditioning model in which heterosexual stimuli, initially producing no erections (CS), were followed repeatedly by deviant stimuli which normally did produce erections (UCS). After repeated pairing in this way erections (CR) occurred to the heterosexual stimuli alone.

This type of classical conditioning procedure was combined with a progressive modification of the CS in the treatment of a heterosexual paedophiliac (Beech, Watts, and Poole 1971). The original UCS was a slide of a pre-pubertal girl. The first CS was a girl slightly older. As conditioning proceeded the CS would systematically become the UCS for the next, more 'mature' CS slide.

Two further techniques for increasing heterosexual responses have been reported. In the first paper (Barlow and Agras 1971) the technique was called 'fading'. The homosexual treated in this study produced erections when shown selected slides of male nudes. Slides showing female genitalia produced a feeling of disgust in him. In the 'fading' procedure the female slide was superimposed on to the male slide with, initially, a fraction of the light intensity of the male picture (e.g. 5 per cent female, 95 per cent male). Provided that a satisfactory erectile response occurred (i.e. 75 per cent of full erection) the light intensity of each slide was altered, the female becoming relatively brighter (e.g. 10 per cent female, 90 per cent male). This process continued until the female slide alone was projected. The result was an increase in heterosexual fantasies as well as erections to heterosexual stimuli. It is comparable in its gradual modification of stimuli and monitoring of change by measuring of erections, to the 'shaping of fantasies' procedure, described by Bancroft (1971). (See p. 45.)

The second method (Herman, Barlow, and Agras 1971) was based on the notion that simple exposure to strong heterosexual stimuli, which it was claimed are usually avoided by homosexuals, would lead to increased heterosexual response. In this case the subject was exposed to a film of a seductive nude female for 10 minutes in each session for a total of 33 sessions. This again resulted in increased penile erection to heterosexual stimuli and increased reporting of heterosexual fantasies. It should be noted that in this case film was used as the sexual stimulus. Erotic films have been shown to be more effective than either erotic slides or fantasies in producing sexual arousal (Bancroft and Staples 1974).

4 *Comparative Studies*

ALTHOUGH aversion therapy has now been used fairly extensively in treating sexual deviance it was not until 1969 that any systematic attempt to evaluate its efficacy was reported (McConaghy 1969). Since then a number of comparative studies have been carried out and some of the questions relating to aversion therapy are beginning to be answered.

In general there are two types of approach in evaluating any behaviour modification technique: group comparisons and single case studies. The methodological issues involved have been well discussed by Yates (1970). The necessary conditions for a satisfactory group comparison he listed as follows:

1. Experimental (or specific) and control (or nonspecific) treatment groups should be chosen that are matched carefully on all relevant variables.
2. Several sources of information should be drawn on to measure the results of treatment, including both specific and general behaviour being assessed.
3. Measures should be taken before, during, and at the end of treatment, and for an adequate period of time following the termination of treatment.

In the single case study, the criterion of success is not improvement or 'cure' but rather whether it can be shown that changes in the patient's behaviour are lawfully related to the experimental operations which were intended to produce them. Thus the single case study proceeds with a series of hypotheses which are tested and modified accordingly. The methodology in such an approach has received less attention than in the case of group studies. The best tried approach is that derived from operant conditioning methodology, in particular the 'baseline–change–reversal-to-baseline' paradigm. Thus once a stable pattern of behaviour is established, some condition or variable is changed. If this results in a deviation of the behaviour from the established baseline and if by restoring the changed condition to its original form the behaviour also returns to the baseline, then this suggests a causal relationship between modifying the condition and modifying the behaviour.

Yates having presented these two approaches rejects the first, the group comparison approach, in favour of the second. In fact he adopts a peculiarly extreme view in considering that the essence of behaviour therapy is the experimental investigation of the single case and any other approach regardless of technique is not really behaviour therapy, or, to put it another way, is not substantially different from any other psychological method of treatment. (For further discussion, see Chapter 7.)

Yates extreme view is not generally accepted. However, the extent that one can generalize from a group comparison study depends not only on the degree of matching of the groups compared but also on the similarity of these groups to any other group of subjects to which the method may be applied. Matching is undoubtedly difficult and nearly always far from ideal, and in practice can only be done on a small number of variables. It is often difficult to know which are the most important variables to be matched.

In addition, Yates is justified in stressing the extent to which single case study methodology has been neglected hitherto. In the present author's view, both types of approach can be valuable and may complement one another. In particular if specific techniques are explored carefully in single case studies, their general usefulness can then be most effectively assessed by means of group comparisons. In this chapter therefore we will consider both types of study, although as yet satisfactory single case studies are as rare as satisfactory group comparisons. In considering the various studies, the criteria of good methodology, suggested by Yates, will be applied.

GROUP COMPARISON STUDIES

Chemical or electrical aversion

Much has been written about the superiority of electrical methods of aversion over chemical methods (Barker 1965; Rachman 1961). There are problems with both types, as indicated in an earlier chapter, but certainly electric shock is a more convenient and generally more acceptable method. However, in only one study, that reported by McConaghy (1969) has any comparison of these two types of aversion been attempted.

McConaghy treated forty homosexuals with either apomorphine aversion or aversion relief using electric shock. His precise apomorphine technique was described on p. 33. The aversion relief was very similar to the method first described by Thorpe, *et al.* (1964) (see p. 37), except that the homosexual words were presented as slides. Fourteen homosexual slides were presented at 10-second intervals followed by a heterosexual slide, the 'relief word', which was presented for 40 seconds. This series of 15 slides was repeated five times in each session, with a different order of homosexual slides and a different relief word each time. Three such sessions a day were given for 5 days. This was compared with 28 sessions of apomorphine aversion in 5 days, the sessions in this case being represented by single injections of apomorphine given at 2-hourly intervals. The forty patients were randomly allocated to the two treatment groups, each group consisting of ten who received their treatment straightaway and ten who waited for 3 weeks. This was designed to provide a comparison after 3 weeks of those who had completed and those who were about to start treatment.

Two measures of change were used. The first involved measurement of penile erections in response to a series of short film sequences, ten showing nude males, ten nude females. The method of measuring erection was a form of volumetric plethysmography similar to that first described by Freund (1963). For some reason, presumably technical, it was not possible to calibrate the machine and therefore measurements between testing sessions were not comparable. Instead a nonparametric method using the Mann–Whitney *U* test (Siegel 1956) was employed.

For each session two groups of ten scores, (ten male and ten female) were combined and ranked in order of decreasing size. The value of *U* was given by the number of times the responses to the female nudes were greater than the responses to the male. A *U* score of 100 indicated maximum heterosexuality (all ten heterosexual scores being greater than any homosexual scores) and 0, maximum homosexuality. If the *U* score was less than 24 or more than 76 the difference between the two groups of ten scores was significant at the 5 per cent level. Results of this measure were given as *U* scores before and after treatment.

In addition to this measure, patients were asked to indicate whether their homosexual or heterosexual desire was 'increased', 'possibly increased', 'unchanged', 'possibly reduced', or 'reduced' after treatment. Also recorded was whether heterosexual relationships were improved or unchanged, and whether homosexual acts had occurred or not. No details were given of how such assessments were made.

These two indicators of change were recorded 2 weeks after treatment and again at follow-up, varying from 1–3 years after treatment. (The follow-up results are given in a later report, McConaghy 1970*a*.) Thirty-five of the forty were followed up in this way.

As far as the penile measurement was concerned, there were eighteen in each treatment group for whom satisfactory measurements before and after treatment were obtained. There was a change from a 'homosexual orientation' (i.e. *U* score less than 50) to a 'heterosexual orientation' (i.e. *U* score more than 50) in eight of the aversion relief group and four of the apomorphine group. Four of the latter group showed a change in the opposite direction. No comment is made about the significance of these changes. No significant difference was noted between the *U* scores at the end of treatment and at follow-up but using the Wilcoxon test of paired replicates, there was a significant difference between the pre-treatment and follow-up scores ($p < 0{\cdot}05$). Unfortunately no details are given of the follow-up scores or how they differed in the two treatment groups.

The subjective reports of sexual interest and behaviour for the two groups are given in Table 4.1.

There are a number of criticisms to be made of this study.

First in allocating patients to treatment no attempt was made to balance for any important variables, such as age or previous heterosexual interest, nor were any details given that enable the reader to compare the groups on such variables. The only relevant information given is in the pretreatment *U* scores; nine patients receiving apomorphine had *U* scores of over 40 whereas only four in the aversion relief group did so.

TABLE 4.1

	After 2 weeks		*At follow-up*	
	Aversion relief	*Apomorphine*	*Aversion relief*	*Apomorphine*
Heterosexual interest 'increased' or 'possibly increased'	6	3	11	7
Heterosexual relations improved	0	1	6	5
Homosexual interest absent	3	4	0	0
Homosexual interest reduced or possibly reduced	7	9	10	9
Homosexual relations absent	13	19†	4	7

† $p = 0{\cdot}05$ (exact test).

The measures used to indicate change after treatment were unsatisfactory. By not calibrating the penile plethysmograph no parametric statistics could be used. The use of the Mann–Whitney *U* score tells us very little about the degree of change of erection and there is no really satisfactory procedure for testing the significance of change in two *U* scores. Furthermore the author reported an exceedingly odd policy in measuring erections. Some patients showed a mean decrease in penile volume to both the male and female stimuli. For some reason which is not explained, these negative responses were considered to have the same significance as the positive responses in other subjects; the greater the decrease in erection the more attractive a stimulus. Even this policy was not consistent and varied in the same subject from one testing session to another. It is not surprising that some unexpected changes in the *U* scores were found, but it is virtually impossible for the reader to assess their significance. The main objective measure of change in this study is therefore of very limited value.

The other measure of change, the subjective report, also leaves much to be desired. No details of how the assessment was made are given. The behavioural change was not quantified so that once again the amount of change may have differed significantly with the two treatments and not have shown as such. The only significant difference between treatments is in the number who had resumed homosexual relationships within 2 weeks of treatment. There is a tendency for the apomorphine group to have shown greater reduction in homosexuality and the aversion relief group to have shown greater increase in heterosexuality. These directions of change do fit in with theoretical and common-sense expectations. However the results are inconclusive and the relative superiority of electrical and chemical aversion remains unclear.

Anticipatory avoidance learning, classical aversive conditioning or psychotherapy

MacCulloch and Feldman, having reported the best results in the treatment of homosexuals (1967*a*), placed considerable emphasis on their use of the avoidance learning paradigm in achieving these results. There were good theoretical reasons, they suggested, why their method should work so well. This theoretical point will be discussed more fully in a later chapter. However, commendably, these workers set out to prove their point. They accepted that it was a possibility that classical conditioning may have played a part in their anticipatory avoidance procedure. They thus embarked on a further study in which their avoidance technique was compared with a classical conditioning procedure. They also wondered whether 'the enthusiasm of the therapist was being communicated to the patient; this together with the fact that a good deal of reinforcement was given in the form of reassurance and praise for reported improvement could be construed as constituting a form of psychotherapy'. Thus they also included a psychotherapeutic procedure in their study (Feldman and MacCulloch 1971.)

The anticipatory avoidance procedure was largely similar to their original method described on p. 36 except that the reinforcement schedules were systematically altered during treatment so that successful avoiding (and hence closer similarity to the nontreatment situation) could be more consistently achieved. They also removed some of the flexibility of the earlier procedure in order to equate with the classical conditioning group such technical parameters as the number of slides used during treatment. The classical conditioning procedure was described on p. 63. The psychotherapeutic procedure carried out by MacCulloch consisted of exploration and discussion of the patient's sexual and associated personality difficulties, expecially the patient's attitudes to females, including attitudes of aversion and fear. Formal systematic desensitization was not used.

Each aversive procedure (avoidance learning and classical conditioning) was given for 24 half-hour sessions. The psychotherapy was given for 12 one-hour sessions. This difference was justified on the grounds that total treatment time should be equal for the three methods, half an hour being too short a period for a psychotherapy session.

Patients were included in the trial provided they were less than 40 years old, not suffering currently from a psychotic illness or 'psychosyndrome', had no personality disorder other than a 'self-insecure type' on the evidence of the initial testing, did not suffer from epilepsy, alcoholism, or drug addiction and had an I.Q. of more than 80. Five patients were excluded on one or more of these grounds. Thirty patients were treated in all, allocated randomly to the three treatments, ten in each group.

Before treatment each patient completed a lengthy historical questionnaire together with Cattell 16PF test, the Eysenck personality inventory (EPI) the Mill Hill vocabulary scale and the Sexual Orientation Method (Feldman *et al.* 1966) (see Chapter 8). The initial interview and later assessment interviews were carried out by a separate assessor not involved in treatment (Feldman).

The procedure after entering the trial was complex. After 24 sessions patients were designated improved or unimproved on the basis of the change in their sexual orientation method (SOM) scores (12 points or more decrease in the homosexual score was the criterion of improvement). Those who did not reach this criterion were crossed over to one of the other treatment procedures. However, on the basis of their review of the literature of psychotherapy in the treatment of homosexuality it was decided that those patients who had failed to respond to one of the aversive methods 'should not be exposed to psychotherapy; but that those who had had psychotherapy should have the opportunity of receiving a learning treatment'. Thus the failures with psychotherapy were randomly assigned to either the anticipatory avoidance or the classical conditioning technique. Those who had failed initially with one of the aversive techniques were assigned to the other aversive procedure. In stage 2 of the experiment therefore, the initial 'failures' received a further 24 sessions. At the end of stage 2 any patient who had again failed to achieve the criterion of success in the SOM score and who had not received both learning treatments was given the third treatment in stage 3.

Patients were followed up at 2-, 4-, 6-, and 12-week intervals. The longest follow-up was 58 weeks, the shortest 12 weeks. Twelve weeks was considered long enough, the authors assuming that a relapse, if it was to occur, would happen within that period.

In assessing the results the only quantifiable measure of change is the change in the SOM score. The analysis of variance of these changes for the three treatment groups (presumably the initial treatment groups) failed to show any significant difference between the groups in either homosexual, heterosexual or combined scores. Not satisfied with this method of analysing the results these workers then looked at the treatment groups in terms of the numbers of patients who had reached the criterion of success (i.e. reduction in 12 or more of the SOM *homosexual* score), after the first 24 sessions of treatment.

They then divided their patients into primary and secondary homosexuals. Primary homosexuals by their definition are those who deny any previous interest in heterosexuality. Two of these were in the anticipatory avoidance group, three in the classical conditioning group and four in the psychotherapy group. Secondary homosexuals are those who have experienced some heterosexual interest, however slight, at some stage in the past. Only one of the primary homosexuals reached the criterion of success and he was in the classical conditioning group. Of the secondary homosexuals, six of the eight treated by anticipatory avoidance, five of the seven treated by classical conditioning, and two of the six treated by psychotherapy reached the criterion of success. Not surprisingly, with such small groups there was no significant difference between the three groups, or between psychotherapy and the two aversion groups combined. However of the two psychotherapy cases who did improve, one relapsed and the other failed to return for further interview, whereas only one of the eleven secondary homosexuals who improved following one or other of the aversive techniques relapsed. These workers therefore concluded that this represented 'clear evidence of the superior efficacy of a learning technique over psychotherapy in the treatment of secondary homosexuals'.

The changes in those initially failing and subsequently treated with alternative techniques were also reported. Of the four secondary homosexuals who were unimproved after psychotherapy, three were improved by the same criteria after aversion, two after classical conditioning, and one after avoidance learning. The fourth failed to respond to either technique. Of the four secondary homosexuals who failed with the initial aversion technique, two did not receive the treatment to which they had been reassigned. Of the other two, one showed a successful response to classical conditioning having failed with anticipatory avoidance, the other failed to respond to either. In the group of nine primary homosexuals, six proceeded to an alternative method, five failed to respond. One who had failed with psychotherapy responded to anticipatory avoidance but relapsed during follow-up.

It should be pointed out that in assessing the results of the second and third stages of treatment the criterion of success (i.e. 12 point change in SOM score) was taken as a change in SOM score from before the *first* treatment to after the *last*. If the criterion was attained the success was attributed to the last treatment given.

Information about sexual practices at the end of follow-up is also given. However, because of the cross-over design it is not possible to judge the effects of psychotherapy alone in this respect.

Details of homosexual and heterosexual practices are given in Table 4.2.

The details for heterosexual behaviour are less easy to interpret as it is not clear what the level of heterosexual behaviour was before treatment in the various groups (i.e. no cross-over and cross-over groups). Once again however there was no appreciable difference between the two aversive conditions.

Unfortunately, the usefulness of this study is lessened by a series of errors in the design and analysis. This particularly applies to the comparison of psychotherapy with the aversive techniques. A number of factors militated against the efficacy of psychotherapy. First, the constitution of the three groups;

TABLE 4.2
Sexual practice at follow-up

Practise	*Avoidance learning*		*Classical conditioning*	
Homosexual	*a*	*b*	*a*	*b*
Strong fantasy	1	5	2	2
Mutual masturbation	0	0	0	0
Anal intercourse	0	0	0	1
Nil	7	1	5	3
Heterosexual				
Strong fantasy	1	0	1	1
Dating	1	1	1	1
Kissing	1	0	2	1
Petting	2	0	3	1
Sexual Intercourse	3	1	0	0
Nil	0	4	0	2
Total	8	6	7	6

a = no cross-over. *b* = cross-over (last treatment indicated).

once again no balancing of important variables was attempted. The authors expressed regret at not having matched for or even excluded primary homosexuals, but the prognostic significance of this group was not appreciated by them until after the trial was under way. The level of previous heterosexual behaviour was to some extent less, and the number of primary homosexuals slightly greater in the psychotherapy group. The number referred by the courts was lowest in the avoidance group. Age was difficult to compare from the data provided and the mean ages could have differed between groups by as much as seven years. Only in relation to current psychiatric treatment did the anticipatory avoidance group appear to be at a disadvantage. In most other respects they appeared to start off better than the other two groups, in particular the psychotherapy group. In addition these workers were faced with a difficult problem in relation to the length of treatment sessions. Their decision to equate 12 hourly sessions of psychotherapy with 24 half-hourly sessions of aversion therapy is an arguable one. In this writer's opinion this decision probably placed the psychotherapy procedure at a further disadvantage.

The cross-over design reveals an extraordinarily low expectation of success for psychotherapy compared with the other techniques and indicates an unacceptable degree of experimenter bias, which is inconsistent with their rationale for including it, in which the enthusiasm of the therapist was considered to be of possible therapeutic importance. Even if these workers had been justified in drawing their conclusion from the literature of psychotherapy—and the present author's review drew different conclusions (Bancroft 1970*c*)—there could be no ethical objection to crossing over from a treatment of presumed effectiveness to one of presumed ineffectiveness if the reverse procedure is ethically justified.

The psychotherapy method is further disadvantaged by their criterion for determining a successful response, the change in the SOM homosexual score. Apart from being a measure of attitude only, and not reflecting with any certainty the level of sexual behaviour (see p. 191), a reduction of homosexual attitude is used to judge on the one hand, two methods directly aimed at reducing homosexual interest and on the other hand, a method with no such aim but rather an increase in heterosexual interest. If an increase in the heterosexual SOM score had been taken as a criterion of success, in many ways a more satisfactory criterion, the psychotherapy method may have compared more favourably. The mean increases in heterosexual scores for the three treatments are shown in Table 4.3.

It will be seen from these figures that not only was the heterosexual change score in the secondary homosexuals similar for psychotherapy and the aversive methods but also was noticeably greater for psychotherapy in the primary homosexuals.

It would thus seem that the only justifiable conclusion from this study is that, as carried out, there was no significant difference in efficacy between these three treatment methods.

Avoidance conditioning versus 'placebo' conditioning

An ingenious experiment comparing an avoidance learning procedure with a 'placebo' conditioning procedure not involving shocks, has been reported by Birk, Huddleston, Miller, and Cohler (1971).

Eight homosexual subjects were treated by each method. An important difference from other comparative studies is that all subjects received their conditioning treatment in the midst of long-term group psychotherapy. The behaviour modification technique was, therefore, part of a wider therapeutic approach. After about 1 year of group therapy the conditioning treatment

TABLE 4.3
Changes in heterosexual SOM scores (From Feldman and MacCulloch 1971).

	Primary homosexuals			*Secondary homosexuals*		
	n	Mean	s.d.	*n*	Mean	s.d.
Avoidance learning	2	1·0	1·41	8	11·0	6·0
Classical conditioning	3	2·66	4·03	7	8·71	10·44
Psychotherapy	4	7·00	9·41	6	8·0	4·69

was started, together with a short period of individual therapy. The sixteen patients were in two therapeutic groups of eight, with half in each group receiving one of the conditioning treatments and half the other. The conditioning groups were selected 'randomly'.

The avoidance learning method was a modification of that described by Feldman and MacCulloch (1965). The most important difference was that instead of simply switching to avoid a shock, an operant response had to be continued to maintain avoidance. Similarly, this operant response could be used to maintain the presence of a heterosexual stimulus. As in the Feldman and MacCulloch procedure a variety of aversive paradigms was involved. These were 'immediate avoidance', 'classical conditioning' trials (where the shock occurred in spite of the avoidance response), 'delayed escape' trials where they were inevitably shocked but could eventually escape from the shock, and 'delayed avoidance' trials. Approximately half the trials were of the immediate avoidance type. Successful avoidance or escape was immediately followed by the presentation of a female slide.

The 'placebo' conditioning method was identical except that instead of receiving a shock, a light was switched on in front of the subject. This could be 'escaped from' or 'avoided' in the same way.

Twenty to twenty-five half-hour sessions were involved over a period of about 6 weeks.

Three methods of assessing change were used:

1. Kinsey ratings based on clinical interviews. (See p. 198.)
2. Blind clinical evaluations and ratings by 'outside' psychiatrists (nine of the sixteen subjects were separately rated by two outside psychiatrists).
3. Sexual behaviour questionnaires giving response frequencies of homosexual 'cruising', petting and orgasm experiences, as well as equivalent heterosexual behaviour and masturbation.

The results were presented in four ways. First anecdotal reports; five of the eight receiving avoidance conditioning reported marked changes in their sexual feelings (in the expected direction) coinciding with treatment, usually after about 12 sessions. None of the eight 'placebo' group did so. However, only two of the changed subjects maintained their improvement. Secondly, during the 2 months following treatment, the 'shocked' group showed a total of 22 points change in the Kinsey ratings, the 'placebo' group only 2 points. This difference is significant at the 1 per cent level. When changes in Kinsey ratings were looked at 1 year after treatment, however, the difference was no longer significant (12 points and 5 points respectively). Thirdly, behavioural ratings showed significantly greater reduction in homosexual cruising and petting in the 'shocked' group than in the 'placebo' group. This finding must be qualified, however, by the fact that there was a much higher level of homosexual behaviour on these measures in the 'shocked' group before treatment and hence more scope for change. Changes in heterosexual ratings were not significantly different. Finally clinical ratings by outside psychiatrists of the subjects themselves were considered. On a variety of nonsexual scales (e.g. depression, isolation, feelings of inferiority) the 'shocked' group had apparently done less well than the 'placebo' group. Similarly with the ratings of homosexual and heterosexual behaviour change the difference between the groups was slight and not significant though generally in the expected direction.

This study, though a useful one, has a number of flaws. The combination of conditioning procedures with other techniques such as group therapy is a sensible one but it does mean that the effects of the conditioning treatment will be confounded by any effects of the other treatment. For this reason, it was important to carry out careful assessment of change immediately following treatment and during the first few months, which was the time when any difference in the effects of the two specific methods would have been most noticeable. In fact, the most careful assessment was not made until at least a year after treatment.

The selection of the two groups on a random rather than on a balanced basis led to them showing important differences before treatment and this fact rendered the scores for change in the sexual behaviour difficult to interpret. Although the 'shocked' group did show a much greater reduction in homosexual behaviour than the 'placebo' group the level of behaviour following treatment was similar in the two groups. There is little doubt that when one is trying to reduce the frequency of an existing behaviour, it is easier to bring about a drop from a high to a moderate level than it is to produce a comparable reduction from a moderate level to virtual cessation of the behaviour. It is also surprising, considering that these workers were using a modification of MacCulloch and Feldman's technique, that they gave no information about the proportion of cases denying any previous heterosexual interest or behaviour, a prognostic factor the importance of which has been greatly stressed by MacCulloch and Feldman (1967*a*).

The use of external clinical raters is certainly a useful addition to their assessment procedure and one which has been lacking in most other studies. The importance of such independent raters is reinforced by the discrepancy between the reported results and those reflected in the behavioural ratings scores.

Nevertheless, it is probably justifiable to conclude from this study that the incorporation of shocks in the conditioning procedure resulted in more immediate change in the level of homosexual interest and behaviour than a similar procedure using innocuous stimuli in place of shocks. At the present time this is the only clinically relevant evidence available on this point.

Aversion or desensitization

So far results of comparative studies, though by no means conclusive, have suggested that the precise method of aversion used does not make much difference to the outcome. In reviewing the literature of psychotherapy and aversion therapy for homosexuality Bancroft (1970*c*) came to the conclusion that although results varied from study to study, when they were grouped together the outcome was similar for the two types of treatment, with approximately 40 per cent showing improvement in both groups.

This raised the possibility that a proportion of homosexuals who presented for treatment responded whatever method of treatment they received, being mainly affected by nonspecific factors in the treatment situation. Bancroft (1970*c*,*d*) therefore attempted to disprove this null hypothesis by comparing two treatment methods which were entirely different in their approach, assumed mechanisms of change and immediate aims, whilst showing similar ultimate aims. The two methods were aversion therapy and systematic desensitization. If the specific technique in each case was of crucial importance, then one would expect some differences between them in their immediate effects. Both were techniques in which the therapist had more or less equal expertise and expectancies of success. Both permitted the incorporation of a number of measures of change before, after and during the course of treatment which enabled a direct comparison to be made. The study was designed in such a way as to make sure as far as possible that the treatment received was similar except for the specific techniques involved. One therapist (the author) acted throughout. Both methods involved 30 sessions of treatment on an outpatient basis, each session lasting approximately 1 hour with usually 2 sessions a week. The average duration of treatment was approximately 4 months. The patients were only offered treatment if they were prepared to accept either method after each one had been explained to them, and they were allocated to either one or other treatment group in such a way as to match the two groups as equally as possible for age, normality of the EPI and degree of previous heterosexual experience. This was done, where possible by pairing them and in fact eighteen of the thirty patients were paired into nine pairs, the remaining twelve being randomly allocated to the two groups. The comparison of the two groups on these variables is shown in Table 4.4.

TABLE 4.4

Comparison of the two groups

	Aversion	*Desensitization*
n	15	15
Mean age	30·7	28·3
Age range	19–46	20–38
Age 35+	4	2
EPI score outside normal range	9	9
Previous heterosexual experience.*†		
Category 1	4	2
Category 2	1	4
Category 3	5	5
Category 4	5	4
With heterosexual partner at onset	5	3

Number of matched pairs: 9. None of the differences between groups reaches significance at the 5 per cent level.

*† For definitions of categories see text.

The categories of heterosexual experience used in Table 4.4 were defined as follows:

1. Unable to recall any heterosexual interest or fantasy since puberty. (This is comparable to the primary homosexual as defined by Feldman and MacCulloch (1971).)
2. Heterosexual interest at some stage since puberty but no attempt at genital contact with a female (i.e. touching the female genitalia or sexual intercourse).
3. Genital contact attempted but always with anxiety, revulsion, or impotence.
4. Achieved genital contact at some stage with no anxiety, revulsion or impotence.

Twenty-three of the thirty patients completed the full 30 sessions of treatment: four dropped out of the desensitization group and three out of the aversion group. Most of the results given will be for the patients who completed treatment—twelve in the aversion group, eleven in the desensitization group.

Two types of aversive procedure were used in the aversion group. For the first 15 sessions the 'punishment of erection' procedure, described on p. 39, was employed. For the last 15 sessions the 'punishment of fantasy' procedure described on p. 39 was used. In this case four key deviant fantasies were chosen for each patient. Each fantasy was dealt with in blocks of 10 aversive trials. The desensitization method was described on p. 47.

The measures of change used in both groups are described below.

Sexual behaviour ratings. Here complex rating scales were used which were developed on an *ad hoc* basis and which covered several areas of sexual interest and behaviour: the noticing of men or women as sexually interesting, frequency of sexual thoughts, frequency of masturbation, dating, kissing, and intercourse on the heterosexual scale and the homosexual equivalents on the homosexual scale. (This was a more complex version of the author's rating scale described in Chapter 8.) The average score on the heterosexual scale for a normally active heterosexual male would be about 25 and the same on the homosexual scale for a normally active homosexual male. These ratings were given retrospectively for four periods preceding treatment, as well as during follow-up and between sessions. The results of these ratings are reported in two ways: behaviour before and after treatment and behaviour between treatment sessions.

Sexual attitudes. The modification of the semantic differential technique for measuring sexual attitudes, developed by Marks and Sartorius (1968) was used. This included sexual evaluation and anxiety scales (see Chapter 8). The patient was asked to fill in these ratings for 2–4 homosexual concepts and the same number of heterosexual concepts together with concepts such as 'myself', 'my psychiatrist' and a few others. The first semantic differential booklet was completed before the patient knew which treatment he was going to receive. Further ratings were made after 15 sessions, at the end of treatment and during the follow-up period.

Erections. These were measured by means of a penile plethysmograph (Bancroft *et al.* 1966), a simple mercury and rubber strain gauge which can be fitted by the patient and worn unobtrusively under his normal clothes. (See Chapter 8.)

Before each patient was allocated to the treatment group he was asked to select pictures of men and women which he found attractive and put them in order of preference. Whilst wearing the plethysmograph he was asked to look at the first five male and the first five female pictures of his choice alternating the sexes and whilst doing so to produce an erotic fantasy in association with the picture. Any changes in the size of the penis were then measured.† The initial testing of these homosexual and heterosexual erections occurred before he knew which treatment he was to receive; the final testing was at the end of the last session of treatment.

Apart from these measures of erection before and after treatment, similar measures were taken during each treatment session, with one homosexual and one heterosexual stimulus presented at the beginning of the session, and one heterosexual stimulus at the end. The first fifteen homosexual pictures of the patient's choice were also used as stimuli during the 'punishment of erection' procedure in the first half of the course of aversive treatment.

The follow-up period was short, the average being approximately 9 months, but because the direct effects of the two methods were under consideration the first 6 months following treatment were considered to be the most important. The results will be presented as follows:

1. Changes in the sexual behaviour ratings from before treatment to after treatment.
2. Changes in sexual attitudes from beginning to end of treatment and to follow-up.
3. Changes in erections from beginning to end of treatment.
4. Changes during the course of treatment in:
   (*a*) sexual behaviour ratings between sessions;

† For details of the measurement technique see Appendix.

(*b*) homosexual erections at the start of each session;
(*c*) heterosexual erections at the start and finish of each session.

Changes in sexual behaviour are shown as mean changes for each treatment group in Fig. 4.1 and Table 4.5. There is virtually no difference between the two treatment groups in behaviour ratings either homosexual or heterosexual. (The change in homosexual behaviour in both groups reached significance. The change in heterosexual ratings did not reach significance in

TABLE 4.5
Group mean changes in sexual behaviour ratings from before treatment (2-year period) to follow-up (first and last 6-month periods)

	First 6-month follow-up			*Last 6-month follow-up*		
	Hetero	*Homo*	*Combined*	*Hetero*	*Homo*	*Combined*
Aversion ($n = 15$)	+2·7	+9·4	+12·1	+3·2	+8·9	+12·1
Desensitization ($n = 14$)	+3·25	+9·4	+12·65	+3·75	+9·0	+12·75
Difference between groups	N.S.	N.S.	N.S.	N.S.	N.S.	N.S.

N.B. An increase in heterosexual rating and decrease in homosexual rating were both considered + changes.

either group. When the last available 6 months of follow-up are compared with before treatment, the heterosexual change does reach significance in the desensitization group, though not in the aversion group.)

Fig. 4.2 and Table 4.6 show the mean attitude change for the two treatment groups. Here again there was no significant difference between the two groups. The change at the end of treatment was significant in each case except for the homosexual change in the desensitization group. At follow-up, the heterosexual change was no longer significant in the aversion group. Thus the maximum attitude change in each group was in the expected direction, that is reduction of homosexual attitudes with aversion and increase in heterosexual attitudes with desensitization.

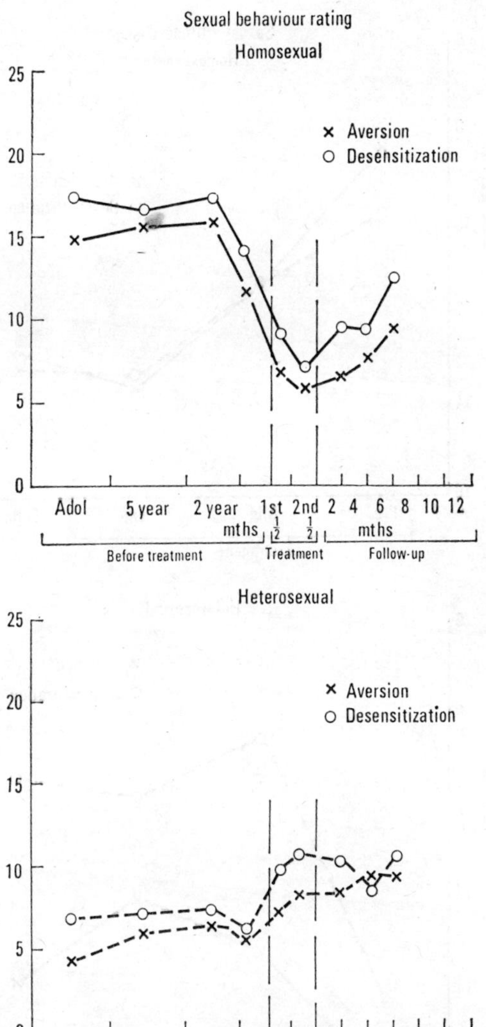

FIG. 4.1. These graphs show the mean ratings for the two treatment groups (aversion and desensitization) for homosexual and heterosexual behaviour. The first four points represent the pre-treatment periods ('adolescence', '5-year period', '2-year period', and '2-month period'). Between the vertical lines are the two scores for the first and second half of treatment. Following this are the follow-up scores for the 2-monthly periods. (From Bancroft 1970*d*.)

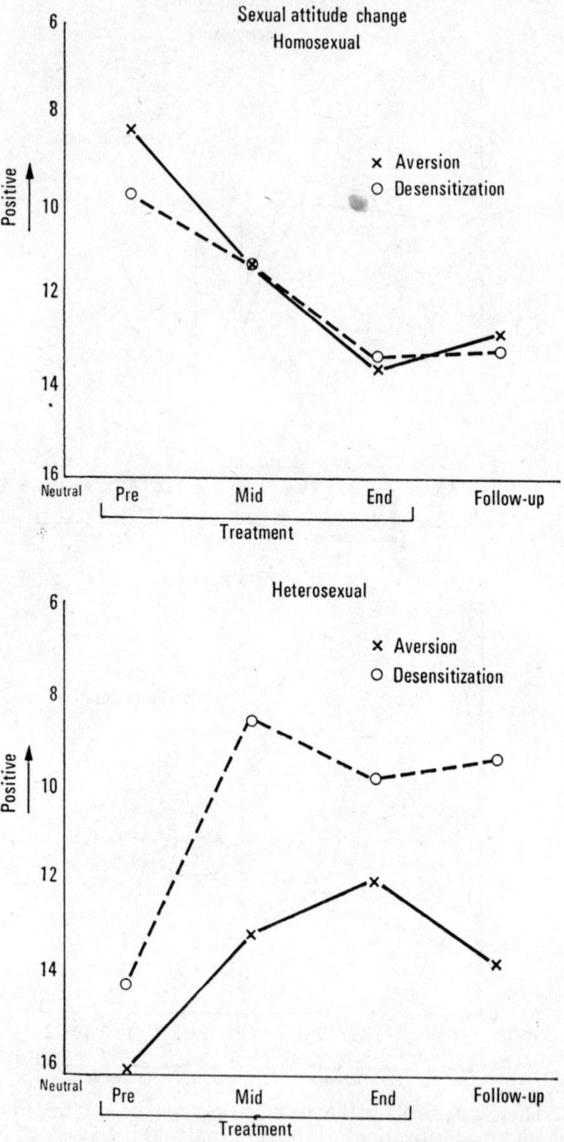

FIG. 4.2 These graphs show the mean scores for the sexual scales on the semantic differential for the four occasions of testing (start of treatment, mid-treatment, end of treatment and follow-up). A neutral score is 16, anything less than this reflects a more positive attitude. (From Bancroft 1970*d*.)

TABLE 4.6
Group mean changes in sexual attitudes
1. From beginning to end of treatment and
2. From beginning of treatment to follow-up
(treatment group minus drop-outs)

	1. Beginning to end of treatment		*2. Beginning to follow-up*	
	Hetero	*Homo*	*Hetero*	*Homo*
Aversion ($n = 12$)†	+4·1	+5·3	+1·99	+4·75
Desensitization ($n = 11$)	+4·5	+3·53	+4·95	+3·36
Difference between groups	$t = 0{\cdot}23$ N.S.	$t = 0{\cdot}875$ N.S.	$t = 1{\cdot}62$ N.S.	$t = 0{\cdot}65$ N.S.

† $n = 10$ at follow-up

N.B. A decrease in heterosexual scores and an increase in homosexual scores were both considered + changes.

Fig. 4.3 and Table 4.7 show the mean homosexual and heterosexual erections for the two groups before and after treatment. Once again there is no significant difference between the treatment groups; all the changes within groups from before to after treatment are significant, except for the reduction in homosexual erections in the desensitization group.

Fig. 4.4 shows sexual behaviour ratings during the course of treatment itself. These are ratings given for the period covered

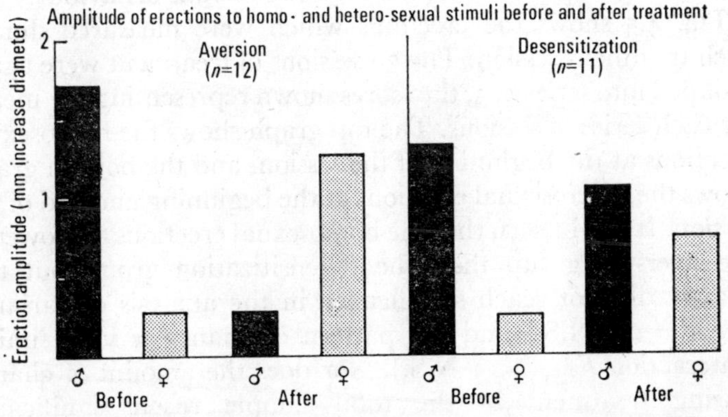

FIG. 4.3. These histograms show the mean increase in erections to homosexual (shaded) and heterosexual (unshaded) pictures, before and after treatment in the two treatment groups. Increases in erection are measured as millimetres increase in diameter of the penis. (From Bancroft 1970*d*.)

by 5 consecutive sessions. These 5-session scores were compared by an analysis of variance which showed that there was no significant difference between the treatment groups ($F_{1,21} < 1$, N.S. for both homosexual and heterosexual ratings) although the amount of change in the total sample did reach significance

TABLE 4.7

Group mean changes in erection to heterosexual/homosexual stimuli from before to after treatment (drop-outs excluded).

	Group mean change†	
	Hetero	*Homo*
Aversion ($n = 12$)	+1·018	−1·45
Desensitization ($n = 11$)	+0·491	−0·276
Difference between groups	$t = 1·11$ N.S.	$t = 1·53$ N.S.

† Means expressed as mm increase in diameter.

($F_{5,105} = 3·1$, $p < 0·05$ for both homosexual and heterosexual ratings). The pattern of change was very similar in the two groups except for the first 5 or 10 sessions, where changes followed the expected direction—in the aversion group there was more reduction in homosexual behaviour and in the desensitization group more increase in heterosexual behaviour.

Fig. 4.5 shows the erections which were measured during each treatment session. The 30 sessions of treatment were again grouped into series of 5, the scores shown representing the means for each series of sessions. The top graph shows the homosexual erections at the beginning of the session, and the bottom graph shows the heterosexual erections at the beginning and end of the session. It can be seen that the homosexual erections are lower in the aversion group than the desensitization group but this change did not reach significance in the analysis of variance ($F_{5,21} = 2·8$ N.S.) and the pattern of change is very similar (interaction $F_{5,105} < 1$ N.S.). Nor does the amount of change during treatment in the total sample reach significance ($F_{5,105} < 1$ N.S.). Looking at the heterosexual erections, however, it can be seen that those at the beginning and end of the desensitization session and the beginning of the aversion session were all very similar, whereas the erections at the end of the session in the aversion were much higher. The difference between the beginning and end erections in the desensitization group was not significant ($F_{1,240} = 2{\cdot}7$ N.S.), but the difference between the beginning and end erections in the aversion group was highly significant ($F_{1,319} = 24{\cdot}8$, $p < 0{\cdot}001$). Thus it

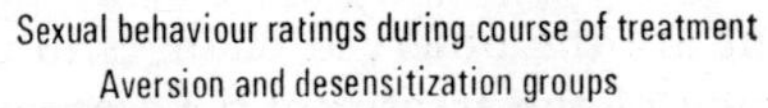

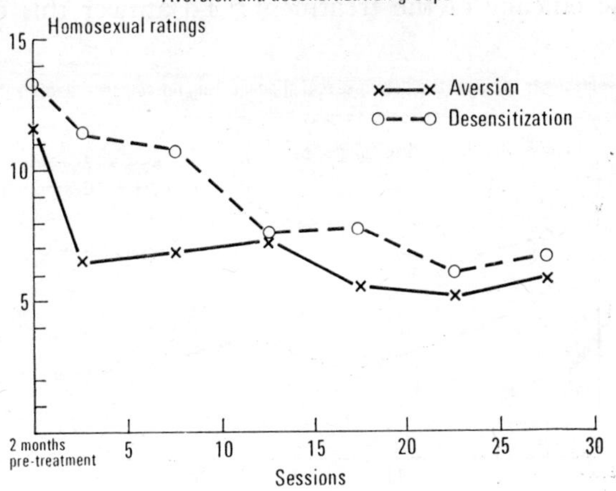

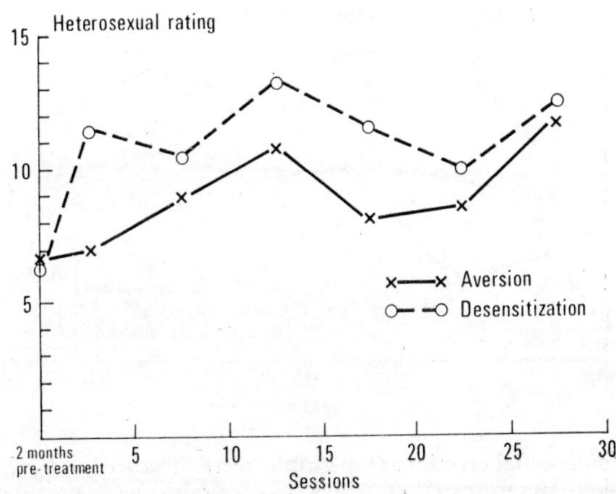

FIG. 4.4. These graphs show the mean sexual behaviour ratings during the course of treatment in the two treatment groups. Each point indicates a mean score for a period covered by 5 treatment sessions, adjusted to represent one of 6 periods of equal length. (From Bancroft 1970*d*.)

seems that in some way the aversion method resulted in a facilitation of heterosexual erections during the course of the session.

To summarize the comparison of the two methods, therefore, there was only one significant difference between the methods, and that was the facilitatory effect on the heterosexual erections during each session, which has just been described.

How relevant are the observed changes to clinical outcome or to the efficacy of the treatment? To answer this question

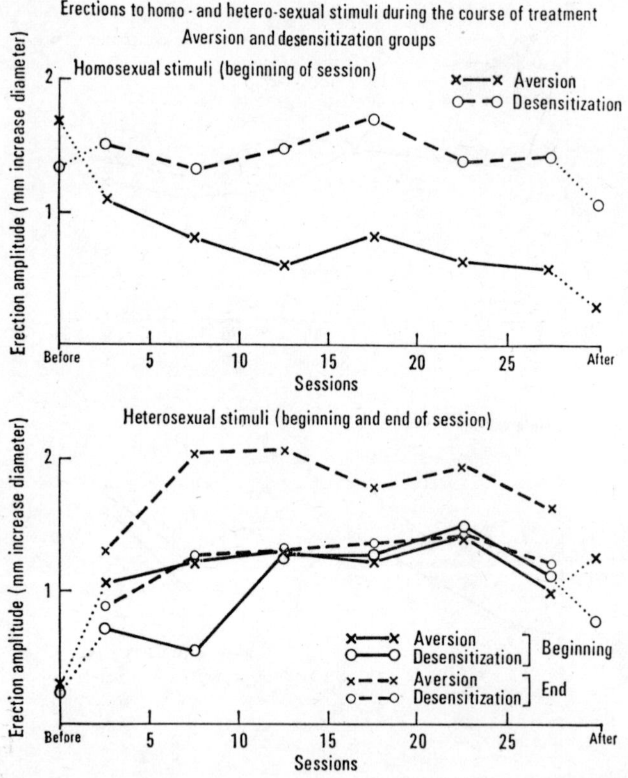

FIG. 4.5. Homosexual erections (top graph) were measured at the beginning of each session. Heterosexual erections (lower graph) were measured at the beginning and end of each session. Each point represents a group mean for 5 consecutive sessions. The mean values for the initial and final testing (as in Fig. 4.3), shown as 'before' and 'after', are connected to the main graph by dotted lines. (From Bancroft 1970*d*.)

the total patient sample was redivided into two groups according to clinical outcome; 'improved' and 'unimproved'. A comparison of these variables was then made in the two outcome groups in exactly the same way as for the two treatment

TABLE 4.8

Mean group changes in attitudes from beginning to end of treatment in outcome groups (minus drop-outs).

	Beginning to end of treatment	
	Hetero	*Homo*
Improved ($n = 11$)	+6·45	+6·22
Unimproved ($n = 12$)	+2·25	+2·83
Difference between groups	$t = 2{\cdot}28$	$t = 1{\cdot}75$
	$p < 0{\cdot}02$	N.S.

groups. First, sexual behaviour change scores were calculated by comparing the scores for the 2 years before treatment with the 6 months following treatment. Reductions in homosexual ratings and increases in heterosexual ratings were taken as positive change scores. By taking a score of 15 for the combined

TABLE 4.9

Mean group changes in erections to heterosexual and homosexual stimuli from before to after treatment in outcome groups (minus drop-outs) †

	Beginning to end of treatment	
	Hetero	*Homo*
Improved ($n = 11$)	+1·271	−0·885
Unimproved ($n = 12$)	+0·303	−0·895
Difference between groups	$t = 2{\cdot}24$	$t = <1{\cdot}0$
	$p < 0{\cdot}05$	N.S.

† Means expressed as mm increase in diameter.

homosexual and heterosexual behaviour change scores as the cut-off point, the twenty-three completed patients fell conveniently into two outcome groups the same size as the treatment groups—eleven improved and twelve unimproved.

Fig. 4.6 and Table 4.8 show mean attitude change in the two outcome groups and here the difference in heterosexual but not homosexual attitude change reaches significance.

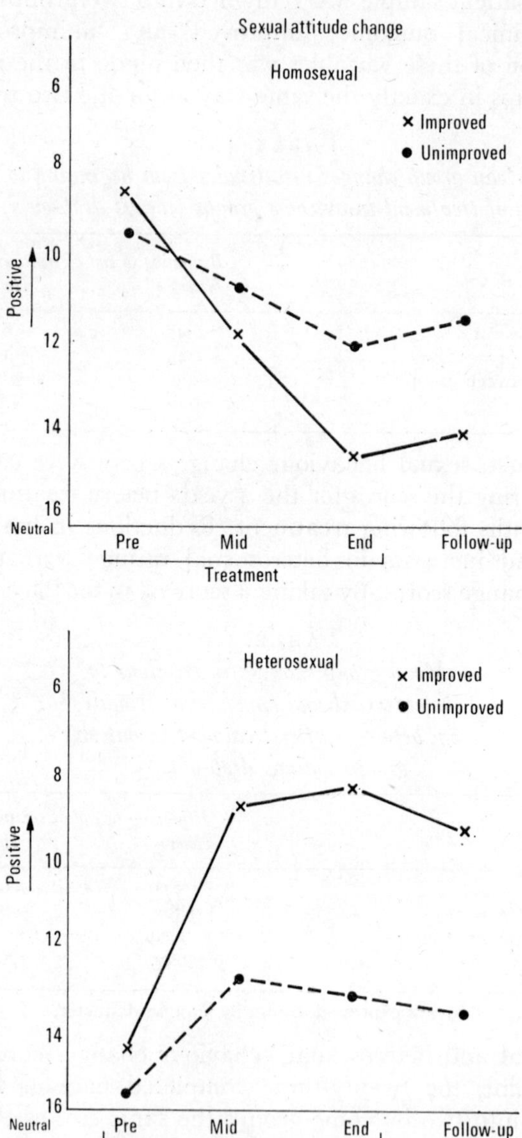

FIG. 4.6. As in Fig. 4.2 except that outcome groups rather than treatment groups are shown. (From Bancroft 1970*d*.)

Fig. 4.7 and Table 4.9 show erections at the beginning and end of treatment in the outcome groups. Here it can be seen that the change in homosexual erections was virtually the same for the two outcome groups and therefore one must conclude that any superiority of aversion in suppressing homosexual erections on this measure was not related to behavioural change. However, the improvement in heterosexual erections is

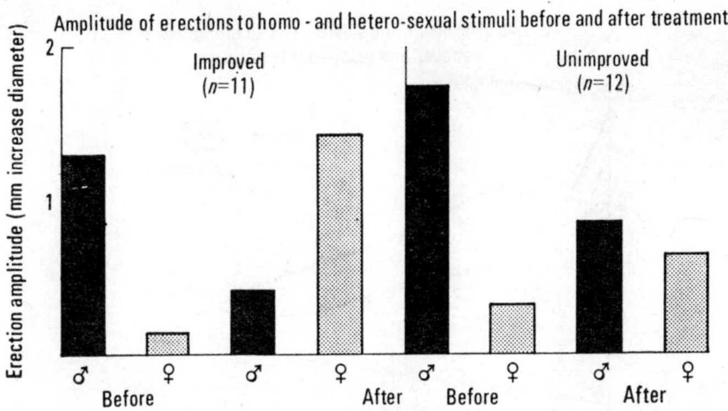

FIG. 4.7. As in Fig. 4.3 except that outcome groups rather than treatment groups are shown. (From Bancroft 1970*d*.)

significantly greater in the improved group and therefore the slight superiority of aversion in increasing heterosexual erections may be related to outcome.

Fig. 4.8 shows the sexual behaviour during the course of treatment in the two outcome groups. The homosexual behaviour is not significantly different between the two groups ($F_{1,21} < 1$ N.S.) whereas the difference in heterosexual behaviour is highly significant ($F_{1,21} = 15{\cdot}1$, $p < 0{\cdot}001$). It can also be noted that the slight superiority of the improved group in terms of homosexual behaviour was not shown until the last 5 sessions of treatment whereas their superiority heterosexually was shown right at the beginning of treatment. It could thus be predicted that if a patient is to improve with either of these methods he is likely to show some heterosexual improvement early in treatment.

Fig. 4.9 shows the erections measured during the course of each session. Once again there is no significant difference between the groups in the level of homosexual erections

($F_{1,21} < 1$ N.S.), but the difference between the beginning and end heterosexual erections is highly significant in the improved group ($F_{1,290} = 43{\cdot}8$, $p < 0{\cdot}001$) and does not reach significance in the unimproved group ($F_{1,319} < 1$ N.S.). Therefore, the facilitatory effect on heterosexual erections described earlier in the aversion group appears to be related in some way to clinical outcome.

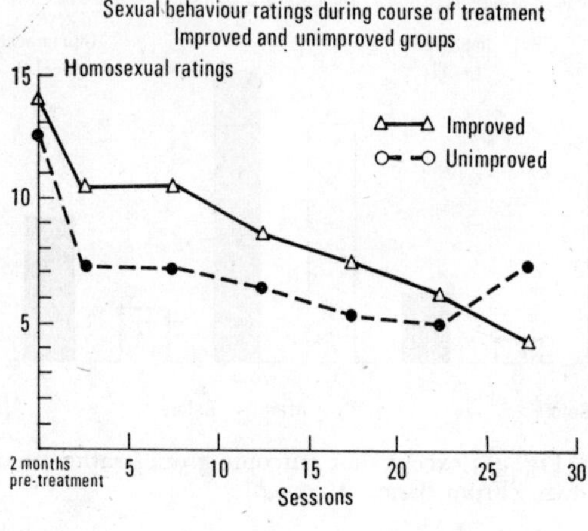

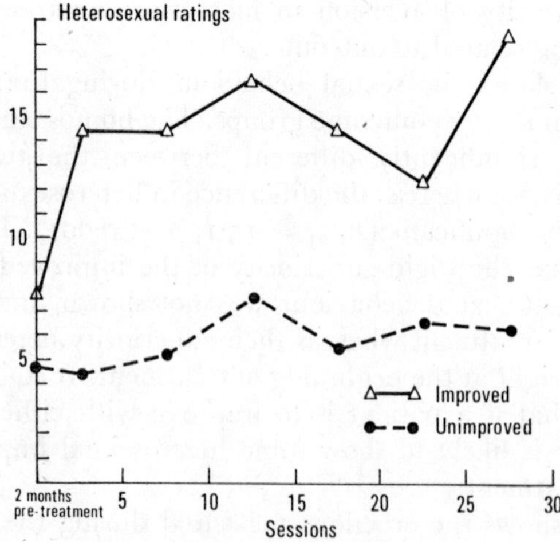

FIG. 4.8. As in Fig. 4.4 except that outcome groups rather than treatment groups are shown. (From Bancroft 1970*d*.)

Thus the point can be made that as far as this study is concerned all the significant differences between the outcome groups are found in heterosexual variables, and it should be remembered that the criteria for clinical improvement involved both homosexual and heterosexual change and in fact there was

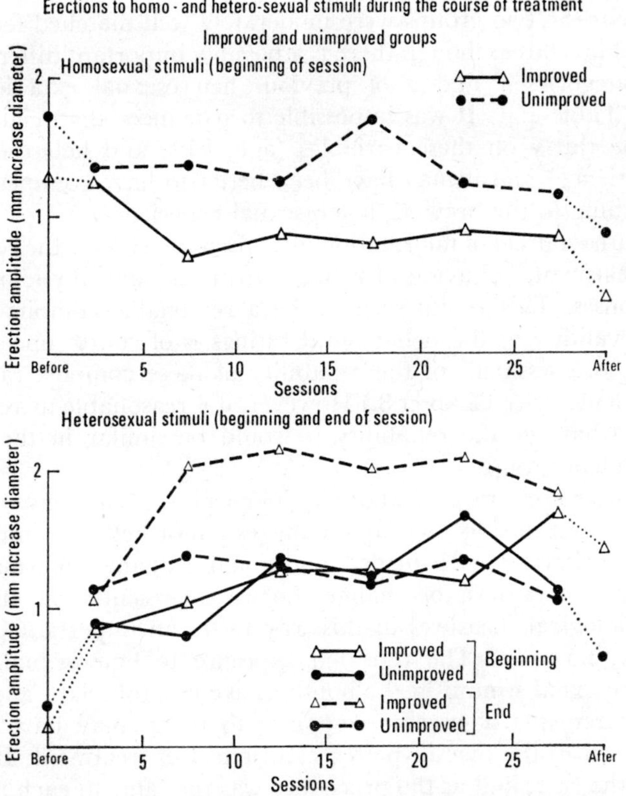

FIG. 4.9. As in Fig. 4.5 except that outcome groups rather than treatment groups are shown. (From Bancroft 1970*d*.)

much more of the former. It seems possible, therefore, that it is the heterosexual effects of treatment which are mainly responsible for the reduction of homosexual behaviour outside treatment. Furthermore, it can be concluded that the only differences in the effects of the specific methods themselves which were related to clinical outcome were firstly changes in heterosexual attitudes which were greater though not significantly so in the desensitization group, and secondly the changed in heterosexual erections from beginning to end of each session, maximal in the aversion group. How does this study satisfy Yates's criteria and what conclusions can be drawn from it?

First, the two groups were moderately well matched for the variables chosen though there is a possibly important difference in categories 1 and 2 of previous heterosexual experience. (See Table 4.4.) It was impossible to pair more than eighteen of the thirty on these variables (age, EPI, and heterosexual experience) and it may have been better to have confined the matching to the previous heterosexual experience.

Three sources of information were used to measure the results of treatment, behavioural ratings, attitudes, and physiological responses. This would seem to be a reasonable combination. The validity of the behavioural ratings is of course uncertain and no assessment of the reliability of these complex ratings was made. (See Chapter 8.) However, it is reasonable to assume that whatever the reliability it would be similar in the two treatment groups.

Behavioural ratings and physiological measurements were carried out during each treatment session or between consecutive sessions. This provided additional valuable information about the pattern of change during treatment. The use of physiological measures in this way raises an important possibility, however. The repeated exposure to homosexual and heterosexual stimuli in the non-aversive control trials, and the measurements of erectile responses to them, may have contributed to the overall pattern and effect of treatment. If this was the case, and as the procedure was the same in each treatment group, its use would increase the similarity between both the pattern and the amount of change in the two groups.

The follow-up period was short but probably long enough to compare the initial effects of the two treatments. The most serious criticism of this study is that the treatment and the measures of change were carried out by the same person, thus introducing the possibility of experimenter bias. It would have been preferable to have had at least some of the measures and ratings made by another independent blind assessor. Unfortunately, for practical reasons, this was not possible. The absence of a no-treatment control (a point which would probably be criticized by Paul (1969)) is considered acceptable as the particular issue involved was the direct effects of two contrasting techniques rather than the therapeutic efficacy of either.

In drawing conclusions from the results the following questions may be posed: 1. Did each method produce similar results by means of the same mechanism (in other words, was the specific technique used irrelevant to the total outcome)? *or* 2. Did it so happen that the two techniques were producing a very similar amount of change by means of different mechanisms? *or* 3. Was each treatment operating through some final pathway of change with each specific method making a useful but not indispensable contribution? The answer to the first question is presumably in the negative because there were some differences in the effects of these treatments which were related both to outcome and to method. But the opposite alternative that they produce the same change through different mechanisms is also not tenable because there was so much similarity in the pattern as well as the degree of change, and it is difficult to avoid the conclusion that much of the change was produced in the same way in the two methods. It is suggested therefore that the third alternative is the most acceptable; that a proportion, possibly a major proportion of the clinical change that occurred was dependent on mechanisms other than those resulting from the specific methods themselves but that the specific methods also played a part.

Thus it remains a possibility that certain specific methods may be more suitable for some patients than others, even though the potential for change may be the same. The specific technique therefore would not seem to be irrelevant but one of the factors determining outcome, the others being relatively nonspecific. The mechanisms operating will be considered in detail in a later chapter.

SINGLE CASE STUDIES

The single case study approach has been well described by Barlow, Leitenberg, and Agras (1969) and Barlow, Leitenberg, Agras, Callahan, and Moore (1973). In the first report the study of two patients was described, one a heterosexual paedophiliac, the other a homosexual. The effect of covert sensitization (as described on p. 43), in which a 10-second sexually arousing image was followed by a 30-second nauseating image, was compared with an extinction procedure in which the 10-second sexually arousing image alone was involved, leaving the 30-second 'nauseous' interval blank.

Three measures of change were used: first a daily count by the subject of deviant sexual urges, secondly, the rating on a 0–4 scale of sexual interest in a series of sexually deviant scenes written on cards, and thirdly, skin conductance changes measured at the beginning of alternate sessions whilst imagining a series of six deviant scenes. These were recorded for a number of days in which no treatment was given; this provided a baseline period. This was followed by a series of 'acquisition' sessions in which the covert sensitization was involved, a series of 'extinction' sessions and a final series of 're-acquisition' sessions. The three measures were continued throughout.

The results shown in the frequency of urges and total score on the card sort, demonstrated a reduction in deviant interest during the 'acquisition' phase, a return of interest during the 'extinction' phase, and a further reduction with 're-acquisition'. Skin conductance changes were less convincing.

In the later study (Barlow *et al.* 1973) these workers went on to test the importance of therapeutic instructions in this type of procedure. They wondered if the combination of therapeutic instruction and the clear relevance of the acquisition procedure may have led to greater expectation of success in that phase compared with the rather negative extinction phase. Four further homosexual subjects were therefore given a 'baseline placebo' procedure in which they were told that homosexual scenes described alone during deep relaxation would be therapeutic. A rationale for this suggestion was offered (i.e. that relaxation would counteract the tense state usually produced during sexual arousal). This was followed by an 'acquisition with negative instruction' phase in which the subjects were told to expect an increase in sexual arousal response ('it is important that we replicate this effect'). Then came an extinction phase with positive therapeutic instructions ('it is time now to return to the therapeutic phase of treatment'), and finally a re-acquisition phase with therapeutic instructions ('it seems that in your case pairing the nausea and vomiting with a homosexual scene is helping you the most so we will continue with that').

The measure of change used in this study was penile erection in response to slides of nude males. By combining the mean erectile change in the first 2 sessions, the middle 2 sessions and last 2 sessions of each phase, the results showed that the acquisition condition (pairing of homosexual with noxious image) was more effective than the placebo treatment in spite of being combined with negative therapeutic instructions ($p < 0{\cdot}05$). In one case, however, the positive therapeutic instruction substantially increased the effect of the 'acquisition procedure' when used for the second time, suggesting that therapeutic instruction may sometimes interact with the method used to produce greater effect.

This is an ingenious approach but there are difficulties in controlling for variables such as therapeutic instruction which are not convincingly overcome in this study. To what extent did the subject's expectation match the instructions, for example? A further methodological flaw in these two reports is that the duration of the various phases varied from subject to subject. No explanation was given why this was so, except in one case, in which it was stated that the phase was prolonged 'to check on a trend'. Clearly it is essential that the duration of acquisition and extinction phases should be determined at the start and not according to how the patient responds.

Callahan and Leitenberg (1973) have compared the efficacy of covert sensitization and a punishment of erection procedure. They used a similar approach to Barlow *et al.* (1969) in treating six subjects including two exhibitionists, two homosexuals, one paedophiliac, and one transvestite. The two treatment procedures, both used in each case, were as follows. Covert sensitization was based on Cautela's (1967) procedure. In each session six sexually deviant scenes were imagined; four of these led simply to an imagined aversive consequence, and in two the subject could escape from the aversive consequence by imagining a normal heterosexual scene. The aversion procedure was similar to that described by Bancroft (1969). Five slides of deviant sexual interest were shown in each session and the subject asked to fantasize appropriately. Electric shocks were given whenever penile volume exceeded a level of 15 per cent of a previously measured full erection. Thus the criterion for shock varied between subjects and there was no limit to the number of shocks administered, in contrast to Bancroft's procedure.

Two types of measure of change were used: penile erection to normal and deviant slides, at the beginning of each session (before shock electrodes were attached) and self reporting of frequency of sexual urges and masturbation.

The two treatments were each given in blocks of sessions either 6 or 10 in number. In each case a baseline for each measure was established before the first treatment was given. Three of the patients received covert sensitization first, the rest starting with the aversive procedure. However, more blocks of covert sensitization sessions than aversive sessions were involved.

There was no apparent difference in the procedures in their suppression of erections to deviant stimuli. However, suppression of self reported sexual urges and fantasies did appear to be greater with covert sensitization, although the data does not permit any definite conclusions on this point. Within these limits, covert sensitization appeared to be more effective than punishment of erections.

However, this report underlined some of the difficulties in interpreting the results of single case studies of this type. The changes in such measures during treatment may well follow a pattern which is determined by factors other than the specific treatment procedure. In Bancroft's study (1970*d*) (see above) the pattern of change was similar in each type of treatment, though such patterns are difficult to demonstrate with certainty. If such patterns do occur, however, the apparent effect of a particular method may depend on at what stage in the course of treatment it is used. This factor can be excluded in a balanced design either by using a group rather than a single case study, or by using sufficiently short periods of treatment with a sufficiently long over-all duration to balance for quadratic effects. Such a procedure would create its own problems in terms of therapeutic acceptability. More information could have been obtained from this study, if the treatments had been administered in a more systematic way in the group of six patients.

A similar single case cross-over design was used in the studies investigating 'fading' (Barlow and Agras 1971) and exposure to strong heterosexual stimuli (Herman *et al.* 1971). Their results have been repeated with other subjects (Barlow—personal communication).

'CROSS-OVER' DESIGN

An interesting study involving the 'cross-over' principle has recently been carried out by Rooth and Marks (1974). They treated twelve exhibitionists using three treatment techniques. Each subject received all three treatments, with the order of treatment according to a balanced design. This represents a combination of group and single case study methodology. The three treatments were: electric aversion, 'self-regulation', and relaxation. The complete course was given on an inpatient basis over a 3-week period, each technique involving 8 sessions of approximately 45 minutes duration during 1 week of treatment.

The details of the methods are as follows: in the aversion technique electric shocks were associated with both fantasies of exposing (as in the punishment of fantasy procedure; see p. 39) and the simulation of exposing behaviour in which the subject 'exposed' in front of a mirror whilst verbalizing an actual exposing situation. At some stage during this simulated exposure a shock would be given.

The self regulation procedure was based on the principle of an impulse–response chain in which the 'exposing' response would tend to occur as a predictable consequence of a chain of impulses and events. By intervening with an alternative response sufficiently early in the chain, the deviant behaviour might be avoided. This technique, therefore, aimed at clarifying the early stages of the chain and practising a repertoire of alternative responses. These were both overt (e.g. removing oneself from the situation or reading a newspaper) or covert (e.g. carrying out mental arithmetic). The relaxation procedure involved a combination of muscular relaxation (Jacobson 1964) and the principles of autogenic training with concentration on heaviness and warmth (Schultz and Luthe 1959). In all three techniques the therapist would answer any questions or comments by the subject in a way that he considered to be therapeutic.

When the first six subjects had completed treatment a preliminary look at the results suggested very little difference between the methods. For the remaining six subjects, therefore, the three procedures were 'intensified'. In each case the subject was asked to carry out each day 2 sessions on his own, in addition to the therapist's session. With the aversion technique this included 1 session of self shocking of deviant fantasies and one session of going out into tempting situations for 1 hour and self shocking when an urge to expose occurred. In the self regulation method one session involved covert sensitization (without a therapist, but otherwise similar to the technique described on p. 43) and 1 hour of going out into tempting situations and practising the self regulation procedure learnt with the therapist. With the relaxation method 1 session involved relaxing on one's own and the other practising relaxation whilst in the tempting situation.

For measure of change a series of self ratings were evolved. These included rating ten deviant situations on a 200–4 scale for interest, rating scales 1–7 for the assessed risk of exposing, the time thinking about exposing and pleasure in exposing, and semantic differential scales (Marks and Sartorius 1968) for the concept 'how I feel about exposing'.

The results showed that there was no difference between the first six and second six patients on any of these variables. The only variables to show significant change from the beginning to end of the whole course of treatment were the ratings of interest in exposing situations ($p < 0{\cdot}01$), the assessed risk of exposing ($p < 0{\cdot}01$) and ratings of pleasure in exposing ($p < 0{\cdot}01$). Of these three variables only one, 'pleasure in exposing' showed a significant difference between treatments, with aversion producing significantly more change than either of the other two methods ($p < 0{\cdot}05$ in each case).

Further analysis showed that aversion was more effective than both of the other methods on two other variables (sexual evaluation and time thinking about exposing) and self regulation was more effective than relaxation on one variable (time thinking). The results suggested that self regulation was more effective when it followed aversion.

Aversion therefore appeared to be more effective than self regulation though the differences were not marked. If each treatment had been given for longer the differences may have been greater. It is also possible that if these treatments had been given quite separately to three similar groups of patients the differences would have been much greater. In that case, not only would each method have had longer to show its worth but any interaction between the patients expectations of success and the method used would not be confounded. It may be, for example, that if a subject has expectations of success from aversion and regards the other two procedures as complementary to aversion, the effect of these subjects' expectations will be spread over the course of treatment as a whole, or at least during that part of the treatment when maximum change most often occurs. There was a tendency in the study for most change to occur in the first week, regardless of treatment, though the differences between the weeks did not reach significance. In Bancroft's study (1970*d*) maximum change occurred in the first half of treatment.

5 *The Effects of Treatment, Predicted and Observed*

NEGATIVE EFFECTS

In the early days of modern behavioural modification we were repeatedly warned of the dangers of failing to apply learning theory principles. In 1969 Eysenck wrote the following in relation to aversion therapy.

Punishment may be effective provided certain conditions are fulfilled. The conditions are quite strict, and relate to such technical matters as stimulus–response asynchronism; when they are disregarded as unfortunately they usually have been in the past by practitioners ignorant of the principles of conditioning and learning theory—results may easily lead to worsening rather than improvement.

Franks in 1963 stated that to be optimally effective aversion therapy must be planned and executed in accordance with known principles of conditioning.

If one looks at the experimental literature of aversive conditioning, however, the findings are exceedingly complex and frequently contradictory. The effects of negative reinforcements are in general much less predictable than the effects of positive reinforcements and as Estes (1969) has pointed out, there has been little clarification of the effects of aversive stimuli in recent years in spite of a substantial increase in the amount of research using such stimuli. The complexity of the problem has been summarized by Bandura (1969):

the degree of control exerted by punishment is largely a function of the intensity, duration and distribution of aversive consequences, their temporal relations to the behaviour to be modified, the strength with which punished responses are concurrently reinforced, the availability of alternative modes of behaviour for securing rewards, the level of instigation to perform the negatively sanctioned behaviour and the psychological characteristics of punishing agents.

Nevertheless, there are three principle effects of aversive stimulation reported in the experimental literature which have been considered relevant to behaviour modification. These are classical conditioning of anxiety or the conditioned emotional response (CER), suppression of a punished response, and acquisition of an avoidance response. It is not the purpose of this chapter to review the relevant experimental literature. This has already been done satisfactorily by Church (1963), Solomon (1964), Azrin and Holz (1966). Bancroft (1966) and Rachman and Teasdale (1969) have considered the literature specifically in relation to aversion therapy and Bandura (1970) provides an over-all review which for our present purposes is the most balanced and useful so far available.

There are important problems in extrapolating from animal experiments to the human clinical situation which are all too often overlooked. In this chapter some human experiments which are of direct relevance to aversion therapy will be briefly reviewed. In addition, evidence arising from the study of aversion therapy itself will be considered. In this way the relevance to behaviour modification of these three experimental effects will be critically assessed. Two other basic concepts derived from the experimental literature, generalization and intermittent reinforcement, will also be considered in relation to behaviour modification techniques.

Classical conditioning of anxiety

This effect follows the association of a previously neutral stimulus (the conditioned stimulus or CS) with a noxious stimulus (the unconditioned stimulus (UCS)). If this association is repeated in the correct order (i.e. CS–UCS) with a suitable time interval between the CS and UCS (optimal interval being 0·5 seconds) some portion of the response to the noxious stimulus (the unconditioned response or UCR) will eventually be elicited by the neutral conditioned stimulus alone. This fractional response is then called a conditioned response or CR. Thus, if the sequence CS–UCS–UCR is repeated enough times in an appropriate manner, the sequence CS–CR will eventually occur when CR will be similar to UCR.

The response to a noxious stimulus is a combination of subjective fear, physiological changes associated with fear, any physiological changes specific to that particular stimulus (i.e. nausea and vomiting produced by an emetic) and usually some overt escape or other coping response. It is, however, the first two types of response which constitute what is normally called conditioned emotional response (CER) or conditioned anxiety.

The simplest form of the classical conditioning procedure in aversion therapy occurs when a 'neutral' (or rather positive) external stimulus is associated with a noxious stimulus (e.g. the pairing of a picture of an attractive sexual object with a shock). The predicted effect would be that after such a procedure the previously 'positive' stimulus elicits an unpleasant CER. This may be sufficient to eliminate the attractiveness of that stimulus and hence the unwanted behaviour associated with it.

The conditioned emotional response may be established in other situations, however. In a punishment procedure, for example, where the noxious stimulus follows not a stimulus but a particular response, the CER may still be conditioned to the stimuli preceding the punished response and to various kinaesthetic and proprioceptive stimuli produced by the response. This CER to these external and internal stimuli, it is presumed, when elicited outside the treatment situation, will then serve to neutralize any 'positive' consequences of the 'treated' response. The behaviour is therefore no longer reinforced or maintained and is hence 'extinguished'. Alternatively another response may be learnt which avoids a noxious stimulus, and hence the noxious CER, and which is itself incompatible with the 'treated' response. In other words an avoidance response is learnt which is reinforced and maintained by the fact that it either avoids or reduces the duration of the CER associated with the punished response. This is the 'two-factor theory' explanation of avoidance learning. Thus it can be seen that in some theoretical models the classically conditioned emotional response or CER is an integral part of the process of suppressing a response or learning an avoidance response.

There are a number of major difficulties in applying the classical conditioning model to behaviour modification. First, in the experimental situation, classical conditioning is typically short-lived and has to be periodically reinforced by re-presentation of the unconditioned stimulus if extinction is to be avoided. If such conditioning occurs during the course of aversion therapy, therefore, it must be associated with some other mechanism if it is to contribute in a long-lasting way to the effects of treatment. It is for the same reason that the original 'two-factor theory' of avoidance learning was unsatisfactory as it did not explain how the CER, which was an integral part of the postulated mechanism was itself maintained without reinforcement. (See D'Amato (1970) for a recent discussion of these theoretical issues.)

The further major difficulty is the effect that awareness has on classical conditioning in human subjects. This has been well reviewed by Rachman and Teasdale (1969) and Bandura (1969). With very few exceptions the evidence suggests that awareness of the CS–UCS relationship increases the likelihood of a conditioned response, a form of conditioning which is sometimes called 'pseudo conditioning' because with such awareness it can occur so readily and does not follow the 'laws of classical conditioning'. More important however is the equally consistent finding that awareness that the UCS (or shock) is no longer going to occur results in a rapid if not immediate 'extinction' of the 'pseudo-conditioned' response. In the aversion therapy situation it is extremely difficult to avoid such awareness and usually no attempt is made to do so.

However, an important difference between aversion therapy and human aversive conditioning experiments is the far greater number of aversive trials involved in the former, with many more conditioning sessions. It is difficult enough to get human volunteers to accept electric shocks in the experimental situation but far more difficult if large numbers over many sessions are involved.

A recent experiment which to a large extent gets round this difficulty and which was specifically designed to assess the role of classical conditioning in aversion therapy was reported by

Hallam (1971). Fourteen male volunteers were shown two slides of abstract designs, one of which was associated with shock. Skin conductance, heart rate, and respiratory rate changes were recorded. When the results of one such session were analysed it was found that a conditioned GSR developed to the slide associated with shock and discriminated between the two slides. This conditioned response extinguished rapidly when the threat of shock was removed. The heart rate and the respiratory changes did not show any clearcut conditioning pattern. This part of the experiment therefore confirmed the findings in most earlier studies. The second part of the experiment, however, was more crucial. In this, five of the original subjects agreed to undergo a further 9 sessions. This meant that they received a total of 205 shocks. This is a situation much closer to aversion therapy than any other similar experiment. In addition, these subjects were tested without the use of shock or shock electrodes 1 month and 6 months after the main experiment ended.

In this second part of the experiment the ability to discriminate reinforced and nonreinforced slides by means of the GSR declined and was lost by the tenth session. The amplitude of GSR also showed a significant decrease as 'treatment' continued. Thus any evidence of conditioned GSR disappeared with continued trials which is of course quite contrary to the expectations of the classical conditioning model.

Heart rate changes in the form of a decrease, and increased shallowness of respiration did become more marked as more sessions were given, significantly so in the former case. At follow-up the heart rate change significantly discriminated between the two slides after 1 month but not after 6 months. These changes at 1 month, however, 'assessed under favourable circumstances (in the same experimental room) were very small in size (change of 2 to 4 beats per minute) and proved very sensitive to experimental conditions' (Hallam 1971).

Therefore, not only was there little evidence of a significant conditioned emotional response, but there was evidence of a reduction in autonomic arousal as the aversive sessions continued. This study in addition underlines the complexity of using autonomic physiological changes as indicators of subjective anxiety or conditioned emotional response and reminds us that it is not justifiable to generalize from one autonomic response to another. It also illustrates how methodologically difficult it is to demonstrate the presence or absence of a classically conditioned CER. It is not surprising that the literature of aversion therapy contains so little satisfactory evidence on this point.

However, following on this experiment, Hallam, Rachman, and Falkowski (1972) carried out a further study involving actual aversion therapy. This was specifically designed to test the hypothesis that after aversion therapy subjects display conditioned heart rate and galvanic skin responses to deviant stimuli as well as reporting subjective anxiety towards such stimuli. In this study ten alcoholic patients were given electric aversion therapy in which, whilst looking at slides of drinking scenes, they were asked to imagine themselves drinking in those situations. Shocks were given when the fantasy was signalled. The group was compared with a control group of eight alcoholics who received other forms of treatment (e.g. group therapy, AA meetings). Both groups were given identical assessment sessions before and after treatment in which the slides and fantasies used in the aversion method were involved, together with some neutral slides. Attitudes to these slides were measured, using semantic differential, and physiological responses (heart rate and skin conductance) to both fantasies and slides were recorded.

There were no significant differences between the groups on any of these measures except that the semantic differential ratings of taste became significantly more distasteful following aversion therapy. This 'distaste' however was not related to clinical outcome. Although recovery of skin conductance level after the slides took longer following the drinking slides than following the neutral slides, and reduction in heart rate during slide presentation was less during the drinking slides, this result applied to both treatment groups.

When the successes (six out of ten aversion cases and two out of eight controls) were compared with the failures at 4 months follow-up there was a significant difference in the degree of adaptation of heart rate response to the drinking slides, the successful group showing less adaptation or even an increase in response. This again was irrespective of treatment.

In both these experiments, therefore, there was a failure to demonstrate convincing physiological evidence of classically conditioned anxiety. Such reliance on peripheral physiological responses as evidence of such conditioning has been criticized by Rescorla and Solomon (1967) in their attempt to defend the role of classical conditioning in avoidance learning. They have suggested that aversive conditioning may alter 'common central states' without necessarily altering peripheral states. D'Amato (1970) in attempting to retain objectivity prefers to call such alterations of central state 'fractional anticipatory fear responses'. Either way it is difficult to see how we can avoid relying on subjective reports from human subjects for evidence of such conditioning. In these two studies by Hallam and his colleagues the only measure of subjective experience, the semantic differential, also failed to provide evidence of an effect which was related to both the aversive procedure and successful clinical outcome.

These studies, nevertheless, provide the only systematic investigation of classical conditioned anxiety in aversion therapy of any type. For the rest of the literature, including that dealing with sexual disorders, we are confined to anecdotal or incomplete evidence. However, there is consistency between these various bits of evidence and it is therefore worth looking at them briefly.

In the case of chemical aversion, it has been assumed by most workers that the response to be conditioned is nausea and vomiting rather than anxiety. Although such methods are badly suited for producing the optimum classical conditioning procedure, their use in treating alcoholism has led to some reports of an apparent conditioned aversion, whereby following treatment the sight or taste of alcohol may induce nausea or even vomiting (e.g. Hammersley 1957). The proportion of cases showing such effects has not been reported, however, nor has any association between such effects and clinical improvement been demonstrated.

In the treatment of sexual problems the reporting of nausea as a conditioned response to the deviant stimulus after chemical aversion is rare. Pearce (1963), in particular, comments that whilst his transvestites, following chemical aversion, sometimes reported disgust in association with cross-dressing or fantasies, none of them reported nausea. On the other hand, Hallam *et al.* (1972), describing the subjective experience of alcoholics following electric aversion, reported four out of six patients in whom the smell or taste of alcohol had altered in an unpleasant way. Three of them said it was now repulsive and the fourth that the taste and smell had become bitter. Marks and Gelder (1967) found that fetishists and transvestites most commonly reported lack of interest rather than negative feelings about the deviant stimuli after successful aversion treatment.

Thus it seems that any subjective experience following aversive conditioning depends as much on the nature of the behaviour being modified as on the nature of the noxious stimulus. This raises an important theoretical issue: is aversion therapy more likely to be successful if the noxious stimulus is 'appropriate' to the behaviour in question? Seligman and Hager (1972) have questioned the assumption of equipotentiality of association between various types of stimuli and response and suggest the concept of 'preparedness', in which the conditioning of certain types of response is considered more likely when associated with certain types of stimulus. They cite in particular the work of Garcia and Koelling (1966) with rats, in which nausea induced by radiation sickness was paired with both a taste and an audio-visual stimulus. Only the taste became aversive. Similarly when these two stimuli were paired with electric shock only the audio-visual stimulus became aversive. Wilson and Davison (1968) related this work specifically to aversion therapy but as yet we await relevant evidence from the treatment situation.

A type of noxious stimulus which fortunately has been used to a very limited extent, and again only with alcoholics, is scoline-induced apnoea (Campbell, Sanderson, and Laverty 1964). The factor which distinguished this particular method from other aversive procedures is not just that complete paralysis of respiration is an exceedingly unpleasant experience, but in this case it was quite unexpected by the patients. The fact that several of these patients did subsequently feel anxious in the treatment situation is not surprising, and the report suggests that the conditioning was far from specific to the alcohol, but was associated with the total situation including the therapist.

It is conceivable that if an electric shock of equivalent unpleasantness and given with similar surprise was used, conditioned anxiety would result in at least some patients. This is a theoretical point, however, as such a procedure would not be justifiable whatever the consequences.

MacCulloch, Feldman, and Pinshoff (1966) reported heart rate changes in two homosexuals treated with an anticipatory avoidance method involving electric shock: one was a successful outcome, one a failure. The successful case did show some evidence of conditioned heart rate change but the pattern, as is often the case with this variable, was complex and difficult to interpret. Cardiac acceleration was associated with the onset of the deviant stimulus but was followed by deceleration in spite of continuation of the stimulus.

In the author's experience of sixty cases of aversion therapy, only one has shown conditioned anxiety which has generalized outside treatment. This case is of considerable interest and will be described in some detail. The patient was a 37-year-old highly intelligent scientist who had a somewhat anxious and mildly obsessional personality (Bancroft 1969, patient C). This man's subjective anxiety ratings during treatment are shown in the top half of Fig. 5.1. It will be seen that not only did anxiety during aversive trials mount as the number of treatment sessions increased but so it did also in the non-aversive trials in which the patient, disconnected from the shock electrodes, knew he was not to receive a shock. By the eighth session of treatment he was finding himself increasingly tense before the session started. Following the eleventh session he found himself looking at an attractive man with his usual interest but with an uncomfortable feeling in his stomach and great uneasiness. By the fourteenth session he was consistently feeling a twinge of discomfort when seeing attractive men. The degree of discomfort and anxiety during the actual session was becoming extreme, tension and headaches remaining with him for the rest of the day. By the twenty-first session he was beginning to adapt to this phobic response. 'Most men don't interest me now.' Anxiety was less frequent, a feeling of indifference prevailing.

Outside treatment it was noticeable that the anxiety was associated with the awareness of sexual attraction. By rendering the stimuli no longer attractive the anxiety was avoided. Considerable anxiety generalized to the treatment situation, however, and in the later stages of treatment he would feel mounting anxiety on approaching the hospital. This continued for several

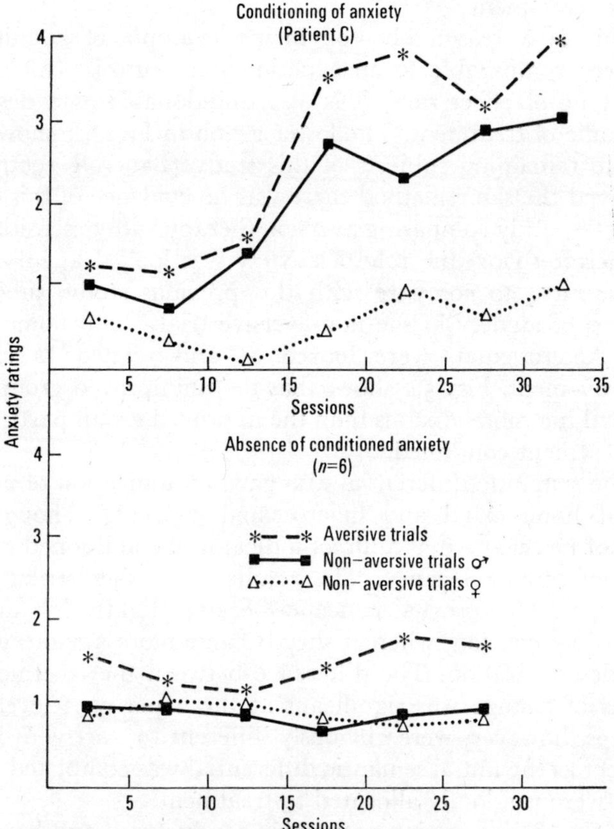

Fig. 5.1. This compares the anxiety ratings during the course of treatment in one patient who showed evidence of conditioned anxiety (top graph) with those of the rest of the group none of whom showed this effect. Each score is the mean rating for 5 consecutive sessions. For details, see text.

months after stopping aversion therapy. This phobic pattern remained for approximately 2 years. During that time there were a number of occasions when a homosexual approach was made to him. These incidents would invariably produce acute and severe anxiety forcing him to leave the situation at once. During this time he was unable to overcome his anxiety towards women and eventually as the homosexual phobia began to wane some evidence of homosexual interest unaccompanied by anxiety began to return although never as strong as before treatment.

This is a reasonably convincing example of conditioned anxiety comparable to an experimental neurosis. Not only is this type of effect rare, it is also questionable as a desirable outcome of treatment. The lower graph in Fig. 5.1 shows that in the remaining subjects of this study (Bancroft 1969) who received the same method there was no evidence of this effect.

In the study comparing aversion therapy with desensitization (Bancroft 1970*c*) the role of anxiety was looked at in various ways. First, to compare with this previous study, subjective ratings of anxiety in the non-aversive trials, both homosexual and heterosexual, were looked at and related to clinical improvement. Fig. 5.2 shows that the unimproved group were if anything more anxious than the improved group particularly as treatment continued.

The semantic differential also gave an indication of anxiety about homosexual and heterosexual concepts. Though this cannot be regarded as a direct indicator of conditioned anxiety it is of some relevance. The results are rather striking (see Fig. 5.3). Homosexual concepts became slightly less anxious following aversion, whereas they became more anxious following desensitization. The difference between the treatments in terms of change was significant at the 2 per cent level. The groups, however, were obviously different to start with in this respect as the initial semantic differential was completed before they were randomly allocated to treatment.

In six of the aversion group skin conductance and heart rate were monitored during the course of treatment. Skin conductance levels were then looked at in non-aversive trials. The 30 seconds preceding the first non-aversive homosexual trial was taken as a baseline and compared with the first 30 seconds of the homosexual trial and the first 30 seconds of the heterosexual trial immediately following it. If conditioning of the anxiety to the homosexual stimuli was to occur one would expect these three measures to change differentially as treatment proceeded with levels in the homosexual trials habituating less or even increasing. In fact, as shown in Fig. 5.4, all three changed in a similar fashion. The conductance levels correlated significantly with the subjective ratings of anxiety during these

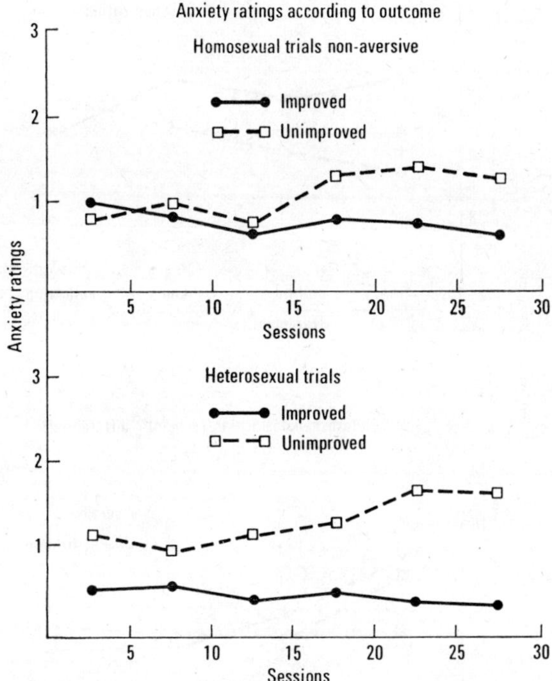

FIG. 5.2. Patients receiving aversion (Bancroft 1970*d*) were divided into two groups, improved ($n = 5$) and unimproved ($n = 7$), according to the amount of behavioural change following treatment. This graph shows the mean anxiety ratings (for 5 consecutive sessions) for the two outcome groups in the homosexual non-aversive trials (top graph) and the heterosexual trials (bottom graph). The unimproved group became slightly though not significantly more anxious as treatment continued.

trials ($r = 0{\cdot}52$). This pattern of decreasing skin conductance as treatment proceeds is similar to that reported by Hallam (1971) in his experimental study. The heart rate was sampled less often but it was possible to compare the mean rates for these same time intervals in the first, tenth, and fifteenth sessions. (See Fig. 5·5.) Once again, there was a decrease in heart rate similar in the three variables, as treatment continued.

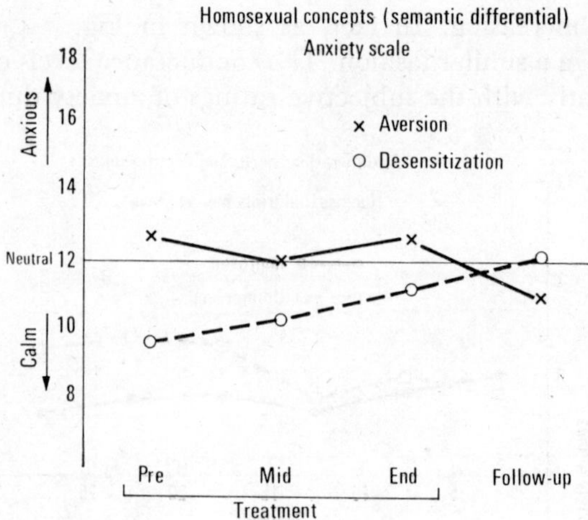

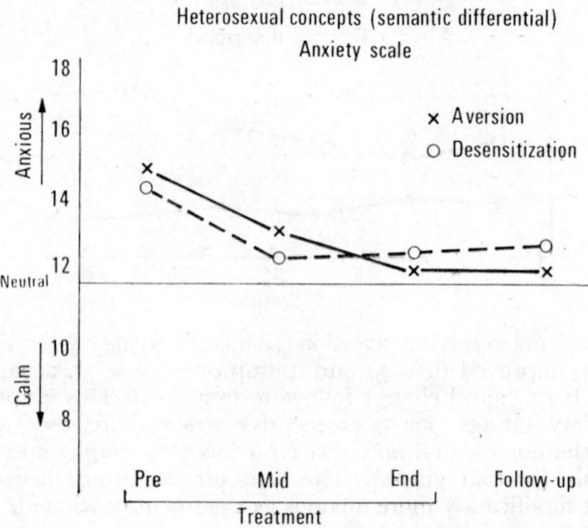

FIG. 5.3. These graphs show the mean scores for the anxiety ratings on the semantic differential for each treatment group. Concepts rated for anxiety are homosexual (top graph) and heterosexual (lower graph). A score of 12 is neutral, greater than 12 more anxious, less than 12 more calm. The greater initial anxiety to homosexual concepts in the aversion group cannot be explained as a result of the method as those ratings were made before the method was allocated.

In considering conditioned anxiety let us finally look at anecdotal evidence of phobic responses outside treatment. Five patients in this comparative study (Bancroft 1970*c*) did report such effects but they were always transitory, occurring at most on three or four occasions. Examples of these reactions were as

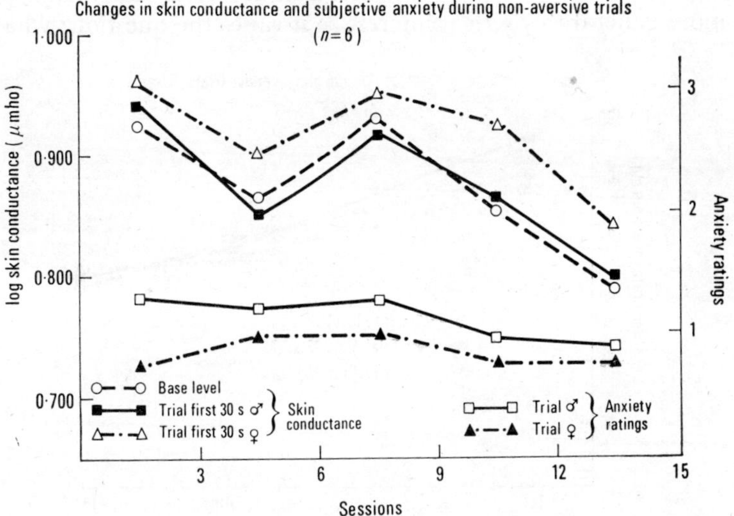

FIG. 5.4. The upper part of the graph shows mean skin conductance levels for the following time periods; 30 s preceding the non-aversive homosexual trial (base level), the first 30 s of the non-aversive homosexual trial, and the first 30 s of the first heterosexual trial. Scores shown are means of 3 consecutive sessions. The lower graph shows anxiety self ratings for the same homosexual and heterosexual trials.

follows: seeing pictures of naked men in the shop window and feeling a slight fear; finding it 'distinctly unpleasant to contemplate anything homosexual' after a particularly anxious treatment session; experiencing a slight revulsion on seeing certain men who reminded him of pictures used in the treatment; experiencing 'distinct, distasteful, unpleasant feelings' more like depression than anxiety on seeing attractive males on television. Three of these five patients were in the improved group. In addition to these reports, however, two of the desensitization group reported comparable experiences: in one, intense and unusual anxiety when a homosexual approach was made; in the other, anxiety whenever homosexual thoughts intruded into masturbation fantasies. These reactions might have been considered as conditioned anxiety if aversion therapy had been involved.

It therefore appears that conditioned anxiety, if it occurs at all, is usually transient and not clearly related to clinical improvement. The rare exception that has been described is of more general theoretical interest as it raises the question: what

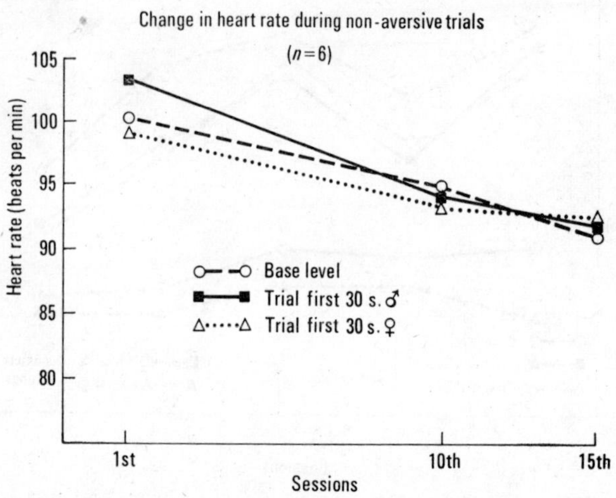

Fig. 5.5. In the same subjects involved in Fig. 5.4 heart rate was monitored during the first, tenth, and fifteenth session. The mean rates for the same 3 time periods in each session are shown. For further details, see text.

are the individual characteristics that result in the production of such experimental phobias and what relevance do they have to phobic conditions in general?

It is convenient at this point to briefly consider other aspects of anxiety in aversion therapy. Whether 'conditioned anxiety' occurs or not, is anxiety during treatment a pre-requisite for a successful outcome? Evidence from animal experiments suggests that any response which was originally motivated by anxiety or, in other words, associated with anxiety reduction during its acquisition, would be facilitated rather than suppressed by aversive (anxiety-provoking) stimuli. Beech (1960) suggested that this might be the case in treating writer's cramp with aversion therapy, and Eysenck and Rachman (1965) suggested that highly anxious patients might respond badly to aversion. The available evidence does support these suggestions.

Schmidt, Castell, and Brown (1965) reported higher anxiety scores on the Taylor manifest anxiety scale in the unimproved group than in those who improved following aversion. Marks *et al.* (1970) found that anxiety about self as measured by the semantic differential was negatively correlated with successful outcome. Solyom and Miller (1965) measured their six patients treated with electric aversion therapy on the IPAT anxiety scale. All were highly anxious and all did badly.

In the author's comparative study (Bancroft 1970*c*) those showing high anxiety about 'myself' on the semantic differential at the start of treatment showed less behaviour change following aversion (correlation between anxiety ratings and homosexual and heterosexual behaviour change both reached significance; hetero, $r = -0{\cdot}56$, $p < 0{\cdot}05$; homo $r = -0{\cdot}57$, $p < 0{\cdot}05$). In the desensitization group the correlations were not significant but were in the opposite direction; (hetero $r = +0{\cdot}20$, homo, $r = +0{\cdot}25$). These findings therefore suggest that people who are generally anxious do less well with aversion. They do not indicate, however, whether high anxiety during the session is a good or bad thing.

Some patients may be highly anxious before treatment starts and yet be relatively free from anxiety during the treatment sessions. One of the patients reported by Bancroft (1969, case E) showed this contrast dramatically. He was intensely anxious about his sexual problems and the prospect of aversion therapy before treatment started. During treatment, however, he appeared calm and consistently rated zero for anxiety.

In the comparative study (Bancroft 1970*c*), ratings for anxiety (on a 0–4 scale) were given for each aversive trial. The mean score for the whole aversion group for all sessions was 1·5. For the five improved cases the mean was 1·31; for the remainder 1·65. In both groups, however, the individual mean scores varied considerably. Two of the improved patients rated zero throughout treatment; the other three were quite anxious. This mean anxiety rating, although it correlated significantly with anxiety score for 'myself' at the start of treatment did not correlate with behavioural change scores. When these results are added to those of the earlier study (Bancroft 1969) they provide no evidence that anxiety during the sessions is related to outcome.

Five patients in the comparative study and one in the earlier study (Bancroft 1969, case E) reported general anxiety between sessions. In one, this took the form of attacks of severe sweating and anxiety in church or restaurants. He reported five attacks during the course of treatment and had only experienced one such attack previously. He reported none during the follow-up period. This man consistently rated zero for anxiety during aversive trials. Two others reported well circumscribed attacks of anxiety (not related to obvious homosexual stimuli) whereas in the other three there was a general heightening of pervasive anxiety lasting for days at a time. It is possibly relevant that five of these six did well.

The relationship of anxiety to outcome is therefore far from simple and may only become comprehensible when the cause of the anxiety is taken into account. There may be many factors in addition to the pain of the electric shock operating in this respect.

Suppression of the punished response

Punishment, as used here, is defined as the application of an aversive stimulus contingent upon a particular response. The more widely used definition, that of Azrin and Holz (1966), requires the future probability of the occurrence of that response to be reduced by the aversive stimulus. In other words the procedure is only called punishment if it is effective. For our purposes it is necessary to consider punishment procedures that may be ineffective.

The aversive component of punishment may involve the application of a noxious stimulus or the withdrawal of a rewarding stimulus (i.e. 'time out' from positive reinforcement). It is the first type that concerns us here, and apart from aversion therapy itself, relevant studies involving human subjects have been few. They include experimental studies with normal children in which the noxious stimulus is symbolic (e.g. a sharp rebuke, as in Aronfreed and Reber 1965) or a loud unpleasant noise (Walters and Demkow 1963), and 'analogue' studies with adult volunteers (e.g. the punishment of smoking behaviour with electric shock; (Powell and Azrin 1968)). There are also a number of case reports of the use of punishment in controlling the behaviour of autistic or otherwise severely disturbed children (e.g. Birnbrauer 1968; Lovaas and Simmons 1969). These various studies have been reviewed by Bandura (1969) and Johnston (1972). Unfortunately they have limited relevance to aversion therapy of sexual problems, particularly those studies involving children. The child's perception of the aversive situation must differ in important ways, either because he is not aware of being in an experiment (e.g. Walters and Demkow 1963), or because the aversive procedure is forced upon him in an environment over which the therapist has more or less complete control (e.g. Lovaas and Simmons 1969). Nevertheless it is worth noting that in the experimental studies with normal children, punishment appeared to be more effective when given earlier rather than later in the sequence. With the control of smoking in volunteer adults the aversive procedure was more effective as the strength of the aversive stimulus increased, though the effect did not generalize and led to withdrawal from the experiment and early return of the behaviour to pre-treatment levels. With the disturbed children the punishment was effective and was associated with other desirable changes in behaviour but again did not generalize. In none of these studies was it possible to comment on long-term effects.

In the aversion therapy of sexual disorders three types of response have been involved in the punishment procedure; overt behaviour (e.g. the cross-dressing of transvestites), fantasy, and erections. These represent three different classes of response, the first motor, the second a 'thinking' response, and the third an autonomic response.

In the case of suppression of motor behaviour there is no relevant and systematically collected data to discuss. The suppression of erection and fantasy, however, do justify further consideration.

The punishment of erection procedure, in which the noxious stimulus is made contingent upon the erectile response to a deviant stimulus, would appear to be a good punishment model, as one can punish a precise response promptly. Various levels of erection as the response to be punished can be used although the author's experience has been mostly with low levels, representing changes of which the subject is only just aware. The only other workers who have reported using this method are Callahan and Leitenberg (1973) who used a higher level, representing approximately 15 per cent of a full erection, as the response to be punished.

The predicted effect is a gradual suppression of erectile responses to deviant stimuli, generalizing outside treatment so

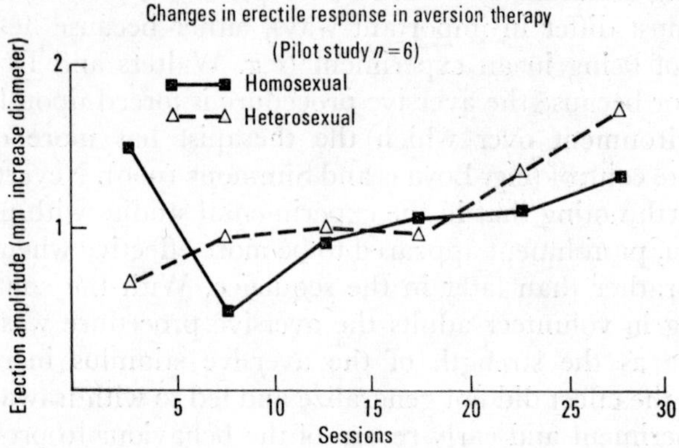

FIG. 5.6. This graph shows the change in erections during the course of a punishment of erection procedure (Bancroft 1969). Mean scores for 5 consecutive sessions are given. There was an initial suppression of punished erections (i.e. to homosexual stimuli) with later recovery as treatment continued. This recovery was associated with an increase in erection to heterosexual stimuli.

that a state of erectile impotence or at least an inability to get erections to deviant stimuli ensues. So far, in only one patient has anything comparable to this predicted effect been observed. (Bancroft 1969, patient A). During the treatment of this man there was a period of 3 weeks when in the initial stages of any homosexual contact he would produce an erection but lose it as soon as the homosexual act started. This was not associated with any anxiety or revulsion. During this time he was continuing to have frequent and satisfactory intercourse with his wife. He eventually 'broke through' this 'conditioned impotence' by getting his homosexual partner to relate a heterosexual situation to him. However, the rest of the patients in that study showed initial suppression followed by later recovery of homosexual erections whilst treatment continued. (This pattern of recovery during relatively mild punishment has been well described in animal experiments (Azrin and Holz 1966).) This recovery was also associated with an increase in heterosexual erections (see Fig. 5.6). This was satisfactory as far as achieving heterosexual change was concerned but it was not achieving the treatment goals of homosexual change. When aversion was compared with desensitization (Bancroft 1970*d*), an attempt was made to exploit this heterosexual facilitation

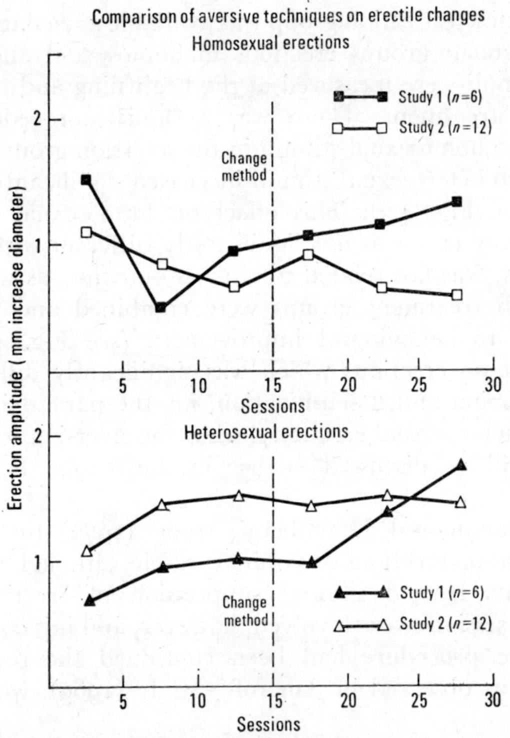

Fig. 5.7. Changes in erections during aversion are compared in two studies (Bancroft 1969; 1970*d*). The scores shown are means for 5 consecutive sessions. The change in method at session 15 applies to study 2; punishment of erection gave way to punishment of fantasy. For further details see text.

effect, whilst at the same time avoiding the homosexual 'recovery' phase, by changing the aversive procedure halfway through the course of treatment. This predicted effect was observed although it was by no means certain that it resulted from the change in procedure. Fig. 5.7 shows a comparison of erectile changes in these two studies, study 2 representing the aversion group of the comparative study. At the mid-point in study 2 in order to avoid the recovery phase, shock was made contingent upon fantasy rather than erection. Although this recovery did not take place the reduction in homosexual erections in study 2 did not reach statistical significance. The heterosexual responses did increase significantly although they did not show the late increases seen in study 1. In the second study the desensitization group was available as a control and in both treatment groups erections to homosexual and heterosexual stimuli were measured at the beginning and end of the course of treatment. There was a significant reduction in erections to homosexual stimuli in the aversion group, whereas erections to heterosexual stimuli increased significantly in both groups (see Fig. 4.3). This effect on homosexual erections, which in any case was not significantly different with the two treatments, was not related to clinical outcome, as was shown when both treatment groups were combined and redivided according to behavioural improvement (see Fig. 4.7). The only effect on erections which was significantly different between aversion and desensitization, i.e. the paradoxical facilitation of heterosexual erection during the aversion session (see p. 74), will be discussed further in the second half of this chapter.

In Callahan and Leitenberg's study (1973) the effect of punishment on erections was quite variable, although two of the six patients treated showed suppression of erections. Few treatment sessions were involved, however, and it is conceivable that if the procedure had been continued the recovery of erections, as observed in Bancroft's study (1969), would have occurred.

Further work is needed to untangle the effects of punishment of erections as both their facilitation and suppression may result and as yet the reasons for one rather than the other are not clear.

The suppression of punished fantasies was first reported by McGuire and Vallance (1964). Systematic investigation of this effect has been carried out by Marks and Gelder (1969), Marks *et al.* (1970) and Bancroft (1970*c*). In this work, suppression of fantasies has been arbitrarily defined as the inability to produce a clear mental image within either 2 or 3 minutes. The procedure is first to describe the fantasy to be imagined in clear detail. The patient is then told to begin and to signal by pressing a button or tapping as soon as he has the image clearly in his mind. The variable measured is the time from the therapist's signal to begin, to the patient's signal of fantasy present—the response latency. If, after say 2 minutes, the patient has not signalled, the fantasy is considered suppressed and after an interval the next trial is started. Increase in the response latency can be regarded as a measurable form of partial suppression.

The following case is a good example of suppression of fantasy which is of interest for several reasons. The patient was a 49-year-old businessman who solicited males in public lavatories in order to practise fellatio on them. He was a man of some social standing who constantly feared exposure and humiliation. The effect of punishment on his deviant fantasies is shown in Fig. 5.8. Four fantasies were treated in sequence. With the first fantasy there was a gradual onset of suppression which became complete in the thirteenth session of treatment after 144 aversive trials. The remaining three fantasies were involved in treatment at later stages but in each case suppression developed more rapidly so that in session 14 all fantasies were totally suppressed. In other words, at this time there was a generalization of suppression through all treated fantasies. In the first fantasy, in spite of removal of the shock electrodes, complete suppression continued for a further 8 sessions; in the other three fantasies, extinction occurred although suppression (re-acquisition) quickly developed again.

The treatment was effective in that he stopped thinking homosexual thoughts and consequently stopped making his previous contacts. One year later, and rather suddenly, his previous pattern returned and he came back for more treatment. The second course of treatment, identical to the first, was given and the effects on the same fantasies are shown in Fig. 5.9. Once again the results were very similar except that fewer trials to suppression were required for the first fantasy and more for the remaining three. Once again, the treatment was effective for a further eighteen months, relapse occurring eventually.

This case demonstrates that suppression can occur in a convincing way. But in what proportion of cases and with what relationship to clinical outcome? Thirty-three patients who had received a punishment of fantasy procedure were looked at with this question in mind. This group was a mixture of fifteen homosexuals, fourteen transvestites, and four cases of various sexual deviations. In most of these cases the results of treatment

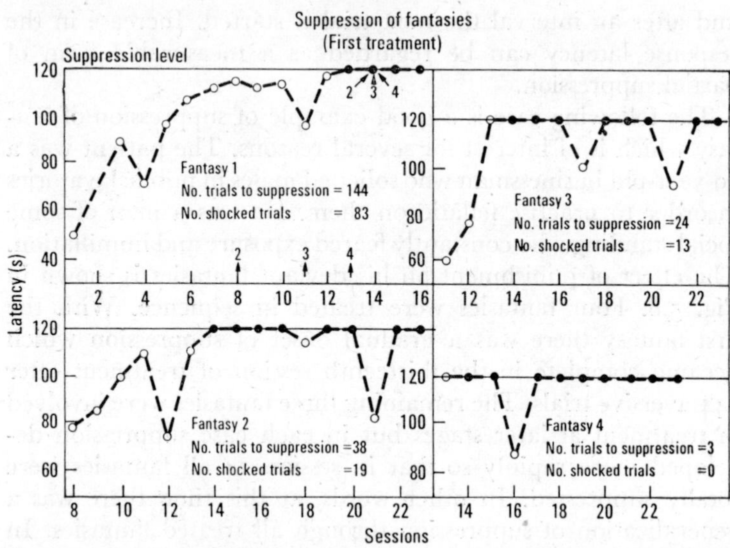

FIG. 5.8. This shows the response latencies of deviant fantasies during the punishment of fantasy procedure. Treatment started with fantasy 1. Fantasy 2 was introduced in session 8, fantasy 3 in session 11, fantasy 4 in session 13. Fantasy 1 became suppressed in session 13, the remaining 3 all became suppressed during session 14. The filled circles at 120 s indicate non-reinforced suppressed trials, i.e. no shock electrodes in place. Intermittent reinforcement was used during aversive trials. 'Number of trials to suppression' indicates the total number of aversive trials; 'the number of shock trials' indicates the number in which shock was delivered.

have been reported previously (Bancroft and Marks 1968; Marks *et al.* 1970; and Bancroft 1970*d*). Each case was looked at for evidence of either complete or partial suppression (for this purpose partial suppression was defined as an increase in the mean response latency of more than 50 per cent in the second half of treatment). Clinical improvement defined in terms of change in behavioural ratings and lasting at least 6 months was

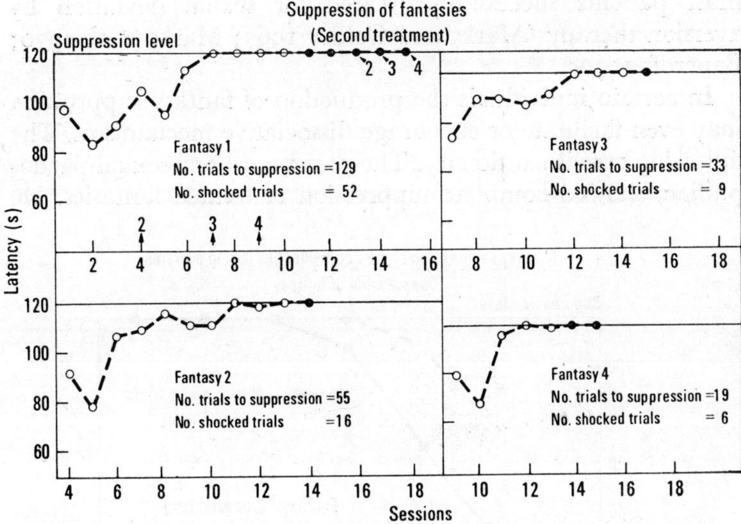

FIG. 5.9. This shows the fantasy response latencies during the second course of treatment with the same patient as shown in Fig. 5.8. The interval between courses was 1 year. For further details, see text.

also looked for. The relationship between suppression and clinical improvement is seen in Table 5.1.

It is apparent that although some degree of suppression is quite common it is just as likely to be associated with therapeutic failure as success. Indeed, from the long-term point of view it is questionable whether complete suppression is to be encouraged. What it implies is that the deviance is avoided by not thinking about it. What would seem to be more desirable is the ability to think about the deviant behaviour without feeling the original interest, the type of change described by

TABLE 5.1

Relation of fantasy suppression to clinical outcome

Outcome	*Complete suppression*	*Partial suppression*	*No suppression*	*Total*
Improved	3	5	11	19
Not improved	3	4	7	15
Total	6	9	18	33

most patients successfully treated for sexual deviation by aversion therapy (Marks and Gelder 1967; Marks *et al.* 1970; Bancroft 1970*c*).

In certain individuals the production of fantasy suppression may even facilitate or encourage dissociative mechanisms. The following case is cautionary. The patient, a homosexual paedophiliac, showed complete suppression of treated fantasies. He

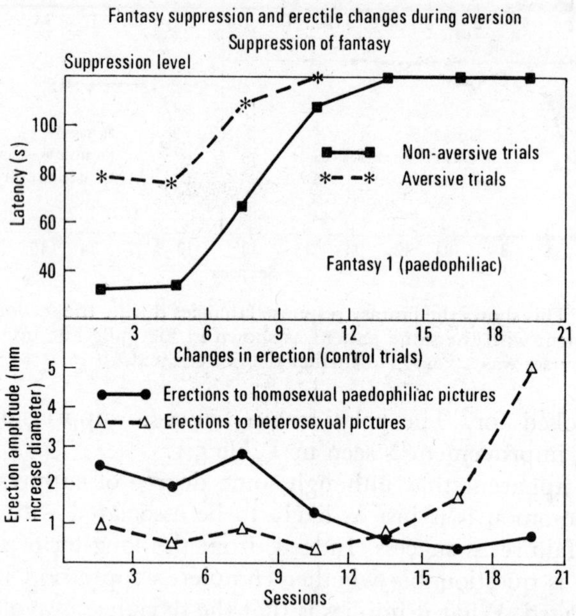

FIG. 5.10. The top graph shows suppression of deviant fantasies in aversive and non-aversive trials in a paedophiliac treated with a punishment of fantasy procedure. The lower graph also shows reduction in erection to paedophiliac pictures (during non-aversive trials) and increase in erections to normal heterosexual pictures as treatment continued. Scores given are the means of 3 consecutive sessions.

also showed increased heterosexual erections towards the end of treatment. (See Fig. 5.10.) The suppression also generalized to untreated fantasies. Following treatment any fantasy, sexual or otherwise, was suppressed if it included one of the boys involved in the treated fantasies. If it included any other boy it would only be suppressed if it were a sexual fantasy. (See Fig. 5.11.) On the face of it this seemed to be a good therapeutic response. The patient reported virtually no deviant interest at the end of treatment. In the follow-up period he continued to report no interest, yet his wife repeatedly complained that he was staying out longer than he should and would often spend long periods in public lavatories while she was waiting for him. He continued to deny any homosexual interest until eventually

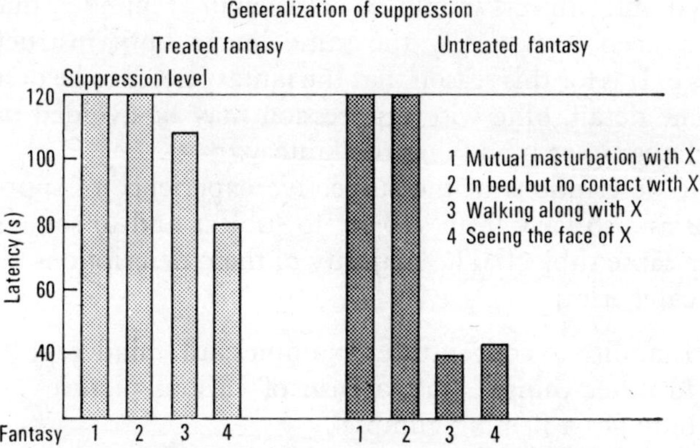

FIG. 5.11. These histograms show the mean response latencies for various fantasies following treatment in the paedophiliac referred to in Fig. 5.10. When the post-treatment fantasy included a boy who had featured in one of the punished fantasies during treatment, suppression was complete if the post-treatment fantasy was in any way sexual whereas non-sexual fantasies were only partially suppressed. Suppression generalized to any fantasy in which paedophiliac activity was involved (1 and 2) even if the boy concerned had not featured in treated fantasies. There was no suppression, however, if such a boy was featured in a non-sexual fantasy (i.e. 3 and 4).

a homosexual offence came to light. It is impossible to say whether this man was deliberately misleading us or was rather deceiving himself by means of dissociative mechanisms, but the latter should be considered a possibility. Suppression of fantasies in his case was probably unhelpful and certainly misleading.

The mechanism of suppression of fantasies remains obscure although it obviously has interesting implications (Eriksen and Kuethe 1956). Subjects vary in the way they produce the appropriate fantasy, some apparently switching on the image as though it were a photographic slide, others having to build up the required image by working through a sequence of events or gradually adding the components of the final image. These two types of fantasy production tend to be reflected in the initial response latencies, the former being relatively shorter, sometimes as brief as four or five seconds. In some cases as fantasies become more difficult a subject may resort to the 'build-up' process when the 'instant image' starts to fail. If systematic investigation of the suppression of fantasies is to be carried out, subjects should be occasionally reminded that they are to keep to precisely the same image until instructed to change. It is for this reason that the fantasy needs to be described in some detail, otherwise suppression may be avoided by simply changing or modifying the fantasy.

The descriptions of the subjective experience of suppressed fantasies also vary from subject to subject and to some extent in the same subject. The majority of these descriptions fall into four categories:

1. Inability to concentrate; examples are 'mind kept turning to other things', 'just a rush of various pictures', 'I can only get a fleeting glimpse'.
2. Modification of fantasy; fantasies either altered in an apparently involuntary way or the sequence of events lost before the appropriate image was achieved. An example of the former was the persistent image of a flaccid penis when the subject was trying to imagine anal intercourse with a partner.
3. Mental 'switching off'; examples are 'mind goes blank', 'my mind switches off', 'it was like a curtain coming down' 'like waves going through my head and wiping it clear'.
4. Selective loss of imagery; for example 'I can think about it but I can't visualize it'.

In five of the patients experiencing complete suppression of fantasy, physiological monitoring during suppression was carried out. No consistent physiological patterns emerged, although there was a tendency for the skin conductance tracing to flatten out. This is an effect which is also frequently associated with the maintenance of visual imagery, particularly when it is not anxiety-provoking. Other measures, including forearm blood flow, erection, and pulse rate varied unsystematically during the period of fantasy suppression.

At the present time therefore there is very limited evidence of the occurrence of suppression of deviant responses as an effect of aversion therapy. Such evidence as there is, in relation to erections and fantasies, does not show any clear relationship between suppression and appropriate behavioural change outside treatment.

Learning avoidance responses

The investigation of avoidance and escape learning in animals has been well reviewed by Solomon and Brush (1956), Solomon and Wynne (1953), and more recently by Rescorla and Solomon (1967) and D'Amato (1970). (Escape learning is learning a response which terminates or escapes from the shock after its onset; an avoidance response avoids the shock altogether by anticipating it.)

Two experiments involving avoidance learning in human subjects are relevant here. Graham, Cohen, and Shmavonian (1964) used a trace conditioning procedure where the CS was a visual stimulus and the UCS an electric shock. (A trace conditioning procedure is one in which the CS terminates before the onset of the UCS.) The subject could escape or avoid the shock by hitting a punch-ball placed in front of him. Some subjects were told there was something 'that could be done about the shock', the remainder were given no indication of the nature of the experiment except that they would be receiving periodic shocks. The 'informed' group all learnt to avoid. In the 'uninformed' group there was considerable variation: some made no response at all, some escaped but did not avoid, the remainder avoided.

The second study is by Turner and Solomon (1962). Four different types of avoidance training were used, incorporating a delayed conditioning procedure (delayed conditioning is more commonly used than trace conditioning and involves the CS continuing beyond the onset of UCS). Three types of training required movement of the feet as the escape or avoidance response and these varied in their complexity and in the likelihood of their occurrence as part of the 'pain–fear' reaction (UCR) to the shock. The fourth type was called a 'shuttle-box analogue'; a form of switch placed in front of the subject, which when operated turned off the shock. Once again, the subjects were divided into 'informed' and 'uninformed' groups. With the three 'foot' responses, the 'uninformed' group showed little avoidance learning, the 'informed' group considerably more. With the 'shuttle-box analogue' both the 'informed' and 'uninformed' learnt to avoid. These results suggest that where there is a relevant escape or avoidance response of a reflexive nature and a short response latency the human subject may be less and probably no more efficient than the laboratory animal in learning to avoid. Where avoidance obviously involves cognitive processes such as the recognition that the 'shuttle-box analogue' was a switch, the human subject is clearly superior to the dog. In comparing this study with the previous one, it is the 'shuttle-box analogue' which is directly comparable to the 'punch-ball' response. The most striking difference is that all the uninformed subjects avoided with the 'shuttle-box analogue' whereas only half did so with the 'punch-ball'. The reason for this difference is not clear, though it may reflect the more obvious switching mechanism of the 'shuttle-box analogue'.

If this point is taken a stage further and the human subject is told not only that 'there is something that can be done about the shock' but also precisely what should be done, then no new learning is necessary at all. It is simply a question of comprehending instructions.

This point should be borne in mind when we consider the aversive procedure of Feldman and MacCulloch (1965). In this the avoidance response to be learnt was the switching off of a slide. These workers justified their method mainly on the grounds that avoidance learning in animals shows such high resistance to extinction. It is true that a dog will continue with an acquired avoidance response almost indefinitely if the response continues to be apparently effective. If on the other hand the avoidance is prevented and 'reality testing' takes place, i.e. the animal experiences no shock in spite of being unable to avoid, then the response will be extinguished (e.g. Baum 1970). When it is primarily cognitive mechanisms that are involved the human subject in a laboratory can learn and 'unlearn' avoidance responses with relative ease (Graham *et al.* 1964). It is when anxiety is involved, as in neurotic behaviour, that the subject has less control over what he learns and what he 'unlearns'. It is not the 'switching off slide' response that will be relevant outside treatment but the learned need to avoid the types of stimuli that have been encountered during treatment. The important question therefore is not whether Feldman and MacCulloch's patients learn this particular avoidance response but rather whether they condition any anxiety or other emotional response to the slides which then generalizes to other relevant stimuli outside treatment and induces avoidance of these stimuli. They give little evidence on this point, though they do give some details of the changes in escape and avoidance response latencies during treatment in four of their patients (MacCulloch *et al.* 1966). They report that the changes are very similar to those described in dogs with a sudden shift from escape to avoidance (Solomon and Wynne 1953). These observations are difficult to interpret, however, because of the complex procedure involved. In a proportion of trials the subjects were shocked whether they avoided or not. Because of this they were certain to receive some shock. If a normal avoidance paradigm had been used, then the patients could have avoided shock altogether. Here the important conflict would not have been between avoiding shock and looking at an attractive slide but between avoiding shock and receiving it, as the shock must seem to the patient to be the crucial part of the treatment. The patient's motivation to be successfully treated would therefore be involved. It is complexities such as these that make a direct comparison with animal experiments so difficult. It must be concluded that the unusually good response to this particular technique reported by MacCulloch and Feldman (1967*a*) is not adequately explained in terms of avoidance learning and still awaits clarification.

The procedure reported by Abel *et al.* (1970) does however involve an avoidance response which is potentially relevant to behaviour outside treatment. When the deviant stimulus (a tape-recorded sequence) was presented the subject could avoid the shock by verbalizing a normal sexual sequence. This distracted from and counteracted the effects of the deviant stimulation. These workers have only reported limited experience with this procedure which deserves further investigation.

Generalization

This refers to the spread of a learned effect to stimuli or situations similar to but not exactly the same as those in the original learning situation. Thus, if anxiety is conditioned to the photograph of an attractive male during treatment, it may generalize to photographs of similar males or even to actual people of similar appearance. The more like the original photograph or stimulus the new stimulus is, the closer will the anxiety response be to the original conditioned response and vice versa. This phenomenon is known as a generalization gradient.

Clearly, generalization of this type is fundamental to the learning theory explanation of behaviour modification. Anything learned in treatment, be it a conditioned emotional response, suppression, or an avoidance response, needs to generalize to relevant stimuli outside treatment. Generalization can be undesirable if it affects stimuli or situations which are acceptable. In the experimental situation some unwanted generalization can be avoided by 'discrimination training' in which the 'desirable' stimuli are consistently paired with unconditioned stimuli different from those paired with the 'undesirable' treated stimuli. This principle has been used in the modification of sexual disorders by many workers who have for example deliberately presented normal heterosexual stimuli in the absence of any aversive stimuli (e.g. Bancroft 1970*d*). In this way, it has been hoped to avoid any effects such as suppression of erection occurring to both normal and deviant stimuli.

In laboratory experiments, generalization gradients and the effects of discrimination can often be clearly demonstrated (e.g. Hoffman and Fleshler 1964). Do these effects occur in behavioural modification of sexual disorders, however? Unfortunately, there has been very little systematic investigation of such effects and once again we have little more than anecdotal evidence. Some interesting single case studies of suppression of fantasy have been carried out. An example is a sadist treated by Marks *et al.* (1970). This man's fantasy of beating another man's buttocks was repeatedly associated with shock leading to its complete suppression. The subject also had difficulty in imagining the man's buttocks without beating being involved although such non-sadistic fantasies were not completely suppressed. It was found that fantasies of beating other parts of the body were also completely suppressed although they had not been involved in the aversive trials, but in non-sadistic fantasies involving other body parts the degree of suppression depended upon the closeness of the body part to the buttocks. There was thus an 'anatomical gradient' (Marks and Gelder 1969). Generalization of suppression to untreated fantasies was also described in the case on p. 114. This type of effect emerged in a number of cases.

The opposite of generalization, discrimination or specificity of learning also occurs on occasions for no very explicit reason. Marks and Gelder (1967) showed, in a transvestite, suppression of erectile response confined to those garments which had been treated. Why generalization occurs in some cases and discrimination in others is far from clear. It is possible that the explanation lies in the procedure involved, but it may also be due to individual differences in the subjects, including the degree of discrimination learning that had preceded treatment.

Partial reinforcement

This is a further concept derived from animal learning experiments which has been given prominence in behaviour modification techniques (Yates 1970) When a response is conditioned by positively reinforcing (rewarding) it, but the reinforcement is only administered in a proportion of occasions that the response occurs, the resistance to extinction of that response is increased. This is one of the most robust findings in learning experiments. When Lewis (1960) wrote his review of the topic, the prevailing explanation for this effect was that partial reinforcement rendered the acquisition phase more like the extinction phase and hence facilitated generalization of learning. For various reasons this attractively simple explanation has given way to a variety of more sophisticated and less digestible explanatory theories which have been reviewed by Robbins (1971). Of these the principal ones are that of Amsel (1972) involving 'frustration theory' and that of Capaldi (1966) involving a 'sequential hypothesis'. This theoretical confusion, it should be emphasized, applies to the use of partial *positive* reinforcement. When negative reinforcement or aversive stimuli are involved we have not only theoretical uncertainty but meagre and conflicting evidence. D'Amato (1970) has summarized the problem well in relation to escape learning, where partial reinforcement has been shown to have similar effects. He points out that there are two types of procedure, one in which the aversive stimulus is no longer applied (leading to removal of 'primary drive' engendered by the aversive stimulus as well as the 'primary reinforcement' derived from escaping), the other in which the 'primary drive' is maintained (i.e. the aversive stimuli are still applied) but the 'primary reinforcement' is eliminated (i.e. the escape response is blocked). It is not clear which is most effective in increasing resistance to extinction though D'Amato suggests that it is the latter type which is most closely analogous to extinction with positive reinforcement. As far as punishment and avoidance learning are concerned one can find even less guidance in the literature. With punishment the alternatives would seem to be either stopping punishment, or continuing with the aversive stimulus in the absence of the previously punished response. With avoidance learning, where resistance to extinction in the laboratory situation is exceptionally high without any special reinforcement schedule, the alternatives appear to be either preventing the avoidance response and stopping the aversive stimulus, or preventing the avoidance response and continuing with the aversive stimulus. The first procedure is equivalent to the 'flooding' procedure which has been shown by Baum (1970) to be effective in extinguishing the avoidance response. On the basis of the earlier model of partial reinforcement this would thus seem to be the appropriate type of 'non-reinforcement' to use in a partial reinforcement schedule. On the other hand, if D'Amato's interpretation is accepted, then the latter procedure would seem to be appropriate and this was in fact used by Feldman and MacCulloch (1965) in their anticipatory avoidance treatment technique. They introduced a proportion of trials in which the avoidance response was blocked and the patient was shocked.

In other forms of aversion therapy, involving either classical conditioning or punishment procedures, partial reinforcement by withdrawing shocks in a proportion of trials has been generally used. This procedure itself can be interpreted in two ways. First, the subject may be expecting a shock and not get one; secondly, the shock electrodes may be removed and the subject then knows he is not going to be shocked. Although it is this latter condition which can be considered most similar to the situation outside treatment and hence relevant to the extinction phase, it is the first type of non-reinforced trial which has been used as 'partial reinforcement', and which may be possibly more relevant to the current explanatory theories.

Does the use of such non-reinforced trials in fact improve the efficacy of the method? One effect of having a proportion of trials in which the subject expects but does not receive a shock is an increase of uncertainty. This it has often been assumed will increase anxiety and hence may make the procedure more aversive. Experiments to assess the effects of uncertainty on the response to shocks have produced conflicting results however. Deane (1961) and Elliott (1966) both found that whereas uncertainty about the severity of the shock produced anxiety as reflected in heart rate and self ratings, uncertainty about the timing of the shock did not. On the other hand, Jones, Bentley, and Petry (1966), using an operant procedure for obtaining information, found that subjects sought more information to reduce uncertainty about the timing of the shock than about the intensity of the shock. More recently Lovibond (1969) reported that a regular anticipated series of shocks was considered to be less noxious than shocks administered in an irregular fashion.

This issue was investigated further by Bancroft (1970*c*). In a punishment of fantasy procedure four deviant fantasies were involved in each case. Four reinforcement schedules were used (100 per cent, 70 per cent, 50 per cent and 30 per cent, one for each fantasy) but with the subject expecting shock in each trial and with the latency of shock more or less constant. Three variables were looked at: the mean response latency for all aversive trials (reinforced and non-reinforced), the degree of suppression (measured by subtracting the mean response latency for the first half of treatment from the mean for the second half) and the mean anxiety self rating for all aversive trials (on a 0–4 scale). The results are shown in Table 5.2. This data therefore fails to show any difference in the effects of these various reinforcement schedules on any of the three variables examined.

In each treatment session, however, the series of aversive trials for each fantasy was preceded by two or three non-aversive trials in which the electrodes were not attached and

TABLE 5.2

	100%	70%	50%	30%	*Analysis of variance*
Mean response Latency/s	51·1	46·5	44·5	52·8	$F_{3,27} = 3{\cdot}86$ ($p < 0{\cdot}05$†)
'Suppression'/s (Second half–first half)	+14·08	+3·77	+2·19	+7·21	$F_{3,27} < 1{\cdot}0$ (N.S.)
Mean anxiety rating 0–4	1·73	1·64	1·61	1·60	$F_{3,27} = 1{\cdot}10$ (N.S.)

† Tukey test showed no significant difference between any of the pairs of means.

therefore the subject was not expecting a shock. It was also possible therefore that the various reinforcement schedules produced different effects in this different type of 'extinction' trial. If any generalization outside treatment was to occur, it should certainly have generalized to these trials. The results are shown in Table 5.3. On this evidence it would seem that this

TABLE 5.3

	100%	70%	50%	30%	*Analysis of variance*
Mean response Latency/s	38·2	36·0	30·1	44·9	$F < 1$ (N.S.)
'Suppression'/s	+11·4	+2·64	+1·68	+21·71	$F = 1{\cdot}54$ (N.S.)

type of partial reinforcement is no less effective than 100 per cent reinforcement in producing suppression of fantasies.

At the present time therefore, it is justifiable to use partial reinforcement in aversive procedures (i.e. not always giving shock when it is expected), not because there is evidence to show that this is more effective, nor that it increases resistance to extinction, nor that it is more anxiety provoking, but because it appears to be as effective as 100 per cent reinforcement and it seems reasonable to reduce the number of shocks as far as possible.

POSITIVE EFFECTS

Whether aversive procedures are used or not, the goal of treatment in the majority of cases will be an improvement in normal heterosexual behaviour. Some methods are specifically aimed at achieving such a goal (e.g. systematic desensitization). In others there is either no such direct attempt or some procedure is combined with aversion in the hope that it will increase heterosexual responses. Although a clear rationale for such methods has not always been present, changes have been reported and some thought should be given to why they occurred.

The final test of such change is in overt sexual behaviour and such behavioural change may occur first in masturbation fantasy, with a change to heterosexual fantasies, or first in overt behaviour with a heterosexual partner. Behavioural change of this type, however, may be preceded by both attitude change and by measurable change in physiological responses to heterosexual stimuli (e.g. erection).

Let us consider the extent and nature of such changes, first in the course of aversive procedures, secondly with systematic desensitization, and thirdly with methods of positive conditioning. Compared with the negative effects of aversive stimuli, there are relatively few experimental studies on which to base our predictions for such treatment methods.

Positive changes during aversion

The concept of discrimination in aversive procedures has already been mentioned: heterosexual stimuli are consistently not punished in contrast to deviant stimuli. This reduces the likelihood of any punishment effect generalizing to the 'normal' stimuli and responses. Apart from this, however, various reasons have been put forward to explain why such procedures might increase heterosexual responses.

First, the principle of 'aversion–relief' has been proposed (Thorpe *et al.* 1964, see p. 37). Thus, if aversive stimuli are associated with deviant stimuli, then the presentation of a 'normal' stimulus can act as a signal of the cessation of aversive stimulation. The relief from such a signal becomes associated with the 'normal' stimulus. This, it is assumed, serves to reduce anxiety responses usually associated with 'normal' stimuli and hence permits the heterosexual response freer expression. Unfortunately, these workers present no data to show whether the treatment had any such effect in reducing heterosexual anxiety. In McConaghy's comparative study of aversion relief and chemical aversion (1969) there was a slightly greater tendency for increased heterosexual interest in the aversion–relief group but this was not significant, and in any case no evidence was presented to suggest that it was due to an anxiety-reducing effect.

Feldman and MacCulloch (1965) in their anticipatory avoidance procedure associated the presentation of a heterosexual stimulus with successful avoidance of shock in a proportion of trials. They also assumed that a reduction of anxiety would thereby be associated with heterosexual stimuli. Once again, however, no evidence to support this hypothesis was presented.

One of the most striking consequences of the aversive procedure reported by Bancroft (1970*d*) was the increase in heterosexual erections, particularly the paradoxical facilitation of these responses during the course of an aversion session, an effect which was not observed with systematic desensitization. One explanation that can be dismissed is that the 'facilitation' was spurious, owing to the relative suppression of heterosexual erections at the start of the session resulting from the anxious anticipation of the forthcoming aversive procedure. If this were the case the heterosexual erections would have been lower at the start of the session in the aversion group than in the desensitization group; in fact, they were strikingly similar. The 'aversion–relief' principle could again be invoked. A striking contrast in autonomic arousal between an aversive homosexual trial and a non-aversive heterosexual trial is demonstrated in Fig. 5.12. If heterosexual erections had been previously inhibited by the presence of anxiety, then this explanation might account for the change. However, the relationship between anxiety and erection is complex (Bancroft 1970*b*, 1974) and certainly some of the patients in the study were showing erections in spite of intense anxiety. Whilst 'aversion–

relief' remains a possibility, therefore, there is no positive evidence from this study to support it.

The paradoxical facilitation could be likened to the so-called 'punishment contrast' effect observed in animals (Azrin and Holz 1966; Quinn *et al.* 1973); in some situations a response temporarily suppressed by punishment will transiently increase

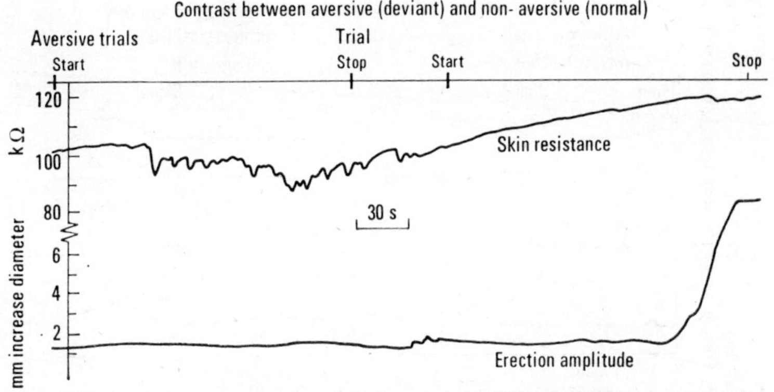

FIG. 5.12. This tracing shows skin resistance and erectile changes during an aversion session involving punishment of erection procedure. Two trials are shown, one an aversive trial in which the erectile criterion for shock is not reached and hence no shock is given, the second is a non-aversive trial involving heterosexual stimuli. In the first, subjective anxiety is high and the skin resistance tracing shows marked activity. In the second, the patient is calm as reflected in the skin resistance tracing, and a full erection occurred. This demonstrates the striking contrast between an aversive trial and a non-aversive trial immediately following it. Such contrasts may serve an 'anxiety relief' function for heterosexual responses.

following punishment even above its pre-punishment level. A further effect probably related is 'behavioural contrast' (Reynolds 1961), in which the strength of response to one stimulus is affected by a change in the amount of reinforcement of responses to a different stimulus (an effect first described by Pavlov (1927) and called 'induction'). In this treatment situation, when heterosexual stimuli are presented following a series of aversive trials involving homosexual stimuli, both effects may be involved. Such observations do not explain the mechanisms underlying these effects but the erectile changes could be homologous and therefore open to investigation in the same way.

An observation that has been frequently made by the author

is a temporary increase in erection following the cessation of an erotic stimulus or fantasy. This occurs whether the erection is being punished or not (see Fig. 5.13). This could be an example of a Sherringtonian 'rebound phenomenon' (Sherrington 1947); during presentation of a stimulus, excitatory and inhibitory

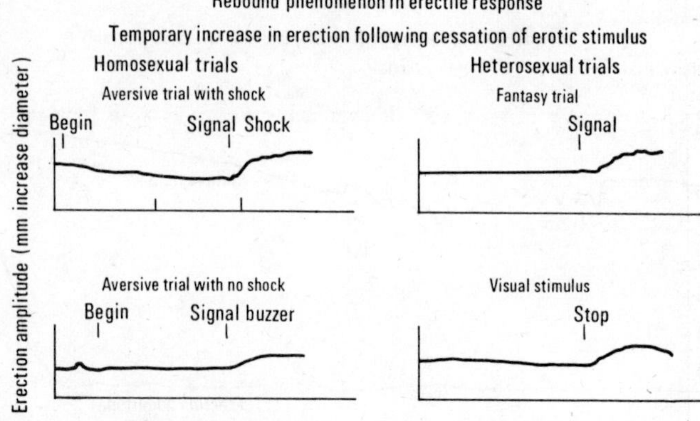

FIG. 5.13. A transient increase in erection (usually no more than 1 mm increase in diameter) often follows cessation of a stimulus. These tracings show the 'rebound' effect in two aversive trials in which the increase followed the signalling of a clear fantasy. In one case the signal was immediately followed by a shock, in the other by a loud buzzer. A similar effect is shown in the heterosexual trial. In one case the increases followed on the signalling of a clear heterosexual image, in the other, the switching off of an erotic slide.

influences may operate on the erectile mechanism and when the stimulus ceases excitation may transiently outlive inhibition. If such a rebound effect was operating, then a comparable mechanism could account for the facilitation from start to finish of the session; throughout the aversive trials a high level of erectile inhibition was presumably operating and was hence counteracted by an even higher level of erectile excitation than would normally be necessary. If the central nervous system adjusted to this level it could have temporarily continued at the same level after the cessation of aversion. If this explanation is correct it would apply to erections to homosexual stimuli also, whereas the avoidance relief explanation would not predict a homosexual facilitation effect.

A further comparable and even more striking effect observed in several patients was an increase in erection following a shock. When this was marked the shock had an apparent 'pumping' effect on erection. This effect was only observed when shock was delivered during the development of an erection and was not simply due to shock induced movement (see Fig. 5.14). This facilitatory effect of a painful stimulus during a state of sexual arousal provides a possible model for the establishment of masochistic responses. Amongst the patients who have shown this effect, two were masochists and in one the aversive procedure was clearly associated with increased erectile responses to deviant stimuli (Bancroft 1971) (see Fig. 5.15). At the moment, however, the relevance of this effect remains obscure although the above findings justify caution in treating masochists with aversion (Marks *et al.* 1970).

Systematic desensitization

Desensitization as a method of treating non-sexual phobias has probably received more controlled experimental study than any other form of psychological treatment (Rachman 1967; Marks and Gelder 1968; Paul 1969). The only systematic study of its use in the treatment of deviant sexual behaviour is that reported by Bancroft (1970*d*). In this case the rationale of the method depended on the concept of homosexuality as a phobia, or fear, of heterosexuality. If the theoretical basis for desensitization of phobias in general is discussed first, the extent to which homosexuality fits the 'heterosexual phobia' model can be considered.

A series of experimental 'analogue' studies has demonstrated that the combination of relaxation and the presentation of a hierarchical series of imaginary phobic situations is more effective in reducing phobic anxiety than either the relaxation or the hierarchical presentation used alone (Rachman 1967). The failure of repeated or hierarchical presentation of the phobic image without relaxation to produce significant improvement has been taken as evidence that simple extinction of a conditioned anxiety response is not the relevant mechanism. Only two significant theoretical alternatives have so far been suggested.

First the explanation given by Wolpe (1958) who was the originator of this technique; he derived the method from his work in producing experimental neurosis in cats. He showed in

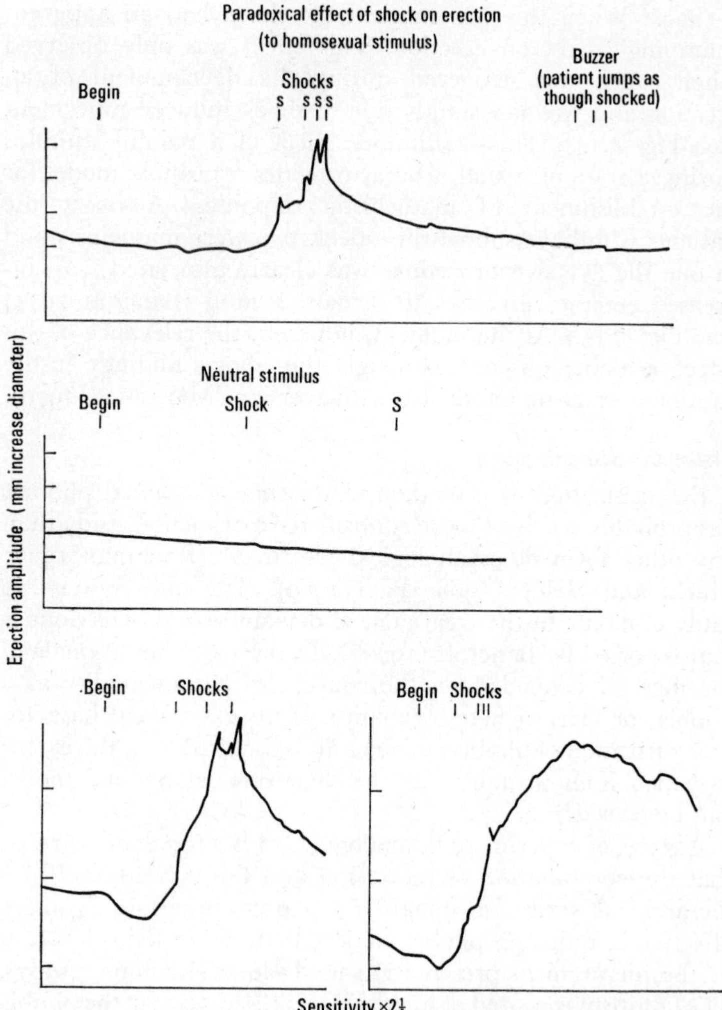

FIG. 5.14. In some instances shock (to the forearm) has produced a paradoxical increase in erection. This is shown in the top graph when each shock is followed by an increase as if by a pumping action. The absence of any such effect when a buzzer sounded, producing a similar movement as the shock, excludes the possibility of a movement artefact. This effect only occurs if an erection is already developing at the time of the shock. This is demonstrated in the middle tracing when shock during a neutral fantasy produced no effect. The lower tracing shows further examples of this paradoxical effect at greater sensitivity.

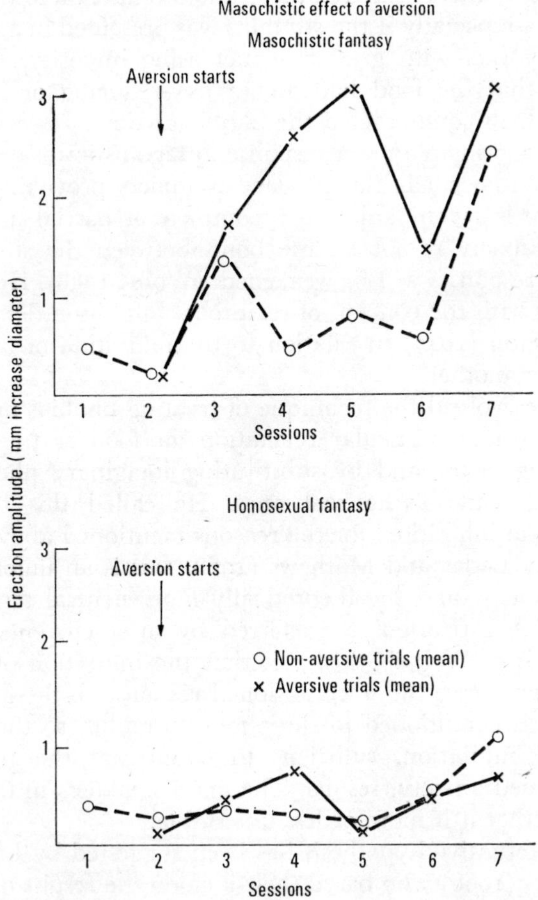

FIG. 5.15. These graphs show the mean erectile responses occurring between the patient being asked to produce a deviant fantasy and his signalling its presence. The mean response for the two types of trial for each session are shown for two different fantasies. In the non-aversive trials, no shock electrodes were attached. In the aversive trials he expected, in a proportion of trials, to receive a shock when he signalled (intermittent reinforcement). In the case of the masochistic fantasy, erections were greater when a shock was anticipated. This was not so with the non-masochistic fantasy. N.B.: Erections measured occurred *before* any shock was delivered. (From Bancroft 1971.)

his cats that the presentation of food at the same time as the phobic stimulus resulted in the gradual reduction in the phobic anxiety—especially if the stimulus was presented in a hierarchical way (i.e. with gradually increasing intensity). He concluded that the food had an anxiety-reducing or inhibiting effect which counteracted the phobic anxiety. He evolved the following principle: 'if a response antagonistic to anxiety can be made to occur in the presence of anxiety-provoking stimuli, so that it is accompanied by a complete or partial suppression of the anxiety responses, the bond between the stimuli and anxiety responses will be weakened' (Wolpe 1958). He drew an analogy with the concept of reciprocal inhibition described by Sherrington (1947) in relation to the inhibition of one spinal reflex by another.

Wolpe evolved the technique of treating phobias in humans by substituting muscular relaxation for food as the anxiety-inhibiting factor and by substituting imaginary phobic situations instead of the real ones. He called this technique 'reciprocal inhibition' for the reasons mentioned above, but as stated by Lader and Mathews (1968) this is an unfortunately loose analogy and the theoretically more neutral term 'systematic desensitization' is preferred by most current workers. The basis of Wolpe's theory is that the inhibition of anxiety which represents the unconditioned response to the relaxation process, is conditioned to the phobic stimulus, so that a conditioned inhibition, sufficient to counteract the previously conditioned anxiety, results. The main weakness in this hypothesis is that it is more or less untestable.

An alternative hypothesis has been suggested by Lader and Mathews (1968) who based their idea on the results of habituation experiments in normal and phobic subjects. Lader (1967) had shown that habituation (i.e. extinction) of the GSR (galvanic skin response) to a repeated auditory stimulus occurred more rapidly when the level of autonomic arousal was low. He postulated that above a certain critical level of arousal the reverse of habituation would take place, leading, with repeated stimulation, to a state comparable to a panic attack. Immediately below the critical level no change in the GSR would result but as arousal fell further habituation would occur and become increasingly rapid.

He found that in the testing situation, 'anxiety state' neurotics and agorophobics maintained a relatively high level of arousal and habituated much less than normals. Patients with specific phobias, e.g. of animals, were nearer to the normals than to the anxiety neurotics and agorophobics in both level of arousal and speed of habituation. Lader and Mathews related this fact to the finding that specific phobias responded better to desensitization than agorophobias (Marks and Gelder 1965), and postulated that desensitization worked by lowering arousal to levels at which maximum habituation could occur. The crucial effect of relaxation, they suggested, was to lower arousal rather than to inhibit anxiety *per se*. This hypothesis is more open to testing than Wolpe's and does generate a number of practically useful ideas but, as Lader and Mathews suggest, habituation, if relevant to desensitization, probably plays only a part in the over-all effect of the treatment.

To what extent does homosexuality fit into the phobic model? Many writers of the modern psychoanalytic schools consider that homosexuality is a reparative pattern which develops to cope with the fear of heterosexuality.†

In some cases the thought of heterosexual behaviour produces a feeling of discomfort or revulsion in a homosexual which could be considered comparable to a phobic response. In such cases, desensitization would seem an appropriate treatment. If it resulted in the ability to imagine heterosexual thoughts with none of the previous discomfort then sexual interest in them would be more likely to occur, especially if previously the appraisal of threat in the situation had inhibited sexual responses (e.g. erections). However, in many homosexuals the thought of heterosexual behaviour does not provoke anxiety—it is rather regarded with indifference. In such a case it is conceivable, though by no means proven, that by adopting a homosexual identity and role one is avoiding the heterosexual situation and hence removing the threat from it. The thought

† The therapeutic relevance of heterosexual anxiety should not, perhaps, be confined to this primary aetiological role. If for other reasons homosexuality predominates initially, then this fact alone would make any subsequent attempt to become heterosexual more difficult, and hence more threatening, for the following reason. The thought 'I am a homosexual' is effective in provoking the fear 'I would fail as a heterosexual' and this fear may block heterosexual progress, or at least lead to anxiety in the heterosexual situation (Bancroft 1970*a*).

of heterosexuality does not provoke anxiety in such a person because the possibility of it happening does not seem to exist. Such a homosexual might come for treatment denying heterosexual anxiety, but if the treatment proved sufficiently effective to make a heterosexual confrontation a real possibility then anxiety might arise.

Even more difficult to fit into this phobic model are those homosexuals who not only deny heterosexual anxiety but also positively enjoy heterosexual contacts. Here the phobic model only fits if it is postulated that for some reason the *exclusively* heterosexual role presents a threat. It was with this last type of homosexual that the rationale of this method in Bancroft's (1970*d*) study was most difficult to justify. In one such case the man had a very effeminate manner and it was suggested to him that the thought of heterosexuality other than with his sexually non-threatening wife would provoke anxiety. He related to other women by his non-sexual 'camp' role and avoided the sexually provocative masculine role. In his case the hierarchy consisted of imagining adulterous exploits and they proved to be effectively anxiety-provoking.

To what extent did the patients in this study of systematic desensitization fit the phobic model? On the basis of the original clinical history five patients expressed fairly obvious anxiety in relation to heterosexuality in general; they were considered to be 'phobic'. Four patients expressed slight anxiety in relation to some aspects of heterosexuality but not all, they were considered 'slightly phobic'. In the remaining six, anxiety about heterosexuality was more or less denied. These clinical impressions were supported by the anxiety ratings for heterosexual concepts on the semantic differential; the mean scores for the three groups being 17·3, 15·2, and 11·8 respectively (a score of 12 being neutral, the score of 21 maximum for anxiety). Of the four patients who dropped out of desensitization treatment in this study, one was in the slightly phobic group, the other three were in the non-phobic group.

Several patients responded to the desensitization process in the way expected of phobic patients in general, i.e. some items would provoke anxiety when imagined but after repeated presentation, would cease to do so. (see Figs. 5.16., 5.17(a), (b)). Of the six who showed the expected desensitization response,

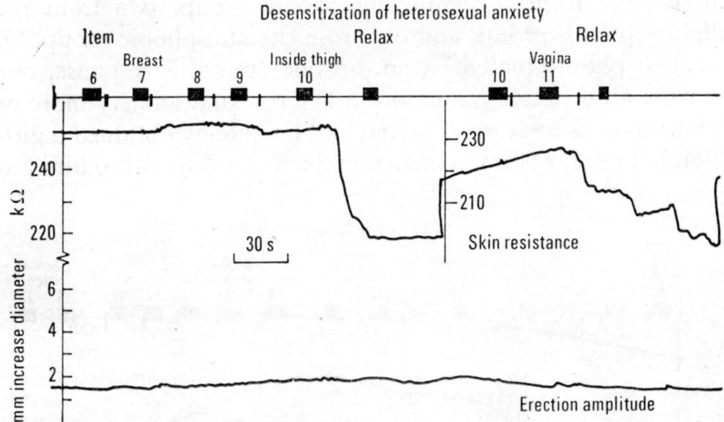

Fig. 5.16. This tracing shows skin resistance and erectile changes during a desensitization session. When item 10 of the hierarchy (touch the inside of the girl's thigh) is presented, there is a marked drop in skin resistance indicating anxiety. The patient is re-relaxed and the item re-presented, this time without anxiety. The next item (touching the vagina) then produces a further marked drop of skin resistance and a report of subjective anxiety.

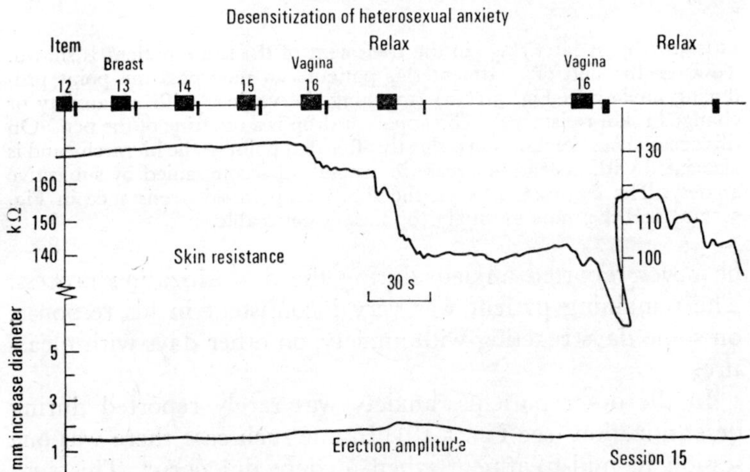

Fig. 5.17(a). This shows part of a desensitization session in which the image 'touching the vagina' provokes anxiety with a sharp drop in skin resistance. After further relaxation the image is repeated but with the same effect. The session is stopped at this point.

three were from the clinically phobic group, two from the slightly phobic group, and one from the non-phobic group. Of the two phobic patients who did not show this response, one showed an effective reduction in heterosexual anxiety more or less as soon as treatment started and he quickly obtained a girl-friend. The fear of impotence remained a real threat to him but

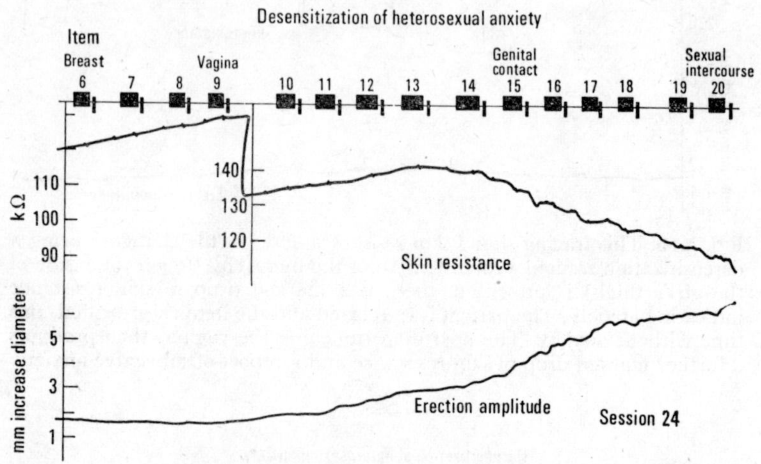

FIG. 5.17(b). A later stage in the treatment of the same patient is shown. Towards the end of treatment this patient can now pass the point producing anxiety in Fig. 5.17(a) (touching the vagina) with no anxiety or change in skin resistance. (The apparent drop is a resetting of the pen.) On this occasion an erection starts shortly after that point in the hierarchy and is associated with a steady increase in arousal, unaccompanied by subjective anxiety. The contrast between the sharp drop in skin resistance in Fig. 5.17(a) and the more gradual drop here is noticeable.

he never reported anxiety during the desensitization process. The remaining patient was very inconsistent in his response, on some days reacting with anxiety, on other days with pleasure.

In the other patients, anxiety was rarely reported during desensitization (see Fig. 5.18). In one such case there was one session in mid-treatment when anxiety did occur. This suggested the emergence of anxiety provoked by the approaching reality of heterosexuality, as mentioned earlier, but in this case, the patient appeared to respond by retreating into homosexuality rather than by overcoming the anxiety.

When the outcome in those who completed treatment was considered, only one of the six who improved was in the non-phobic group. The initial heterosexual anxiety score was 16·5 for the improved and 13·2 for the unimproved groups. The reduction in heterosexual anxiety, however, did not correlate significantly with heterosexual behaviour or attitude change.

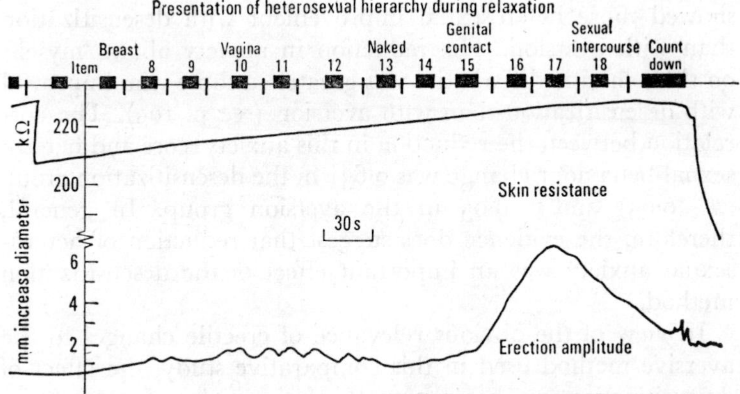

Fig. 5.18. This tracing shows a desensitization session with a patient who only once reported anxiety throughout the whole course of treatment. Characteristically this recording shows a flat skin resistance tracing supporting his report that although he found the image pleasant and developed an erection he experienced neither anxiety nor sexual excitement. This patient showed little change outside treatment in spite of consistent erection during the desensitization procedure.

The presence of the heterosexual 'phobic' element in the *aversion* group and its relation to outcome, should also be considered in relation to the above findings. On the basis of the clinical history before treatment, two of the patients were described as phobic, nine as slightly phobic, and four as non-phobic. The mean anxiety scores for heterosexual concepts (semantic differential) before treatment were 16·8, 15·0, and 12·2 for these three groups respectively. When outcome was considered, three of the slightly phobic and three of the non-phobic were in the improved category, whilst the phobic patients and the remainder were in the unimproved group. The pre-treatment heterosexual anxiety scores for the two outcome groups were 13·1 for improved and 15·4 for unimproved, the reverse of the scores for the desensitization group. Anxiety scores for heterosexual concepts before treatment were correlated with heterosexual behaviour change, the correlation coefficient being 0·3 for the desensitization group and −0·35 for the aversion group. Although neither of these correlations is significant the difference between them just reached significance at the 5 per cent level. In other words those with high heterosexual anxiety initially showed more heterosexual improvement with desensitization than with aversion. The reduction in anxiety about 'myself' on the semantic differential was greater in those who improved with desensitization than with aversion (see p. 105). The correlation between the reduction in this anxiety score and heterosexual behaviour change was 0·631 in the desensitization group ($p < 0{\cdot}05$) and −0·05 in the aversion group. In general, therefore, the evidence does suggest that reduction of heterosexual anxiety was an important effect of the desensitization method.

In view of the obvious relevance of erectile changes to the aversive method used in this comparative study, the effect of desensitization on heterosexual erections also deserves consideration. The erections at the start and finish of the session have already been discussed (see p. 126). In addition erections were measured during the course of the desensitization process itself. There was a general tendency for these erections to increase, particularly in the first few sessions when the desensitization effect was most noticeable. How relevant were these changes to outcome? The mean erectile change for the whole course of treatment for the six improved cases was 1·5 mm increase in diameter; for the five unimproved it was 2·5 mm. Thus a tendency to produce erections during desensitization was, if anything, associated with a poorer outcome. Why should this be so?

The patient who showed the greatest and most consistent erections during desensitization, when it was pointed out to him, remarked that although the hierarchy items involved heterosexual behaviour, the sexual scenes were described by a male voice—in other words he was responding to a homosexual element in the treatment situation. It was later observed by the therapist that of the four patients with the strongest and most consistent erectile response during desensitization, three had expressed fairly strong positive feelings for the therapist, two with barely disguised sexual connotations. The correlation between maximum erection during treatment and sexual evaluation of the therapist on the semantic differential at the end of treatment just failed to reach significance. Thus it seems likely that a homosexual factor was operating in treatment, at least in some cases. If the patient was unaware of this, then the vicarious erection produced may have had a positive effect on the heterosexual interest and attitudes. If, however, the erections were interpreted as being basically homosexual, then this could have had an adverse effect on outcome (the increase in heterosexual erections from the beginning of the course of treatment to the end was correlated with heterosexual attitude change in the desensitization group, $r = 0{\cdot}63$, $p < 0{\cdot}05$).

The specific effect of desensitization is therefore most likely to depend on the reduction of heterosexual anxiety as expected from the method. This is in sharp contrast to the aversive procedure in this comparative study, in which none of the predicted effects of aversion were shown to be related to outcome.

Positive conditioning of heterosexual responses

Apart from systematic desensitization, most of the techniques which have aimed directly at increasing heterosexual responses have relied on the measurement of erections, using the erection either as a response to be directly modified (as in the operant procedure of Quinn *et al.* 1970) or to monitor the response to heterosexual stimuli (as in the 'fantasy shaping' reported by Bancroft (1971) or the 'fading' procedure of Barlow and Agras (1971)). What evidence is there that penile erection is a conditionable response and what is the significance of monitoring erectile change in a therapeutic procedure?

Penile erection is an autonomic response (Bancroft 1970*b*) and the conditionability of such responses is a subject of much current debate. The traditional view was that autonomic responses could be conditioned according to classical conditioning principles, whereas skeletal responses could be learned according to operant principles of reinforcement (Kimble 1961). Miller (1969) and his co-workers challenged this view and there was evidence, at least in animals heavily curarized and reinforced with depth electrodes or aversive stimuli, that autonomic responses could be learned according to operant principles. The relevance of these findings to autonomic learning in man is still uncertain, the main counter-argument being that the autonomic learning is an 'epiphenomenon', the direct effect of reinforcement being the control of cognitive mediating processes that precede the autonomic response. As penile erection is such a measurable autonomic response, and one which is under relatively good control (Laws and Rubin 1969; Henson and Rubin 1971) it is surprising that it has received no attention from autonomic learning experts, although Katkin and Murray (1968) used sexual arousal as an example of an autonomic response which might be spuriously conditioned by rewarding sexually arousing thoughts.

Some experiments have been carried out in human subjects which do suggest that penile erection is readily conditionable by Pavlovian procedures. Rachman (1966) and Rachman and Hodgson (1968) used a classical conditioning paradigm in which an erotic slide was used as the unconditioned stimulus to produce an erection, and a neutral slide (picture of a boot) was used as a conditioned stimulus. Conditioned erections to the boot were demonstrated following this procedure, providing what Rachman called an 'experimental analogue of a fetish'. McConaghy (1970*b*) and Barr and McConaghy (1971), in a more complex series of experiments, associated neutral visual stimuli with both heterosexual and homosexual stimuli in groups of both heterosexual and homosexual subjects. They demonstrated conditioned positive and negative erectile responses, with the homosexual stimuli acting as the negative UCS for the heterosexuals and vice versa. The results, though not always easy to interpret, do suggest a striking conditionability of erections. Quinn *et al.* (1973) and Herman, Barlow, and Agras (1973) reported the use of a classical conditioning paradigm in transferring erectile responses from inappropriate to appropriate stimuli.

Quinn *et al.* (1970) used an operant conditioning paradigm in an attempt to treat abnormal homosexual responses. In this case the reinforcement used was drink given to a fluid-deprived subject. They showed a convincing association between reinforcement of erections and increased erectile response. When we add to these various studies the striking and unexpected erectile changes reported by Bancroft (see p. 126) it remains a distinct possibility that penile erection is readily and perhaps peculiarly susceptible to conditioning procedures and if so, this susceptibility requires further study.

Even if erectile responses can be conditioned in this way, what would be the significance of such responses to the sexual attitudes and behaviour of the subject? In Bancroft's (1970*d*) comparative study there was no correlation between erectile change and attitude or behaviour change in the aversion group, though in the desensitization group the correlation between increase in heterosexual erections and heterosexual attitude change was significant ($r = 0{\cdot}632$, $p < 0{\cdot}05$). It is an obvious possibility that if erections occur in response to novel stimuli, a change in sexual attitude may also occur with the novel stimulus becoming more sexually attractive. However, the correlation between attitude change and erectile change does not indicate which if either of the changes came first. Specific experiments would have to be carried out to test this hypothesis. (See p. 172).

What part does monitoring erections play, as in the 'shaping' (Bancroft 1971)or 'fading' (Barlow and Agras 1971) procedures? It may be that, to be effective, the change of stimulus from deviant to normal must be sufficiently gradual for erections to continue to occur. In this way, the erectile response acts as an indicator of the continuing sexual nature of the stimulus resulting in a gradual weakening of the idea that normal stimuli are not sexually arousing. It was noticeable that in the case of fantasy 'shaping' reported by Bancroft (1971) the subject experienced several crucial and sudden attitude changes which seemed to be periodically precipitated by the gradual stimulus change (e.g. the sudden change from male to female partner in the fantasy and the consequent vigorous maintenance of heterosexual identity; the subject's acceptance that he could take an active role in a sexual relationship rather than merely being acted on in a masochistic way).

The change in sexual attitudes that follows the eliciting and measuring of erectile responses was demonstrated in the patient reported by Beumont, Bancroft, Beardwood, and Russell (1972), a man with hypo-gonadism whose sexual arousability was restored by the administration of testosterone. Before treatment started sexual attitudes were neutral and there were no erections in response to erotic stimuli. Once the testosterone had been administered, sexual attitudes were measured immediately before and after the testing of erections. Although there had been a significant increase in positive sexual attitudes

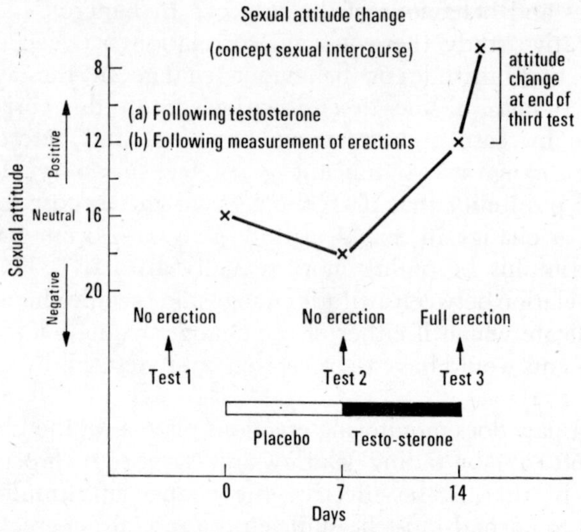

FIG. 5.19. This graph shows the effect that measurement of erection can have on sexual attitudes. The hypogonadal patient, who was treated with first placebo and then methyl-testosterone, showed a response to the latter after 1 week. Initially his attitudes changed significantly. Immediately following the attitude ratings, his erections to erotic stimuli were measured and these also showed a marked change. The semantic differential was then re-administered immediately following the physiological testing and showed a *further* significant change.

in the first of these two measurements (compared with the pre-treatment level), the measurement of substantial erections to erotic stimuli was followed by a further significant increase in attitude immediately after the testing session. (See Fig. 5.19.)

The feedback of behavioural change has been shown to facilitate the behavioural treatment of phobias (Leitenberg, Agras, Thomson, and Wright 1968). This may not only be because of the information imparted to the subject (which in the case of erections he could be aware of without feedback) but also because the information is shared between subject and therapist so that its 'reality' and significance can be less easily denied or minimized. Nevertheless the variable association between erectile change and attitude change that has been observed probably indicates that the consequence of any erectile change will depend on how that change is interpreted by the subject. A spurious or vicarious change in one person may lead to a dramatic attitude change, whilst in another an apparently genuine change is written off as treatment artefact. This general principle of the interpretation of physiological responses is of considerable theoretical relevance to the development of sexual preferences. The interpretation of 'nonspecific' erection by pre-pubertal boys (Ramsey 1943), for example, may influence their further sexual development.

6 *Clinical Findings and Prognostic Factors*

So far the most consistent finding to emerge from the few available studies comparing treatment techniques is that the precise method used makes very little difference to the outcome providing that it is obviously a form of treatment and not some 'placebo' procedure. The general significance of these findings will be discussed in more detail in the next chapter. Apart from such findings, what can be learned from the various uncontrolled studies? Do the results vary according to the type of sexual deviation being treated, and are there recognizable factors that indicate prognosis?

Successes have been claimed for many types of treatment and for most types of sexual deviance, with the possible exception of transexualism. Uncontrolled single case reports or groups of selected cases tell us relatively little except that the condition is treatable at least in some instances, and that the technique is usable in such cases. There are a number of reports, however, in which the results are given for a complete series of cases, so that the success rate can be indicated and characteristics distinguishing the successes from the failures identified.

To compare the success rate in one series with that of another is, unfortunately, rather a crude business. The criteria for improvement are all too often vague or undefined. Sometimes success is determined by reduction in deviance. At other times it is determined by the increase in normal heterosexuality. The length of follow-up varies considerably. Certainly there is a need for methods of evaluating and measuring the effects of treatment which can be used across studies, a problem which will be discussed in Chapter 8.

Within these major limitations let us look at the various results. The following types of deviance will be considered separately: homosexuality; paedophilia; fetishism, transvestism and transexualism; exhibitionism; and sado-masochism. Most reports have involved the treatment of homosexuality. As a number of prognostic factors are probably relevant regardless of the type of sexual deviance involved they will be considered initially in relation to homosexuality. When the other types of deviance are dealt with, any additional prognostic factors of specific significance will then be discussed. In each case representative results with non-behavioural psychotherapy will also be mentioned briefly for comparison.

HOMOSEXUALITY

Clinical results

A summary of the results from the principal studies are given in Table 6.1. The results of the last two studies (James, Orwin, and Turner 1973; Mumford, Lodge Patch, and Andrews 1973) have been kindly given to the author by these workers prior to publication. Both studies involved a precise replication of the Feldman and MacCulloch (1965) technique, except that in the first study (James *et al.*) an automated programming procedure was used, reducing though not eliminating therapist involvement. In this first study thirteen patients dropped out once treatment had started. There were also five 'pilot' cases who were not included in the final analysis and who generally did badly. In the second study (Mumford *et al.* 1973) only two of the three improved showed heterosexual as well as homosexual improvement. There were also two patients whose outcome was described as 'some change', meaning a reduction but not cessation of homosexual activity. In one of these there was heterosexual (marital) improvement.

Although there is considerable variation, seven of the therapeutic teams (Freund; Solyom and Miller; Bancroft and Marks; Bancroft; McConaghy; Birk *et al.*; James *et al.*; and Mumford *et al.*) reported success rates of 33 per cent or less. The remainder, the most notable, are the series reported by MacCulloch and Feldman, and Mellor who was originally working with the

TABLE 6.1

Outcome in behavioural treatment studies of homosexuality

	Number treated	*Improved at end of treatment*	*Improved at follow-up*	*Duration of follow-up*	*Method of treatment*
Freund (1960)	47	—	12 (25%)	5–8 yrs	Chemical aversion
Schmidt, Castell, and Brown (1965)	16	8 (50%)	—	—	Aversion–relief
Solyom and Miller (1965)	6	0 (0%)	—	—	Modified aversion–relief
MacCulloch and Feldman (1967*a*)	43	—	25 (57%)	1–2 yrs	Avoidance learning
Bancroft and Marks (1968)	12	—	3 (25%)	1–2 yrs	Electrical aversion (punishment procedure)
Fookes (1969)	15	—	9 (60%)	3–3½ yrs	Electrical aversion (classical)
McConaghy (1969)	40	—	11 (27%)	1–3 yrs	Chemical aversion or aversion–relief
Bancroft (1970*d*)	15	—	5 (33⅓%)	½–1½ yrs	Electrical aversion (punishment)
	15	—	5 (33⅓%)	½–1½ yrs	Systematic desensitization
Feldman and MacCulloch (1971)	30	—	17 (57%)	3–13 mnths	Avoidance learning, classical aversion or 'psychotherapy'
Birk, Huddleston, Miller, and Cohler (1971)	8	—	2 (25%)	2 yrs	Avoidance learning
Mellor (1972)	27	—	18 (66%)	?	Avoidance learning and classical aversion
James, Orwin, and Turner (1973)	51	—	17 (33%)	2 yrs	Avoidance learning
Mumford, Lodge Patch, and Andrews (1973)	11	—	3 (27%)	2–4 yrs	Avoidance learning
Total	314		127 (40%)		

other two. Fookes' results are more difficult to judge as his report was extremely brief and Schmidt, Castell, and Brown's results applied to the end of treatment when the success rate is usually spuriously high. It was also impossible to judge from their paper whether the criteria for improvement included increased heterosexual feelings or behaviour.

The superiority of the results of the 'Manchester group' (MacCulloch and Feldman; Mellor) remains something of a mystery. They themselves have demonstrated that their particular avoidance technique is not significantly superior to simple classical 'aversion' (see p. 57) and in any case other workers replicating their method have consistently

TABLE 6.2

Refusal and 'drop-out' rate in those offered aversion treatment for homosexuality

Study	*Number offered treatment*	*Number refusing treatment*	*Number of 'drop-outs'*
MacCulloch and Feldman (1967)	45	2 (4·5%)	7 (15·5%)
Bancroft (1969)	16	6 (35%)	0 (0%)
Bancroft (1970*d*)	47	17 (36%)	7 (15%)
James *et al.* (1973)	70	14 (20%)	13 (18·5%)
Mumford *et al.* (1973)	17	6 (35%)	0 (0%)

achieved less satisfactory results (Birk *et al.* 1971; James *et al.* 1973; Mumford *et al.* 1973). One aspect that may be relevant is that of selection. MacCulloch and Feldman (1967*a*) make the point very clearly that in order to properly assess prognostic indices they offered treatment to anyone referred to them. It is noticeable that only two patients declined their offer of treatment. A much higher initial refusal rate has been reported in most other series where relevant data is given (see Table 6.2). Nevertheless it is still difficult to see how this difference could account for their superior results unless it reflects some selection operating at the referring level, which seems unlikely.

If these workers continue to obtain such good results it is to be hoped that the reasons for them become clear. In the meantime, it is probably fair to say that most other workers, using behavioural techniques, have failed to change substantially more than a third of the homosexuals treated by them.

It is interesting at this point to compare these results with those reported using more orthodox psychotherapeutic techniques. The results of the principal series are summarized in Table 6.3. Here again the success rates vary considerably but when outcome at follow-up is considered, the combined improvement rate for the two psychotherapeutic series (Bieber *et al.* 1962; Mayerson and Lief 1965) is 39 per cent, strikingly similar to the over-all combined rate for the behaviour therapy series (40 per cent).

TABLE 6.3
Outcome of psychotherapy for homosexuality

	Number treated	*Improved at end of treatment*	*Improved at follow-up*	*Duration of follow-up*
Ellis (1956)	40	30 (75%)	—	—
Woodward (1958)	48	7 (14·5%)	—	—
Bieber *et al.* (1962) and (1967)	106	44 (42%)	(34%)	5+ years
Mayerson and Lief (1965)	19		11 (58%)	4½ years
combined			(39%)	

It therefore becomes of particular importance to recognize in the ordinary clinical situation those patients who are likely to fall into this 30–40 per cent. Let us therefore consider a number of factors that may have prognostic significance.

Prognostic factors

Motivation. It is assumed by most workers that the subject's desire for change is a necessary prerequisite for success. To many this would seem a superfluous assumption as a treatment can hardly be considered justified if its goals are not desired by the subject. However, as discussed earlier, it is precisely in this area that so much difficulty arises—to what extent can a homosexual genuinely want to become heterosexual rather than be forced to seek such change by the pressures of society? In many cases the motivation of the subject is not always clear and at the outset there may be ambivalence. Evidence of change during treatment and the increasing probability of a final heterosexual adaptation may resolve the ambivalence which previously had stemmed from the fear of being left 'sexless' or 'neither one thing nor the other'. What observations have been made of the relevance of motivation to outcome?

First, what happens to those who accept treatment under pressure from the courts or from other quarters? Freund (1960) clearly separated the twenty cases in his series who were under pressure from courts or other agencies because of homosexual offences. None of them showed any lasting response to treatment. The outcome was also poor in the seven who received treatment under pressure from relatives. Nine of his patients sought treatment because of 'unrequited homosexual love'; it is possible that to seek treatment in such a situation is more a manifestation of despair than a genuine wish to change. As it happened none of them changed. In MacCulloch and Feldman's (1967*a*) series, eleven patients were referred for treatment on an order of the court and seven were seen following a court appearance. Eight of these eighteen improved as compared with seventeen out of twenty-five of the remainder; a difference which is not significant. In Mellor's (1972) study, five out of seven referred by the court were successfully treated as compared with thirteen out of nineteen of the remainder.

MacCulloch and Feldman reasonably point out that a court referral may enable a homosexual to receive treatment that he either did not think was available or was too shy or ignorant to obtain. It would certainly be naïve to assume that because a homosexual has recently been charged with a homosexual offence, his motivation is suspect and that he does not really want to change. The fact that he has been charged may be sufficient to tip the scales against his continuing as a homosexual. This is borne out in a study of psychotherapy reported by Woodward (1958) from the Portman Clinic. Because of this clinic's forensic association, 76 of the original 113 cases (58 per cent) were referred by the courts or by probation officers. Motivation was measured by co-operation, and staying in treatment was greater in those with more convictions for homosexual offences, although recividism associated with non-sexual offences did not show this relationship. Nevertheless there is no doubt that it is extremely difficult to judge a patient's real wishes if pressure from a court is operating. In the author's opinion, treatment to modify sexually deviant behaviour to a more normal pattern should never be undertaken as a condition of a sentence or probation order, except when the treatment is aimed at suppressing dangerous or severely antisocial sexual behaviour. In this latter case the therapist is primarily acting as an agent of society. If, however, the patient is referred by the courts and appears to be motivated to change to a more normal pattern, then treatment should be offered on a purely voluntary and unconditional basis.

However, as already indicated, the absence of involvement with the courts does not ensure unequivocal motivation in those seeking treatment. It may seem strange that a patient would voluntarily undergo such a procedure as aversion therapy if he did not wish to achieve its aims. However, there are other factors which might operate. Some homosexuals, because of a sense of guilt, might wish to demonstrate to themselves and to others that they have left no stone unturned in their attempt to change: having failed they can then accept their homosexuality with an easier conscience. Aversion therapy with its special connotations might be peculiarly effective in this sense. Others may prefer aversion therapy as a technique in which they can take a passive and relatively non-verbal role and yet go through the motions of being treated. Examples of each are described by Bancroft (1970*c*).

Feldman and MacCulloch (1971) assessed the motivation of their subjects at initial presentation. Unfortunately they did not explain how this was done but they rated four as having low, fourteen equivocal, and twenty-five high motivation. The four in the low category were all over 40. There was a highly significant association between these initial ratings and outcome ($p < 0{\cdot}001$).

The problem of motivation remains an important but complex one. The implication is often made that motivation is a matter of degree, some patients wanting to change more than others. It is unlikely to be that simple. Whereas in some cases the deviant behaviour is strikingly ego-alien and the subject's wish to be rid of it clear and unequivocal, in many others there is considerable conflict. The homosexual may recognize all too clearly the advantages of being heterosexual at an intellectual level whereas in contrast he may have already experienced the emotional rewards of a homosexual relationship. Such a conflict may be denied or hidden, or openly expressed; it seems unlikely that the latter would carry a worse prognosis than the former.

Degree of deviant and normal sexual behaviour before treatment. Feldman and MacCulloch (1971) have concluded that the single most powerful predictor of a poor response to therapy is the complete absence of any previous heterosexual interest. They call such individuals 'primary' homosexuals, whilst the reporting of any previous heterosexual interest invokes the label 'secondary' homosexual. They do not make clear whether heterosexual interest or experience before puberty justifies the 'secondary' label but this is presumably the case. By combining their two series they demonstrated a powerful relationship between 'primary' homosexuality and poor outcome (see Table 6.4).

TABLE 6.4

Association between homosexual type (primary or secondary) and success at latest follow-up in response to avoidance learning.

	Primary	*Secondary*	*Total*
Success	5	36	41
Failure	12	10	22
	17	46	63

$\chi^2 = 12{\cdot}21$; $p < 0{\cdot}001$. Reprinted from Feldman and MacCulloch (1971).

On the strength of these findings these workers concluded that 'primary' and 'secondary' homosexuality have a different aetiological basis. The circularity of this type of reasoning has been mentioned earlier (see p. 12). It is difficult to judge the validity of past sexual histories and as in the case of transexualism (Bancroft 1972*a*) there may be a tendency to retrospective distortion to make the past history consistent with the current sexual identity. If such a mechanism is operating it may be of prognostic but not aetiological significance. Prognostically not even this indicator is foolproof; 29 per cent of the 'primary' homosexuals were successfully treated. In Bancroft's study (1970*c*) there were five so-called 'primary' homosexuals. One of these was rated improved (though the follow-up period was short in his case), two slightly improved. In the group treated by Mumford *et al.* (1973) there were three 'primary' homosexuals, one of whom responded to treatment.

In Bancroft's study there was a significant correlation between the amount of reduction in homosexuality following treatment and the level of homosexuality ($r = 0{\cdot}043, p < 0{\cdot}05$) and heterosexuality ($r = 0{\cdot}381, p < 0{\cdot}05$) in the 2 years prior to treatment. The first correlation may simply be reflecting scope for improvement; the second is more difficult to explain though it may indicate that it is easier to relinquish homosexuality when heterosexuality has been recently experienced. There was no correlation between post-treatment change and the highest level of either homosexual or heterosexual behaviour prior to treatment, nor with the number of years of active homosexuality.

Of the various psychotherapy series, Bieber *et al.* (1962) found some heterosexual activity in the period before treatment to be a good sign, especially an attempt at heterosexual genital contact even if the attempt was unsuccessful. The occurrence of heterosexual dream content before treatment was also a favourable sign. Patients who had been overtly homosexual but not heterosexual before the age of 16, were more likely to discontinue treatment. Mayerson and Lief (1965) found that their unimproved group had the earliest onset and longest duration of homosexuality. The same group also had the earliest onset of heterosexual behaviour. In fact the 'much improved' group had the least amount of heterosexual experience before treatment although the difference was not significant. They also found a tendency for heterosexual dreaming before treatment to be more frequent in the improved group. They concluded that 'actual heterosexual performance is not so important a prognostic factor as is heterosexual orientation'. Woodward (1958) drew no conclusion in relation to heterosexual adjustment but she did suggest that a loss of the homosexual impulse was more likely to occur in 'bisexuals . . . who have not started overt homosexuality until their late teens and who do not have a very long habit of activity'. Ellis (1956) stated, rather surprisingly, that the patients with little or no heterosexual activity before treatment improved more, although the figures he gave did not support this.

In summary therefore, the denial of any previous heterosexual interest in the past substantially reduces the likelihood of a successful outcome. The significance of the amount of previous homosexual and heterosexual behaviour, on the other hand, is not at all clear.

Age. It is often assumed that age is an important variable. MacCulloch and Feldman (1967*a*) reported better results in their patients under 30 (sixteen out of twenty-three improved against nine out of twenty in the over-30 group) however, four of the nine patients over 40 did well. Schmidt *et al.* (1965) and Bancroft (1969; 1970*d*) found no association between age and outcome.

Of the psychotherapeutic series, Bieber *et al.* (1962) found that patients over 35 change less but there was no correlation between outcome and age before 35. Woodward (1958) found that increase in heterosexuality was more common in those under 30, whilst Mayerson and Lief (1965) found no such association.

Age is likely to be associated with a number of variables, some of which will produce conflicting effects. Whereas the younger homosexual may find it easier to make the necessary adjustments to a heterosexual role, he may be less motivated to give up his homosexual role which still has a lot to offer him. The older homosexual is losing his appeal, becoming more aware of the disadvantages of his role as he approaches middle age. Also the young homosexual is likely to have a stronger sexual urge (Kinsey, Pomeroy, and Martin 1948) and may find it more difficult to restrain a well-established homosexual habit. On the other hand in Bancroft's study (1970*c*) increase in heterosexual erections was more marked in the younger age group. It is perhaps not surprising that no clear relationship has been found between age and outcome.

Personality. Attempts to define which personality types respond best to treatment are hampered by the serious general difficulties in defining personality. Feldman and MacCulloch (1971) have paid the most attention to this aspect, though their choice of method for classifying personality types is open to criticism. They labelled their patients according to Schneider's (1958) scheme as 'self-insecure type', 'weak-willed type', or 'attention-seeking type'. No data is available for the validity or reliability of such a classification. Although in most cases the clinical judgement was based on the pre-treatment interview, in some it was revised in the light of findings during treatment. A classification as loaded with value judgements as this would be especially vulnerable to observer bias.

In their earlier paper (MacCulloch and Feldman 1967*b*) they were optimistic about selecting favourable cases by means of this obscure clinical procedure. In the more detailed analysis of their two series by Orford (Feldman and MacCulloch 1971) the results justified less optimism, although they still maintained that those with 'self-insecure' personalities had a better prognosis than those with any other type of personality disorder. Bancroft (1969; 1970*c*) divided his patients into those who would be considered in need of psychiatric help for problems other than their homosexuality and those who would not. In his first study he found no difference in outcome between the two groups. In the second study although there was a trend in favour of normal personality it did not reach significance; ($\chi^2 = 3.53$, 1 d.f.).

The various psychotherapeutic series are no more helpful in this respect. Mayerson and Lief (1965) claimed that patients with 'primary diagnosis of personality pattern or trait disturbance' did better than those diagnosed as 'psychoneurotic'. Ellis (1956) reported a better outcome in his less emotionally disturbed males, but in females the reverse applied. Woodward (1958) concluded that 'psychopathic personality' and heavy drinking were associated with a poor outcome. Bieber *et al.* (1962) concluded that personality diagnosis 'was not related to outcome' but they gave few details.

Psychometric tests have been used in a number of studies. Feldman and MacCulloch (1971) tried the 16 PF and failed to demonstrate any useful predictive factors although the C score (ego strength–ego weakness) showed a weak relationship to outcome. The EPI or MPI has been used by Feldman and MacCulloch (1971), Schmidt *et al.* (1965) and Bancroft (1970*c*). The first two studies found an association between neuroticism and poor outcome but this was not demonstrated in the third. The negative association between general anxiety before treatment and response to aversion therapy has also been shown by Schmidt *et al.* (1965) using the Taylor manifest anxiety scale and Bancroft (1970*c*) using 'anxiety about myself' on the semantic differential. These findings were consistent with those of Marks *et al.* (1970) in a group of transvestites treated with electric aversion. Solyom and Miller (1965) measured their patients on the IPAT anxiety scale; all but one were highly anxious and in the neurotic range; all did badly.

General conclusions about the importance of personality factors to outcome are therefore uncertain at the present time. The suggestion is that the more normal and less generally anxious the personality the better, particularly if aversion is to be used. But as yet such a conclusion is of only limited value in the practical selection of cases.

Intelligence. Intelligence is often considered a desirable quality for psychotherapy (Frank 1961). Only Schmidt *et al.* (1965) and Morgenstern, Pearce, and Rees (1965) have measured intelligence in studies of behaviour therapy for sexual deviance. In neither was an association with outcome found. In the psychotherapy series Ellis (1956) reported a tendency for the better-educated man to show more improvement, whilst Mayerson and Lief (1965) found that patients from lower socio-economic groups did slightly less well. It is still possible that intelligence is more of an advantage in orthodox psychotherapy than in behavioural techniques but this point remains to be demonstrated.

Sex of the patient. Only four female homosexuals treated by behaviour therapy have been reported (all by MacCulloch and Feldman), a few more have been involved in the psychotherapeutic series. Ellis (1956) claimed better results with females than male patients although Mayerson and Lief (1965) found no difference between the two sexes. It is therefore not possible to draw any conclusions from the available evidence except that it is unlikely that women carry a significantly worse prognosis.

Sex of therapist. This is a variable of obvious importance which so far has received no attention. In most series the sexes of the therapists are not given though the impression is that mostly male therapists are involved. However, in MacCulloch and Feldman's series of forty-three cases (1967*a*) a female therapist (Valerie Mellor) treated the majority of cases and has gone on working on her own to produce strikingly good results with male homosexuals since that time (Mellor 1972). It was the writer's original assumption that the use of therapists of the opposite sex in the aversion therapy of homosexuality could well be a disadvantage, hindering the development of heterosexual feeling. Mellor's results disprove this point convincingly and furthermore raise the possibility that the superiority of the Manchester groups' results depends to a large extent on the use of a female therapist. This is made less likely by the fact that in the series of James *et al.* (1973) and Mumford *et al.* (1973) most of the treatment was also carried out by female therapists. The problems of using a same-sex therapist in systematic desensitization, discussed on p. 138, suggest that a therapist of the opposite sex may well be preferable for this method. It is high time that therapist variables in addition to sex of the therapist received some attention in behaviour therapy research.

PAEDOPHILIA

Paedophilia, although most commonly homosexual, may also be heterosexual in the choice of partner involved. There is a certain amount of confusion in the literature about the age range of partner although in most cases the term is used when the desired sexual partner is a pre-pubertal child, or one at early puberty before sexual maturity is reached.

There is very little evidence of the efficacy of behaviour modification techniques in this group. Bancroft and Marks (1968) reported the outcome in four paedophiliacs treated with electrical aversion. Only one of these showed any lasting improvement and this was of a limited degree (this case was reported separately by Bancroft *et al.* 1966). Mellor (1972), on the other hand, obtained good results in a group of twelve paedophiliacs, nine homosexual, three heterosexual. The outcome in eight of these was considered to be successful although as in Feldman and MacCulloch's comparative trial (1971) the reported criterion of improvement was a change in deviant score on the SOM (sexual orientation method).

The treatability of this group is of considerable importance as paedophiliac offences incur such heavy penalties. In the author's experience paedophiliac offenders frequently have personalities in which self-deception and deception of others is marked, making treatment extremely difficult to evaluate (see p. 114). At the moment we lack any obvious prognostic criteria in this group.

FETISHISM, TRANSVESTISM, AND TRANSEXUALITY

Most forms of transvestism that come to treatment are fetishes in which the wearing of female clothes has a sexually arousing effect. Fetishism and fetishistic transvestism will therefore be considered together.

The only form of behaviour modification which has been reported for this condition has been aversion therapy. The first series was reported by Morgenstern *et al.* (1965) and included thirteen transvestites treated with chemical aversion (see p. 34 for details of method). Seven of the thirteen stopped cross-dressing completely; in the remaining six there was a considerable reduction. Little information about outcome was given in this report but more details of the first eight cases were presented by Pearce (1963). Conflicting slightly with the later report it was here stated that one case was a complete failure. The remainder were all moderately or markedly successful. The follow-up period was short. Fookes (1969) in his brief report, claimed success in all five of his transvestites treated with electric aversion, success being indicated by the 'unrefuted claim of the patient to have lost the desire for the perversion'.

Marks *et al.* (1970) reported the outcome 2 years after electric aversion in a group of sexual deviants which included nineteen transvestites. Seven of these showed varying degrees of transexualism (i.e. the desire to have the body of a woman and live as a woman, and not merely as part of the fetishistic masturbation fantasy). Outcome was assessed by means of rating scales of deviant fantasies and behaviour. 'Improved' meant a reduction in rating of more than 25 per cent, 'much improved' more than 50 per cent. The patients were split into two groups: the transexuals and the remainder. In the latter group eight (67 per cent) were much improved after 2 years, four (33 per cent) were unchanged. In the transexual group none was improved at follow-up although three (43 per cent) had shown significant change in treatment, relapsing at some stage during the first year. There was relatively little change in normal heterosexual behaviour in these two groups although in eight patients there had already been regular sexual intercourse before treatment. In these the enjoyment of intercourse usually increased following treatment. Of the nine with no previous heterosexual experience only two succeeded in having regular sexual intercourse following treatment.

The change in deviant behaviour was also reported in a group of twelve untreated transvestites (eight simple, four transexual). Two of these (17 per cent) were rated 'much improved', three (25 per cent, one of them a transexual) 'improved', at follow-up. This group can in no way be considered a control group as the reasons for their not receiving treatment were various, in some cases being due to apparent spontaneous improvement. Nevertheless, it underlines our ignorance of the natural history of these deviant patterns and the need for a controlled study in this particular area.

On the face of it the results of this study were encouraging. The most important prognostic factor to emerge was the presence of transexual feelings which clearly carried a poor prognosis. This is of practical importance not only because it provides a usable selection criterion but also because in some cases these transexual tendencies develop after a period of simple transvestism. This transition from fetishism to transexual transvestism has been discussed in more detail elsewhere (Bancroft 1972*a*). As the transexual state is so resistant to treatment and also so disruptive to the lives of the individual and his family it becomes of potentially great importance to treat the fetishistic stage early. Clearly more work is needed in this particular area.

Transexualism in its full-blown form (Stoller 1969), whether it has resulted from earlier fetishism or childhood transexualism, will rarely be presented to the therapist for behaviour modification because it is very much the essence of the condition that if any change is sought it is in a transexual direction. Nevertheless the occasional case may present and at the present time treatment aimed at reducing the transexualism would seem to be futile. A recent case report (Barlow, Reynolds, and Agras 1973) is of interest in this respect. A young transexual was treated with a form of social skills training which directly aimed at making his social behaviour more masculine. This was accompanied by an increase in heterosexual interest. The follow-up is short, nevertheless, and it should be borne in mind that short-lived dramatic reversal of transexual tendencies was reported by Marks *et al.* (1970). A longer follow-up of this case will therefore be of great interest. The social skills training approach, however, has obvious possibilities in helping the male transexual to 'pass' more effectively as a female and the usefulness of such an approach is being currently investigated by the author.

EXHIBITIONISM

Exhibitionism is an example of deviant sexual behaviour in which the sexual object is usually normal, only the method of relating to that object being deviant. This limits the type of procedure that can be used, as visual stimuli, such as slides, are not likely to be appropriate. Attempts have been made to simulate the exposing behaviour in the treatment situation, (Rooth and Marks 1974) but in most cases imagery has been used.

Evans (1968, 1970) employed a modification of Feldman and MacCulloch's anticipatory avoidance technique. Instead of using pictures, he used slides of phrases related to exposing. He reported the results in twenty cases, success depending on the absence of reported exposing during the 6 months following treatment. Ten were deemed successful, ten unsuccessful. He compared these two outcome groups on a number of variables. There was no difference between the groups in age, marital status, or frequency of sexual intercourse. The successful group showed less deviant masturbation fantasies (i.e. fantasies involving exhibitionism, $p<0{\cdot}01$), and a shorter period of exposing and lower frequency of exposing in the 6 months prior to treatment ($p<0{\cdot}025$). In addition, significantly more trials of aversion therapy were needed in the unsuccessful group before the patient stopped exposing, ($p < 0.01$) or ceased experiencing urges to expose ($p < 0.01$). Evans rather naïvely used these results to stress the importance of applying learning principles in the assessment of cases for treatment. The association between normal masturbation fantasies and successful outcome, he concluded, supported the hypothesis of McGuire *et al.* (1965) that such deviant fantasies maintain the 'habit strength' of the deviant behaviour. There is circularity in this reasoning, however; it could as well be concluded that the use of deviant masturbation fantasies is a consequence rather than a cause of the degree of sexual maladjustment. Nevertheless the involvement of normal fantasies during masturbation can be regarded as a useful prognostic indicator even if it is only a measure of 'severity'. In the same way the frequency and duration of the deviant behaviour may be reflecting the intractability of the problem. This association had not been observed consistently in the treatment of other forms of sexual deviation, but there may be an important difference when the behaviour in question is an offence which may result in prosecution. It is well known that the majority of exhibitionists who are prosecuted only appear before the courts once; prosecution is enough to deter them further. There remains a hard core of recidivists who appear resistant to anything the courts or medical profession can offer. It would have been helpful to have had details of the number of offences in these two groups.

These treatment variables are obviously of limited prognostic value although in the absence of a satisfactory early response they may justify terminating treatment. The little evidence on the timing of onset of change in treatment that is available suggests that there should be early signs of progress (Marks *et al.* 1970; Bancroft 1970*d*).

Fookes (1969) used both imagery and actual exposure in treating seven exhibitionists with electric aversion. Six of the seven were regarded as successfully treated on the basis of the denial of urges to expose. Rooth and Marks (1974) used electric aversion and covert sensitization in their cross-over design reported on p. 87. At 12–14 months follow-up much of the improvement was maintained but 7 of the 12 patients had re-exposed at some stage and 4 had been re-convicted. Abel *et al.* (1970) used an avoidance procedure (described on p. 37) to treat three exhibitionists, but few details of the outcome in these particular subjects are given. An individual case of exhibitionism was successfully treated with systematic desensitization (Bond and Hutchinson 1960).

The only prognostic factor of obvious significance in this group is therefore the presence or absence of deviant masturbation fantasies as reported by Evans (1970).

SADO-MASOCHISM

Few cases of sado-masochism have been treated with behavioural techniques. The use of aversive methods was approached with caution by Marks, Rachman, and Gelder (1965) who feared that, for a masochist, electric shock might have positively reinforcing properties. They devised an ingenious technique for testing this possibility. In an operant procedure the subject was able to avoid or induce shock by varying the speed of responding. He avoided shock both in the presence and the absence of sexually arousing stimuli and went on to show an initially favourable response to treatment though relapsing some months later. Following this, five further sado-masochistic patients were treated with electrical aversion (three sado-masochistic, one sadist, one masochist; Marks *et al.* 1970). Three were 'much improved' and two 'improved' at 2-year follow-up (these ratings indicating more than 50 per cent and more than 25 per cent reduction in deviance scores respectively). These results indicate that masochistic tendencies are not a contra-indication to aversion therapy. Bancroft (1971), however, reported a homosexual patient with masochistic tendencies in whom erections to deviant fantasies increased when associated with shock and in whom aversion certainly produced no benefit (see Fig. 5.15). Very little is understood about the factors causing masochistic responses but it seems unlikely that any simple relationship between painful stimuli and sexual arousal is involved. The facilitation of erections that frequently follows shock discussed in Chapter 5, could provide one mechanism for the conditioning of masochistic responses and at the present time aversive procedures contingent upon erectile responses should probably be avoided in subjects with masochistic tendencies. Reports of single cases involving sado-masochistic behaviour which have been treated with non-aversive procedures have been reported by Davison (1968) and Bancroft (1971) (see p. 44).

7 *Theoretical Conclusions*

AT various stages in this book so far the theoretical basis of behaviour modification has been mentioned and in a previous chapter evidence of effects predicted from such theory was looked for and found to be lacking. It is appropriate at this stage to get this theoretical basis into perspective.

If it is accepted that the primary purpose of research in this area is to improve our ability to carry out useful behaviour modification or treatment, then this purpose can be served in two principle ways:

1. By establishing whether a particular form of treatment is effective and whether by modifying the treatment or the selection of subjects to receive it the efficacy can be further improved.
2. By taking a method that has been demonstrated or assumed to be effective and clarifying the processes underlying its efficacy. In this way the processes may be more effectively or more generally applied.

What part does theory play in each of these types of research strategy? In the clarification of underlying processes of treatment (i.e. 2), one is dealing with mechanisms which are inaccessible. The usual approach in such a case is to adopt a theoretical model† which is assumed in some sense to represent the inaccessible mechanisms under study, and which is formulated in such a way that specific empirical propositions can be generated and verified by experiment.

† For a discussion of the different types of theoretical model that are employed in science, see Harré and Secord (1972).

In the first type of strategy (1) the situation is different. The requirements are first that the treatment procedure is defined in operational terms so that it can be applied in a sufficiently standardized manner, secondly that change in the behaviour being modified is measured satisfactorily, and thirdly that appropriate experimental design is employed to demonstrate the relationship between change in behaviour and the method of treatment. Theoretical models are not necessary for any of these three requirements. The measurement of change in sexual behaviour will be considered in Chapter 8, and the appropriate experimental design will be discussed in more detail in the second half of this chapter. Let us now look more closely at the first requirement, the definition of the treatment procedure. This is basically a set of rules indicating how the therapist should behave and what he should ask the patient to do. It should be sufficiently comprehensive to determine most of the therapist's behaviour, although it is clearly impracticable to determine everything that happens in the treatment situation. It should be sufficiently clear to enable different therapists to behave in a like manner, although again it is impracticable to expect identical behaviour. Such a set of rules can be called a *treatment procedure* to distinguish it from the *theoretical model* of the process of treatment. It should be clear that a treatment procedure will be judged using different criteria to those used in judging a theoretical model. However, treatment procedures are usually derived from theoretical models. Not infrequently a procedure is criticized because the theoretical model on which it is based is considered to be unsatisfactory, though it can be highly effective and based on nothing more scientific than acupuncture or witchdoctoring.

Keeping this distinction between *treatment procedure* and *theoretical model* in mind, let us look at the three main theoretical approaches to behaviour modification and consider in each case the relative merits of the theoretical models and treatment procedures that may be derived from them. The three approaches are as follows:

(1) the traditional stimulus–response learning approach;
(2) the operant learning approach;
(3) the cognitive attitude change approach.

The first two will be considered together in order that the relevant differences between them can be clarified.

THE LEARNING APPROACHES: TRADITIONAL STIMULUS–RESPONSE AND OPERANT LEARNING

D'Amato (1970) has discussed the relative importance of theoretical models in each of these two approaches. The key difference is between prediction and control. In this as in most other respects the difference is one of emphasis but nevertheless it has important implications for treatment research. With the traditional approach of learning theorists such as Hull, Tolman, and Guthrie, the emphasis is on prediction and theoretical models play a central part. With the operant approach of Skinner the emphasis is on behavioural control and theoretical models play a relatively insignificant part. Thus in the first case

> the precise control over the behaviour of individual subjects can be sidestepped by the use of groups of subjects and the major research issues become expressible in terms of how the manipulation of one or another independent variable affects each group's behaviour . . . Variability of results from subject to subject is not only tolerated but expected. Little or no attempt—other than maintaining comparable experimental conditions—is made to force comparable performance in the subjects of a group; the lack of such uniformity is attributed to 'individual differences', i.e. to variables over which the experimenter does not at present have control. (D'Amato 1970.)

For this reason statistical evaluation of experimental results becomes essential.

With the operant approach, on the other hand, when the goal is the control of behaviour, principles of behaviour are based on observed associations between specific behaviour, its consequences, and the setting in which it occurs. Repeated observations in specific circumstances generate behavioural 'laws'. Predictions that the same association will occur if the circumstances are repeated can then be made, but such predictions are not based on any theoretical model. This approach leads logically to the study of individuals rather than groups and if satisfactory behavioural control is established, statistics become superfluous. 'They control their relevant variables experimentally, not statistically' (D'Amato 1970).

This difference in emphasis between the two approaches shows itself in other ways. Reinforcement, for example, is central to both approaches, but whereas the traditionalists will theorize about its nature, the operant man will simply define it in terms of its effects (D'Amato 1970). This leads in the latter case to a certain circularity of definition whereby, for example, punishment is anything that reduces the future probability of a response that precedes it.

Let us now consider each of these approaches more closely. The majority of attempts to modify sexual behaviour have so far been based on traditionalist stimulus–response theoretical models. They include the classical and instrumental conditioning models of aversion therapy and the two models (conditioned reciprocal inhibition and optimal habituation) applied to systematic desensitization. These have all been discussed at some length in Chapter 5. To what extent have they served to clarify the 'process' of treatment? In aversion therapy, as previously indicated, there has been very little evidence to support the various postulated conditioning processes as being central to behaviour change. This may be partly due to the practical difficulties in verifying relevant hypotheses in the clinical situation. Where aversive methods are involved it is also difficult to employ suitable analogue procedures. So far, therefore, aversive conditioning has not proved to be a fruitful theoretical model for process research. Positive conditioning (e.g. of erections) has been somewhat more successful in this respect both with the classical conditioning model and the operant approach which will be discussed below.

How satisfactory are these conditioning models, positive or negative, in providing us with a treatment procedure? They do provide very clear techniques which can be incorporated into a procedure but they lack comprehensiveness; they only determine a part of what happens in treatment. Research into the effects of systematic desensitization proved for several years to be a great encouragement to treatment research in general. A logical series of analogue experiments (reviewed by Rachman 1967) examined the various components of the desensitization procedure to assess their relative importance. Not only was this additive approach a good paradigm of experimental improvement of a procedure but, by clearly separating the components, it offered promising opportunities to test 'process' hypotheses. The relevance of these components to the treatment of patients rather than 'volunteers' was never entirely clear, however, and the importance of systematic desensitization has been thrown into question again following the introduction of a theoretically opposite approach, flooding, which is not dissimilar in its effects (Gelder, Bancroft, Gath, Johnston, Mathews, and Shaw 1973). The value of the reciprocal inhibition or habituation models for process research is therefore uncertain at the present time. As a treatment procedure desensitization is more comprehensive than aversion therapy and has the obvious advantage that its basic principle can be applied by the patient to behaviour outside treatment. Nevertheless for psychiatric patients it is relatively unusual for desensitization alone to be sufficient, and it is common for other therapeutic strategies to be combined with it.

The operant approach to modifying sexual behaviour has featured very little so far, but its contribution is currently growing in importance. It so happens that European and South African behaviour therapists have tended to adopt the traditional learning approach, particularly in the treatment of sexual deviance. This has resulted in the treatment of groups of individuals with the same 'condition' receiving the same technique, the results being subjected to statistical analysis. Not only does this conform with the traditionalist approach to experimentation but also with the 'medical' approach to treatment; the so-called 'medical model' (Yates 1970).

In the United States the main contribution to behaviour modification has stemmed from the operant approach.† From the start, Skinner and his followers were concerned with the practical application of their laboratory based 'behavioural laws'. The logical extension in the first place was to subject human behaviour to comparable laboratory control. Thus the 'operant attack' was first directed at the disturbed behaviour of institutionalized children (Lovaas 1966) or adults (Allyon and Michael 1959), with whom adequate environmental

† This transatlantic difference is now fast disappearing. Wolpe and Lazarus from South Africa and Franks from the United Kingdom, are now in the United States and there is an increasing interest in operant methodology in the United Kingdom.

control was possible. In the treatment of sexual behaviour the same degree of control of reinforcement has been confined to the positive conditioning of erections (e.g. Quinn *et al.* 1970), which can only be carried out in the laboratory situation.

A basic operant principle is the careful analysis of behaviour and its consequences and the organization of the environment so that desirable behaviour is more likely to be followed by positive reinforcement and undesirable behaviour by negative reinforcement. This principle has been used as the basis for comprehensive procedures of treatment for a variety of neurotic or maladaptive behaviours (Goldiamond 1965; Bandura 1969; Krasner 1971). Such procedures determine not only how the patient should behave in his normal environment but also how the therapist should behave in relating to the patient; e.g. if the patient behaves appropriately, the therapist 'rewards' him in some way.

The operant exploitation of the single case study approach, already referred to, raises two very crucial issues. On the credit side it has encouraged the use of treatment programmes which are designed to serve the needs of the individual. This is a healthy departure from the usual 'medical' approach. On the debit side it has led to an undue reliance on the single case study to demonstrate cause–effect relationships in treatment. Yates (1970), for example, takes an extreme view in stating 'controlled investigation of the single case is the only unique feature of behaviour therapy that distinguishes it from other kinds of therapy. If this unique feature is abandoned then behaviour therapy will rapidly approximate more and more to a standard medical model, with catastrophic results.' †

Single case studies do have an important part to play in establishing treatment innovations but the extent to which cause–effect relationships can be established is largely limited to those effects that are reversible and hence fit into the 'baseline–treatment–return-to-baseline approach'. It is possible in some instances to use a multiple baseline approach (Baer, Wolf, and Risley 1968), when there are a number of comparable behaviours to be modified, e.g. responses to a variety of fetish

† Yates is at pains to point out that the usefulness of the single case study has not derived solely from the operant approach and he cites in particular the contribution of M. B. Shapiro.

objects as in Marks and Gelder (1967). Baselines can be established for these different responses (a procedure that is not always easy in the treatment situation) before modification of one of them is initiated. In this way, change in the treated response and no change in the untreated responses suggests a cause–effect relationship. The opportunities for this type of design are few and they raise the usually imponderable question of what determines the degree of generalization of treatment effect to allied behaviours. Furthermore, there has been a singular lack of evidence to generate animal-type behavioural 'laws' which enable one to predict control in more than one human individual. Thus when such cause–effect relationships are established in one case they are of uncertain value in planning treatment for another.†

Even if some degree of prediction is possible when good environmental control is obtained, the single case approach breaks down when the operant principles are applied more generally in and out of the treatment situation by both the patient and the therapist. Then there is no more than a vestige of the control that permitted Skinner to render statistics superfluous.

Thus the operant approach does not concern itself with theoretical models of process but it provides techniques of behaviour control which, when homologous to their laboratory origins (as the operant conditioning of erections), lack comprehensiveness as treatment procedures. When the procedures are made comprehensive enough to deal with the problem of deviant sexual behaviour, their relationship to the laboratory origins becomes more analogous and they cease to differ from other treatment procedures in the need for statistical evaluation of group results.

THE COGNITIVE OR ATTITUDE CHANGE APPROACH

As behaviour therapists have gained more experience, they have, sometimes reluctantly, turned more and more attention

† Undue emphasis on the single case has permitted Yates (1970) to make the following anti-clinical statement:

The validity of behaviour therapy is not a function of whether (the individual patient) improves, deteriorates or remains the same in relation to some arbitrary external criterion, but rather whether it can be shown that changes in his behaviour are lawfully related to the experimental operations which were intended to produce them.

to other aspects of the treatment situation, in particular to cognitive processes. The reluctance has been understandable. They are then dealing with not only inaccessible mechanisms but also relatively inaccessible behaviour, relying on subjective reports or 'pencil and paper' tests. Nevertheless, for many, the crucial importance of such inaccessible cognitive mechanisms and behaviour to the understanding of behaviour modification is obvious. Some have been surprised to find so much apparent relevance in the social psychological literature of cognitive consistency and attitude change. Goldstein and Simonson (1971) have tried to analyse why these two disciplines have kept apart for so long. As yet there have been no studies of behaviour modification, involving either sexual or non-sexual behaviour, in which these ideas and mechanisms have been put to the test. Some research has been done in relation to psychotherapy (Goldstein, Heller, and Sechrest 1966; Goldstein and Simonson 1971), but so far this has been minimal. However, as this approach is becoming a prominent source of theoretical models of treatment at the present time, it is appropriate to consider the underlying theories.

Cognitive consistency theories

The concept of man as a 'rational' being has a long history, though it has been out of favour in psychological circles during this century until the late 1940s (McGuire 1966). Then, following the lead of Heider (1946) a variety of 'consistency' theories were proposed, involving concepts such as balance (Abelson and Rosenberg 1958), congruity (Osgood and Tannenbaum 1955), and dissonance (Festinger 1957). They had in common the idea that man behaves to reduce internal inconsistency amongst his beliefs, feelings, and behaviour. Of these various theories, Festinger's theory of cognitive dissonance has been the most influential and has initiated a considerable volume of experimental work. For reviews of this experimental literature the reader is referred to Feldman (1966), Chapanis and Chapanis (1964), and Bandura (1969).

Dissonance, according to Festinger, is a psychologically uncomfortable state which results from inconsistency between beliefs, feelings, or actions. It is thus accorded a motivating status similar to a 'drive', behaviour being directed at reducing it. As a theory cognitive dissonance tries to predict a great deal and gets into very deep water in the process. Bandura (1969) summarizes the complexities as follows:

According to dissonance theory inconsistent action will produce the greatest amount of attitude change under conditions where small incentives, just sufficient to get the person to comply, are employed; there are minimal threats or coercive inducements; few reasons are given for taking the discrepant stand; the person receives a high degree of choice in committing himself to counter-attitudinal performance; there is high expenditure of effort in the attainment of the goal object or in the enactment of the discrepant behaviour; the inducing agent is viewed unfavourably; and the person being influenced displays high self-esteem.

Both the theory and the experiments generated by it have been widely criticized (Chapanis and Chapanis 1964; Harré and Secord 1972). Conceptually it has all the inadequacies which have been demonstrated in other types of 'drive' theories of motivation (Peters 1960). In addition it moves uneasily between the concepts of dissonance as either a special form of logical relationship or an affective state. So far no one has defined dissonance in terms which enable it to be recognized. In order to make predictions in the experimental situation, the experimenter has been driven to ridiculous lengths of deception and it is inconceivable how one would make any firm predictions in the clinical treatment situation.

It thus seems unlikely that cognitive dissonance will provide satisfactory theoretical models of the process of treatment. However, when we consider *treatment procedure* we are able to refer to a considerable range of strategies or techniques based, to varying extents, on the principle of cognitive consistency and used to attempt to modify attitudes and behaviour. Much of this work has had commercial or political implications, as 'consumer' or 'voting' behaviour are both potentially susceptible to persuasion. The early landmarks in this field were the books of Hovland, Janis, and Kelley (1953), and Hovland and Janis (1959). Most of the key papers are referred to by Bandura (1969) and several of them have been usefully brought together by Rosnow and Robinson (1967). The main theoretical issue that has arisen in this field has been the relationship between attitudes and behaviour (Fishbein 1966), and whether by directly modifying attitudes one can induce stable behaviour change. This question remains to a large extent unanswered though it is widely assumed that whether one starts by changing behaviour or attitudes, both must change if the new situation is to become stable. This is an assumption in line with 'consistency theory'.

Under the heading of attitude change, Bandura (1969) has categorized the available strategies into three groups: belief-oriented, affect-oriented, and behaviour-oriented approaches. This is very reminiscent of the clarification of psychotherapeutic methods offered by Frank (1961) which serves to emphasize the relevance of this section of social psychology to clinical behaviour modification. Let us look at Bandura's three categories more closely and see to what extent they might apply to the therapeutic situation.

Belief-oriented approach. This is based on the use of persuasive forms of communication or information. In this approach there are three principle variables: the nature of the communicator, or in what esteem he is regarded by the subject or recipient; the communication itself; and the personality characteristics of the recipient which may influence his response to a given message from a given communicator.

In the therapeutic situation this category offers two different types of strategy: first, that which aims to maximize the effect of some other treatment strategy, making sure the treatment that follows makes sense and that the patient's expectations of this treatment are appropriate; secondly, that which directly aims to modify attitudes relevant to the goals of treatment. Various experiments have been reported in which direct attempts to modify the patient's opinion of the therapist have been made and these have already been alluded to (Goldstein and Simonson 1971). The general assumption underlying these is that the more positive the patient's feelings about the therapist the more effective the treatment will be. The value of the induction interview in preparing the patient for psychotherapy has also been investigated (Hoehn-Saric, Frank, Imber, Nash, Stone, and Battle 1964; Imber, Pande, Frank, Hoehn-Saric, Stone, and Wargo 1970). As yet, however, there is insufficient evidence of this kind to enable firm conclusions to be drawn about the use of such strategies in the treatment situation.

The concept of 'inoculation' (McGuire 1964), suggests a strategy which could have clinical usefulness, and although in some form it probably features in many therapists' repertoires, it has not been systematically evaluated. The principle, using the analogy of physical immunity to infection, is that one can develop resistance to a form of persuasive communication or event if one has been forewarned of its possible occurrence and hence has had a chance to prepare a defence against it. In the treatment situation the most obvious application of this principle is in warning the patient of possible adverse consequences or phases of treatment which otherwise might be interpreted as evidence of failure or relapse.

The second type of strategy in this category, the direct attempt to modify inappropriate attitudes is, of course, very much part of directive psychotherapy (Frank 1961) though the techniques used have never been properly investigated in spite of the wealth of non-clinical experimental data. In behaviour modification techniques, this aspect of treatment has received even less attention although there is no doubt that the majority of behaviour therapists adopt this type of strategy when it seems to be appropriate. Thus they would expect to correct or modify not only simple ignorance but also inappropriate or inhibited attitudes about normal sexual behaviour. A behavioural approach which has underlined the importance of this aspect of treatment is that described by Masters and Johnson (1970) for the treatment of sexual inadequacy.

The belief-oriented approach, as Bandura (1969) has emphasized, is unlikely to be enough on its own but may facilitate behavioural change so that the two change together in a more stable way.

Affect-oriented approach. In this approach a direct attempt is made to alter the affective response to an attitude object. Thus when a deviant sexual object is involved the aim is to produce a negative affective reaction, such as anxiety, fear, or disgust instead of the usual positive affect of pleasure or sexual arousal. In this way, it is assumed, the attitude to the sexual object will change. There is very little experimental work in this category, most of it involving verbal methods of inducing affective change, but there is a great deal of behaviour modification which fits neatly into this framework although this was usually not the model on which such techniques were based. Thus aversion therapy can be seen as a means of producing negative affect in association with a stimulus of normally positive valence. Similarly systematic desensitization, though it can be conceptualized in other ways, can be seen as a way of producing a calm or neutral affective state in association with an image normally of negative valency. Here one is invoking cognitive inconsistency rather than a conditioned emotional response as the mechanism mediating change.

Hoehn-Saric, Frank, and Gurland (1968) reported an experiment in which patients were subjected to focused attitude change. The technique involved modification of affect with ether inhalation followed by direct suggestion aimed at modifying key attitudes. The attitudes were measured before and after each session by means of a semantic differential. This procedure was followed by appropriate attitude change which carried over to some extent from one session to the next.

Attitude change, as measured by the semantic differential, has been reported during the treatment of sexual deviance (Marks *et al.* 1970; Bancroft 1970*c*,*d*). In neither study, however, was a direct attempt made to establish whether attitude change preceded behaviour change. In the first study (Marks *et al.* 1970) attitude change not only correlated with behavioural outcome but was confined to those attitude objects involved in aversion therapy. In the second study (Bancroft 1970*c*,*d*) attitude change failed to correlate with behaviour change in either the aversion or desensitization group.

There are other ways in which affective experience can be influenced. Valins directly modified the autonomic components of the subjective affective experience by providing false feedback of heart rate. In this way, he modified the approach behaviour to phobic objects (snakes) (Valins 1966). In an experiment more directly relevant to our subject he influenced the preferences for pictures of attractive women in a group of men by feeding back falsely increased heart rate whilst the subjects looked at the pictures (Valins 1967). The full therapeutic possibilities of false feedback in treatment remain to be explored.

Behaviour-oriented approach. This involves inducing behaviour in the subject which is inconsistent with and likely to result in a change in the relevant attitudes and hence an increased likelihood of the behaviour being repeated.

An example of this approach in the experimental literature which is most relevant to behaviour modification is role-playing. In this strategy the subject is asked to enact a role which is discrepant with his own attitudes and behaviour patterns. This procedure has been widely used in cognitive dissonance experiments, most commonly involving writing essays or giving talks which convey a particular message. In these cases it is the message which is discrepant but the behaviour involved in delivering the message makes the discrepancy more relevant to the subject.

A good example of the role-playing strategy is that reported by Janis and Mann (1965). In this study, aimed at modifying smoking behaviour, one group played the roles of lung cancer patients who were told the prognosis and plan of treatment by the physician. The control group simply listened to a recording of these role-playing sessions. There was a greater increase in anti-smoking attitudes and reduction in smoking habits in those role-playing, compared with the control group.

Although role playing in the form of psychodrama has been used in clinical situations for some time (Moreno 1946) only recently has it been based on the attitude change model and used as a systematic method (Goldstein and Simonson 1971).

It may also be that some techniques which induce behaviour change within the treatment situation are effective not because the behaviour change generalizes outside the treatment situation but because it provokes cognitive inconsistency and facilitates attitude change. The modification of erections is an example which was discussed in Chapter 5.

Thus the principles and techniques involved in the attitude change approach, whether or not derived from cognitive consistency theory, do offer treatment procedures which are relatively comprehensive though not yet systematically evaluated. Let us now briefly reconsider these three approaches and assess their relative merits. When the objective is 'process' research, the first two, the stimulus–response conditioning and the operant learning approaches, provide testable *theoretical models* which can be applied to limited aspects of the total treatment situation. The third type, the attitude change approach, is at the present time of more doubtful value in this respect, although it remains possible that the relationship between attitude change and behaviour change is testable.

When we turn to *treatment procedures*, we have two functions to consider. The first is the therapeutic function; providing the therapist with a sufficiently simple framework to avoid blinding him with the inherent complexity of the treatment situation and involving a rationale which meets the emotional needs of the therapist to behave in at least a quasi-scientific manner. The second is the research function; providing a procedure which can be applied systematically enough to have its effects evaluated and which can be modified systematically to see if those effects can be improved upon. In both respects, it is clear that any procedure based solely on the stimulus–response conditioning model is not sufficiently comprehensive. Both the operant and the attitude change approach are superior in this respect though each fits certain aspects of treatment better than others. In choosing between them a number of factors are involved. One approach will suit some therapists more than others, similarly patients' reactions to them are likely to vary. For some, a conditioning approach may be either too mechanistic or dehumanizing, for others it may appear more appropriately rational. Therapists will also vary in the extent to which they prefer their treatment procedure to be based on an all-embracing model, so that everything they do can be fitted into one scheme. It is true that most of the strategies of the attitude change model can be reformulated in learning terms; attitudes, for example, can be defined as 'verbal operants' and 'shaped' accordingly. Similarly, many learning procedures can be reformulated in attitude change terms, aversion therapy can be regarded as a means of provoking inconsistency between beliefs and feelings. However, in the writer's opinion there are times when in order to make it fit the situation, a model is stretched too far to be convincing either to the therapist or to the patient. It is also his opinion that the over-all treatment procedure can be eclectic in its derivation from theoretical models. In Chapter 9 is an example of a treatment approach which makes use of both learning and attitude change principles when each seem to be most appropriate. This is an arbitrary matter which does not necessarily detract from the value of the procedure in outcome research provided that the strategies involved can be defined sufficiently clearly to be repeated.

METHODOLOGY OF OUTCOME RESEARCH

When we consider the evidence that has been presented in this book, it is clear not only that progress in understanding the process of change in treatment has been minimal and is likely to be slow in the future but also that we have achieved little in the way of useful outcome research. On the credit side, we now have a variety of techniques each of which has been found to be useful in certain cases, but set against this is the fact that we understand very little of the indications for choosing one technique rather than another and we are very uncertain when deciding which patients seeking treatment are likely to benefit. This uncertainty stems partly from the traditional adherence to the 'medical model'; we have been concerned with treating conditions rather than individuals. The concept of individual variation, which is so basic to psychological understanding, has largely been ignored in medical research and has received little more attention in the behaviour therapy field. We have gone as far as to employ batteries of possible prognostic indicators which are then correlated with outcome. Needless to say, this usually produces a number of significant correlations and some of these have been reported in Chapter 6. In no case has such a correlational prognostic indicator for the treatment of sexual deviance been cross-validated in a further study. In the treatment of phobias, which has received more systematic and extensive study, and where the same correlational approach has been employed, a variety of prognostic indicators (Gelder *et al.* 1967; Marks, Boulougouris, and Marset 1971), have failed to be validated in further studies (Marks, Gelder, and Edwards 1968; Gelder *et al.* 1973).

Closer attention to both the experimental design and the measures of change is therefore required in studies which aim to answer clinically relevant questions concerning the choice of treatment for the individual case. Measures of change in sexual behaviour will be discussed in the next chapter; let us consider further, problems in experimental design.

Authoritative and comprehensive reviews of this topic have been presented by Campbell and Stanley (1963, specifically in relation to education), Goldstein *et al.* (1966), Paul (1969), and Kiesler (1971). The use of the individual case study design has already been considered and it has been suggested that in evaluating comprehensive treatment procedures appropriate for the modification of sexual behaviour we are required to use group research, especially if we wish to clarify prognostic indicators. Here a few further issues which are considered of particular relevance to outcome research will be discussed. These include:

(1) 'no treatment' control groups;
(2) factorial designs;
(3) cross-over designs;
(4) assessing flexible treatment programmes.

'No treatment' control groups. It is often stated (e.g. Paul 1969) that in order to demonstrate a method's effectiveness it should be compared with a no treatment control group. The virtual absence of any such study testifies to the practical and ethical obstacles involved. Patients seeking and needing help are not likely to wait untreated for the sake of research; they will seek help elsewhere. A 'waiting list' control group, which is sometimes used as a substitute, is not satisfactory as it involves special conditions which are likely to influence change in the target behaviour either positively or negatively.

One must conclude, therefore, that group outcome research should involve the comparison of one technique with another. These may be procedures based on quite different theoretical models (e.g. Bancroft 1970*d*) or alternatively systematic variations of one basic procedure. Although it is true, as Paul (1969) says, that the absence of any significant difference between two compared methods may reflect the fact that neither is effective, it should be possible eventually to demonstrate superiority if further systematic comparisons are made. If not, then we should have serious doubts about the efficacy of any form of behaviour modification.

Factorial design. Paul (1969) has rightly stressed that the factorial design is the most powerful for our purpose. A factorial design is one in which each factor, or main source of variation, is examined at more than one level (Maxwell 1958). It has a particular advantage in permitting interaction between factors to be measured and hence avoiding the need to make direct comparisons between groups that are not necessarily comparable in every respect except the treatment method involved. Full use of the factorial design also means that individual differences are no longer completely lost in the error term, but can at least partly be accounted for if subjects can be satisfactorily classified in terms of a particular individual difference prior to the experiment. Factorial design, in addition, may vary from the most simple to the highly complex. An example of a simple design is that used by James, Orwin, and Turner (personal communication) in the treatment of homosexuals. Patients are

	Aversion	Desensitization
Heterophobic	*n*	*n*
Non-heterophobic	*n*	*n*

where *n* = number of patients

FIG. 7.1. Simple factorial design.

first classified as heterophobic or non-heterophobic (a source of individual variation) and then each of these groups is randomly allocated to either aversion therapy or systematic desensitization. The design is shown schematically in Fig. 7.1.

Although direct comparison of the main treatment effects can be carried out, the most important analysis is of the interaction between treatment and conditions, the hypothesis being that heterophobic patients will do best with desensitization.

A more complex factorial design was used by Gelder *et al.* (1973) in the treatment of phobias. This compared three types of treatment whilst controlling type of phobia, level of expectation and therapist. The design is shown schematically in Fig. 7.2.

Although even more complex designs are possible, that shown

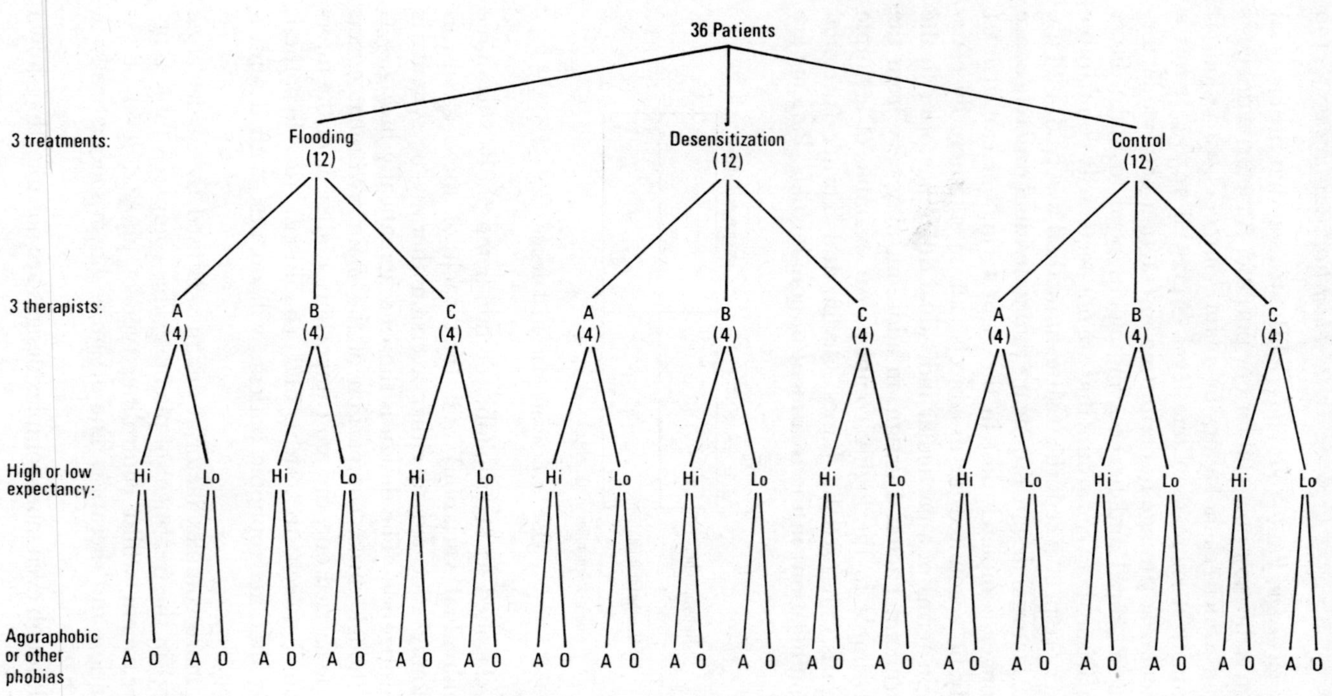

FIG. 7.2. Complex factorial design (Gelder *et al.* 1973).

in Fig. 7.2 is probably as complex as can be practically managed in treatment research. Even so such a design is expensive in both number of patients required and therapist's time and should only be used to answer questions of sufficient importance. There are other designs, not truly factorial, which can be used to answer more limited questions; in particular the cross-over repeated treatment design.

Cross-over design. An example of a cross-over design is that reported by Rooth and Marks (1974) in the treatment of exhibitionists (see p. 87). Some of the disadvantages of this design were discussed in relation to that study. It has the obvious advantage of requiring fewer subjects in order to answer specific questions about main treatment effects. At the same time, however, some information is lost in that a number of rival hypotheses can account for any interaction observed. It is necessary in planning such a design to determine the duration of each treatment block so that improvement is incomplete; obviously if treatment A is followed by treatment B, then treatment A must not be so effective that treatment B has a seriously reduced chance of showing any effect. Only treatments with rapid and simple cumulative effects can be studied in this way. Where there is a possibility of some influence of one treatment on the effects of another, the measuring of a main treatment effect becomes difficult to interpret. Suppose, for example, that treatment A in some way prepares subjects to profit from treatment B, whilst treatment B has the reverse effect on treatment A. This will lead to the false conclusion that treatment B is superior. Finally, it is obvious that the follow-up results cannot be used to assess anything except the effects of a combination of A/B or B/A and there will be, in any case, a number of rival hypotheses to account for such change over time. Repeated treatment cross-over designs would therefore seem to have a limited application to outcome research, and should probably be confined to the study of transient effects.

Assessing flexible treatment programmes. So far the designs discussed have involved the evaluation of clearly defined treatment procedures applied in a standardized manner. As mentioned earlier, however, the clinical approach to the individual patient requires a degree of flexibility that enables the therapist to plan a course of treatment that will suit the individual patient's needs, and also to modify it as appropriate as treatment proceeds. It is mainly this flexibility which distinguishes between what Kiesler (1971) calls 'psychotherapy as an art and psychotherapy as a science of behaviour modification'. Nevertheless if the principles that a clinician follows in making decisions how to proceed are valid, then they should be defined and an attempt made to test them by rigorous experiment.

The experimental validation of flexible treatment programmes does present a particularly important challenge, which so far has not been taken up. Without underestimating the difficulties involved, some possible approaches can be suggested. First, it remains to be demonstrated that a group of patients each treated by a therapist in whatever manner is considered most appropriate would show superior results to a second group, each of which receives a standardized method of known effectiveness. This could be most easily carried out using a simple A/B comparison of matched groups. Although other alternative hypotheses to account for the superiority of one group could not be discounted, the absence of any difference would be a disturbing and important negative finding. In view of the tendency to produce such negative findings in other comparative studies, such a study, relatively easy to carry out in practice, would be worth while. A better design to answer the same question would be a simple factorial design as shown in Fig. 7.1, in which two categories of patients are randomly allocated to either 'free' or 'fixed' treatment.

If one is able to demonstrate the superiority of the flexible approach it then becomes necessary to identify the principles on which that flexibility is based. Here an additive approach could be used in which gradually increasing degrees of flexibility are involved. Thus, one could start with 'one degree of freedom', i.e. one choice between two alternatives, which could then be compared with no choice. If shown to be superior the 'one choice' programme could then be compared with a 'two choice' programme, at each stage the criteria for making the choice being defined. Such an approach would inevitably be time-consuming but at each stage the information obtained would be of immediate clinical relevance. Using a similar approach, principles for changing the treatment programme after it has started could also be established. Thus, if it was proposed that some response to treatment would be evident after x sessions, failure to obtain improvement in that time would be indication for changing to another programme.

It is hoped that other innovations in treatment research designs, as well as these suggested, will be explored in the near future, and that a fair proportion of treatment research effort will be directed at tackling these clinically relevant questions.

8 *Measures of Change*

If behaviour modification techniques are to be properly evaluated, the goals of treatment should be clearly defined and measures used which will indicate the extent to which these goals have been attained. Sexuality, deviant or otherwise, is a complex matter involving the interaction of a number of factors each of which can be separately measured. Following the scheme proposed by Whalen (1966) these factors can be identified as follows:

(1) gender identity and gender role behaviour (Stoller 1969; Bancroft 1972*a*);
(2) sexual preferences and other sexual attitudes;
(3) sexual gratification (i.e. the quality and intensity of sexual pleasure);
(4) sexual arousability (i.e. the capacity to respond to sexual stimulation with increased sexual arousal);
(5) sexual activity, fantasied or real.

The relationship between these components is far from straightforward,† a fact which serves to make the measurement of change more difficult. Let us therefore consider the measuring techniques which have been used for these various components before discussing the extent to which change measured in one component may reflect changes in others.

† For a fuller discussion of the relationship between gender identity and sexual behaviour, see Bancroft (1972*a*).

GENDER IDENTITY

Most attempts to measure gender identity involve questionnaire techniques aimed at establishing the subject's range of interests and preferred activities. First was the M–F test of Terman and Miles (1936) generating an M–F score. This consisted of a combination of tests of word association, ink-blot association, information, emotional, and ethical responses, interests and attitudes to well-known personalities. The test was applied to many different occupational groups for both sexes. In addition it was applied to groups of 'passive' and 'active' homosexuals showing that whereas the 'passive' group were more feminine than some of the females tested, the 'active' group were more masculine than a group of heterosexual soldiers. There is now convincing evidence that sexual passivity is not predictably related to femininity in homosexuals (Hooker 1965; Bancroft 1972*a*) and the M–F test is probably no more than a reflection of conscious sex-typed interests and values that are easily verbalized (Kohlberg 1967) and vary from culture to culture (Mischel 1967). It would not appear to have any value in treatment research.

A further attempt to measure masculinity and femininity as well as characteristics of sexual 'inverts' was made with the MMPI. Scale 5 in the MMPI incorporated some items from the Terman and Miles M–F test. In all, 37 items were found to discriminate between males and females. This particular scale lacks validation more than most in the MMPI and 'it is apparent that considerably more research work is needed if the nature of the sex differences is to be understood' (Dahlstrom, Welsh, and Dahlstrom 1972). Again there are major cultural differences. Feldman (1971) reviewed a number of studies in which the MMPI, the 16 PF test of Cattel, and the Rorschach were used to discriminate between homosexuals and non-homosexuals. In general they were, if anything, less valuable than the more obvious procedure of simply asking the subject what his sexual preferences are. Slater (1944) devised a vocabulary test appropriate to the English culture which was aimed at measuring gender traits on the assumption that men would be more likely to know certain words and women others. Slater and Slater (1947) applied this to groups of homosexual and non-homosexual males and found that the homosexuals knew more feminine words than the normal controls. Clarke (1965), in a further study, showed that the test was highly dependent on age, I.Q., and social class, and that when these were controlled for, the degree of overlap between homosexuals and normals was so great as to make the test of no clinical value.

The dynamic personality inventory (Grygier 1970) is a further European product which is based on the Krout personal preference scale (Krout and Tabin 1954) and aims to measure personality characteristics which would be consistent with psychoanalytic theory. It consists of 325 actions or objects for each of which the subject has to indicate 'like' or 'dislike'. It purports to measure 33 scales including such aspects of personality as hypocrisy, oral aggression, active Icarus complex, ego-defensive persistence, as well as masculine and feminine sexual indentification. A factor analysis study by Kline (1968) suggested only one factor of serious consideration—the 'anal' factor, though the second factor may have reflected masculine interests. Stringer (1970) carried out a further factor analysis and concluded: 'there are 3 bi-polar oral–anal factors and an anal singlet, three phallic factors, two factors of feminine identification, a post-genital (masculine) social sublimation factor and a pre-natal early oral factor'. Once again, it is difficult to see how such a measure will fit usefully into behaviour modification research.

An approach which has more promise is repertory grid technique (Bannister and Mair 1968) based on Kelly's personal construct theory (Kelly 1955). In this technique a series of people (elements) known to the subject are rated on a series of characteristics (constructs) which might include 'masculine', 'feminine', 'like me', 'like I would like to be'. Using the principal components analysis technique devised by Slater (1964) it is possible to examine the position of 'myself' in 'element space' in relation to other people as well as the relationship in 'construct space' between 'like me' and such constructs as 'masculine'. Changes in these relationships can then be measured during the course of treatment (Slater 1965). Such a study was carried out by J. P. Watson (unpublished material). Using a technique described elsewhere (Watson 1970), he investigated three homosexuals undergoing treatment by the author in his comparative study (Bancroft 1970*c*). Grids were administered before, midway through, and at the end of treatment. Watson's main aim was to examine the importance of the therapist and amongst the elements he included 'Dr Bancroft', 'my father', 'my mother', and 'myself'. Changes in the elements space, though interesting, are not relevant here, whilst changes in the construct space are more relevant.

TABLE 8.1

Construct change during treatment: correlations between 'like me' and other constructs

	Patient 1			*Patient 2*			*Patient 3*		
Construct	*Pre*	*Mid*	*Post*	*Pre*	*Mid*	*Post*	*Pre*	*Mid*	*Post*
Worried about sex	0·69	0·92	0·86	0·81	0·87	−0·10	0·73	0·14	−0·71
Like I would like to be	−0·02	−0·11	0·41	0·03	0·25	0·51	0·37	−0·31	0·71
Masculine	−0·43	−0·82	−0·63	−0·03	0·24	0·50	0·29	0·14	0·40
Feminine	0·37	0·85	0·74	0·26	−0·29	−0·37	−0·48	−0·10	−0·53

The correlations between 'like me' and certain other constructs are shown in Table 8.1. These observed changes in correlations reflected independently made clinical observations in an interesting way. Patient 1 was at the outset a markedly effeminate man in mannerism and appearance. He was not well-motivated for treatment but came under pressure from his priest. He did not respond to aversion therapy, but following treatment, 'like me' became more highly correlated with 'like I would like to be' as well as with 'feminine', the correlation with 'masculine' becoming more negative. The suggestion from these changes, that he was more able to accept both his homosexuality and his femininity following treatment, was consistent with clinical observations. Patient 2 started with considerable anxiety about his gender identity. He very much feared being considered feminine although he had no obvious feminine characteristics. He showed a markedly phobic response to heterosexuality and was treated successfully with desensitization. Changes in the correlation with 'like me' showed him to become more 'like I would like to be', more masculine and less feminine. Again this strikingly reflected clinical observations. Patient 3 did not consider himself feminine but worried a great deal about having an inadequate penis. He showed a fluctuating course during treatment going through phases of apparently substantial improvement and then relapsing. At the end of treatment there did seem to be a considerable improvement but the fluctuating course continued through the follow-up period. This is to some extent reflected in the changes in his grid scores which had deteriorated midway through treatment and had improved at the end.

Davison, Brierley, and Smith (1971) reported a case study of a homosexual twin of a discordant monozygotic pair who was treated with aversion therapy. Changes in his element space following treatment suggested a more masculine identification, closer to his heterosexual twin.

There is now increasing interest in non-verbal types of communication and behaviour (Argyle 1969). Some of these behaviours are typically feminine or masculine and may thus play a significant part in gender role behaviour. Women, for example, are more likely to position themselves close to the person they interact with. They generally engage in more eye contact than men and are less likely to adopt relaxed 'asymmetrical' postures during face to face contact. Men are more likely to show high rates of leg and foot movement whereas they touch others less often than women. These various findings have been reviewed by Mehrabian (1972). As yet such evidence is extremely scanty but if gender role behaviour is to be systematically modified, it will be necessary to establish ethological measures of sex-typed behaviour both to clarify treatment goals and to assess their attainment.

SEXUAL PREFERENCES AND OTHER SEXUAL ATTITUDES

Sexual preferences refer not only to the characteristics of one's preferred sexual partner but also to the method of relating to that partner. Distinguishing between homosexual and heterosexual preference and measuring change in this respect is a simple and extreme example. More subtle changes such as in age or shape of one's partner as well as changes from methods of relating which are deviant (e.g. sadistic) to 'socially acceptable' (e.g. assertive) may need to be measured. Techniques of measurement can be divided into 'pencil and paper' tests (attitude measurement) and psychophysiological tests.

'Pencil and paper' tests

The sex inventory. An attempt to devise a questionnaire of sexual attitudes and preferences was reported by Thorne (1966*a*) and called the sex inventory. This consisted of 200 statements about sexual behaviour with which the subject agreed or disagreed (e.g. I feel nervous with the opposite sex; sometimes sex thoughts drive me almost crazy; I always seem to have affairs with older women). Forty of the items were taken from the MMPI and slightly modified. The questionnaire was devised with sexual offenders in mind and, apart from 101 university students involved, was standardized on various sub-groups of prison populations, some sexual offenders, others not. The factor analysis of this base sample (Thorne 1966*b*) generated nine factors which were labelled (*a*) sex drive and interest, (*b*) sexual maladjustment and frustration, (*c*) neurotic conflict associated with sex, (*d*) repression of sexuality, (*e*) loss of sex control, (*f*) homosexuality, (*g*) sex role confidence, (*h*) promiscuity, (*i*) masculinity–femininity. The 101 college students took part in a test and retest reliability study over a 3-month period (Allen and Haupt 1966), in which correlations ranged from 0·67 to 0·89, most being over 0·75. These workers therefore concluded that the sex inventory was a satisfactory measure of stable attitudes. However, this questionnaire has not apparently been used to measure change during treatment. Clearly it would need to be standardized on a more representative population if it was to have wide application. Also, as with most questionnaire tests of sexual attitude, it is probably culture–sensitive and likely to become quickly out of date. It is conceivable, however, that changes in one or other of the scale scores could be a useful measure of response to treatment.

The semantic differential. Marks and Sartorius (1968) reported a modification of Osgood's semantic differential technique (Osgood, Suci, and Tannenbaum 1957). They included standard general evaluative scales (pleasant–unpleasant; good–bad; kind–cruel) and added three approachability scales (friendly unfriendly; approachable–distant; warm–cold), four sexual evaluative scales (seductive–repulsive; sexy-sexless; exciting–dull; erotic–frigid) and three 'anxiety' scales (placid–jittery;

calm–anxious; relaxed–tense). They used these scales to describe a mixture of sexual and non-sexual concepts (elements). This test was administered to a small group of psychiatric patients, half of whom had problems of sexual deviance. Slater's principal components analysis produced three components, general evaluation (81 per cent of the variance), sex evaluation (7 per cent of the variance), and anxiety (4 per cent of the variance). Approachability did not emerge as a separate component but was merged into general evaluation. The test–retest correlations (for a 24-hour period) for the factor scores were all above 0·70 and were considered stable enough to be of clinical value in detecting change with treatment. The semantic differential has the advantage of being easy and quick to adminster (see Fig. 8.1 for a sample form), easy to score and

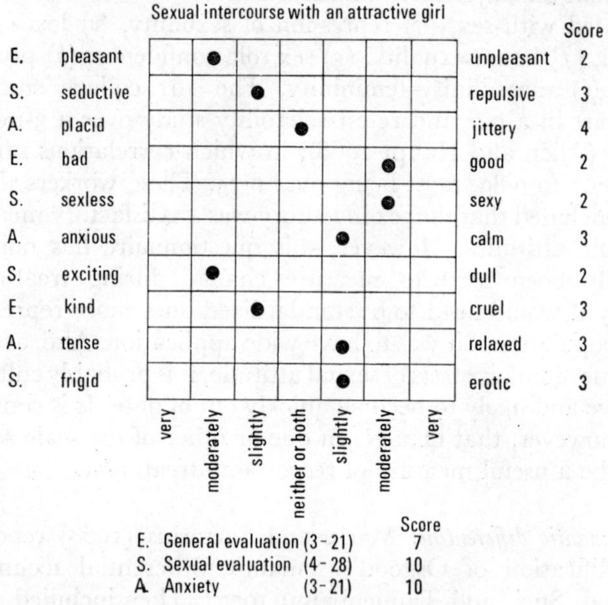

FIG. 8.1. A semantic differential form for the concept 'sexual intercourse with an attractive girl'. The subject's scoring is indicated with a '●' in each line and the score for each scale is given in the column on the right. A score of 1 is most positive, 7 most negative and 4 neutral. The total scores for the 3 factors (E, S, and A), given below the form, are obtained by summing the individual scales for each factor.

flexible in application. It can be used to measure a wide range of sexual attitudes and preferences and can be tailored to suit the individual patient. It has the disadvantage, however, of being easy to dissimulate. It has been used in a number of studies as a measure of change (Marks and Gelder 1967; Marks *et al.* 1970; Bancroft 1970*d*). An example of its use in a single case study is shown in Fig. 8.2.

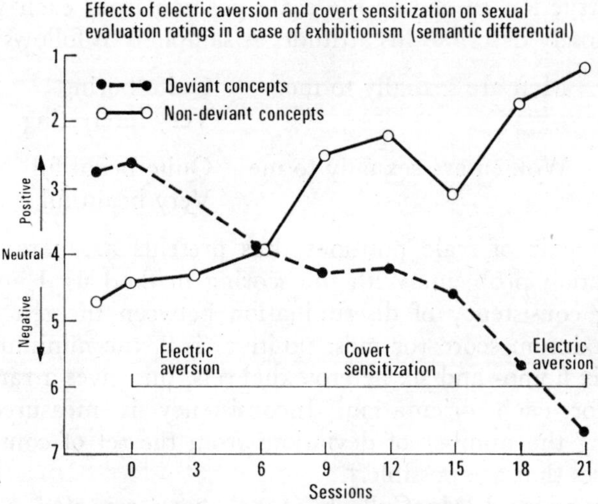

FIG. 8.2. In this exhibitionist patient the semantic differential was administered every third session. The scores here are for sexual evaluation ratings for deviant (i.e. exposing) concepts and normal (i.e. non-deviant) sexual concepts. In this case electric aversion was alternated with covert sensitization. The scores suggested a greater effect from the electric aversion.

The sexual orientation method. This test was devised by Feldman *et al.* (1966) specifically to measure change in homo- and hetero-erotic orientation in the course of aversion therapy. It combines features of the semantic differential (Osgood *et al.* 1957) and the personal questionnaire technique of Shapiro (1961). The method of presentation was devised so as to make use of the scoring system of the latter as well as its ability to detect internal consistency.

Six adjectives and their opposites were taken from the list provided by Osgood *et al.* (1957). These were 'interesting', 'attractive', 'handsome' (or 'beautiful'), 'hot', 'pleasurable', and 'exciting'. These adjectives were applied to two concepts: 'men are sexually to me', and 'women are sexually to me'. Each adjective pair had 5 scale positions: very, quite, neither one nor the other. Each scale position is compared with each of the others making 10 comparisons for each adjective pair. As the six adjectives are applied to the two concepts men and women this makes 12 sets of 10 comparisons, 120 in all. These comparisons are presented to the subject in random order with the instruction to choose the scale position from each which most closely describes his attitude. A sample is as follows:

Men are sexually to me	Quite boring Very interesting
Women are sexually to me	Quite beautiful Very beautiful

Each pair of scale positions thus presents a separate discrimination problem. With the scoring method used and assuming consistency of discrimination between the ten pairs, the maximum score (or most positive) is 8, the minimum, 1. With six homo- and six heterosexual sets, this gives a range of 6–48 for each orientation. Inconsistency is measured by counting the number of deviations from the set of consistent responses that are possible.†

Feldman and MacCulloch (1971) have reported a high degree of internal consistency on this basis. In addition they demonstrated a unidimensionality by carrying out a principal components analysis and finding the vast majority of variance attributable to the first component. Test and retest reliability was approximately 0·8. The validity of this measure was assessed by comparing scores before and after treatment in two groups, improved and unimproved. Prior to treatment the mean scores of the two groups did not differ. Following the treatment the differences were highly significant on both homosexual and heterosexual scores.

Phillips (1968) criticized the scaling method used pointing

† An example of an inconsistency is as follows:

If two adjective pairs are: 'neither interesting nor boring'—'quite interesting', and 'quite interesting'—'very interesting', an inconsistent response would be the choice of 'neither interesting nor boring' from the first pair and 'very interesting' from the second pair.

out that inconsistencies as defined by Feldman and MacCulloch could in fact be consistent depending on the configuration used. He suggested an improvement by reducing the number of discriminations involved. Turner, James, and Orwin (1973) found that in the homosexuals studied by them the degree of internal inconsistency was very much higher than that reported by Feldman and MacCulloch (1971). They also commented on the tediousness of this procedure and how it tends to irritate the subject. As its main advantage would seem to be in avoiding the possibility of 'faking good' which cannot be excluded with simpler methods such as the semantic differential, these criticisms throw some doubt on the usefulness of the measure. Woodward, McAllister, Harbison, Quinn, and Graham (1973) compared the original SOM scoring method with the modification recommended by Phillips. They applied the two tests in two groups of subjects, one unselected normals, the other homosexuals referred for treatment. They found the two tests equally good at discriminating between the groups and the inconsistency score was substantially lower using the Phillips system. This was presumably due to a loss of information with the simpler method. With either method, therefore, the internal validity based on the inconsistency score is uncertain and the simpler method has the obvious advantage of relative brevity. A further limitation of the SOM is that it is simply a measure of homosexual and heterosexual preference. Although it can be easily modified to discriminate another specific preference (e.g. age; Feldman, MacCulloch, and MacCulloch 1968), it nevertheless lacks the flexibility of the semantic differential approach.

Harbison, Graham, McAllister, and Quinn (1973) have modified the sexual orientation method to include some scales indicating anxiety about men and women as sexual partners. They showed this anxiety dimension to be distinct from the sexual preference dimension by means of principal components analysis. These same workers (Graham, Harbison, Quinn, and McAllister 1971) devised a further test based on the sexual orientation method which was designed to assess interest in different types of sexual behaviour with one's partner. Though this was designed for use in investigating sexual inadequacy it could also be applied to deviant sexual behaviour. Five concepts were involved: 'kissing my sexual partner is to me', 'being kissed by my sexual partner is to me', 'touching my sexual partner is to me', 'being touched by my sexual partner is to me', and 'making love (sexual intercourse) with my sexual partner is to me'. The adjective scales were the four sexual scales used by Marks and Sartorius (1968) in the semantic differential. Considering the time and tedium of using this method it remains to be demonstrated that it offers any advantage over the simpler semantic differential.

Psychophysiological tests

A wide variety of physiological measures have been investigated as possible indicators of a sexual response. In the majority the response appears to be nonspecific and hence does not discriminate between sexual arousal and other types of arousal (Zuckerman 1971). Penile erection does appear to be a specific sexual response although occasionally it can be elicited by non-sexual stimuli (Bancroft 1974).†

This measure has now been used extensively to indicate sexual preferences including the discrimination of homo- and heterosexual preferences (Freund 1963; McConaghy 1967; Bancroft 1971; Lee-Evans 1971), and age preferences (Freund 1967). Used simply as a test of sexual orientation, this procedure would appear to be of limited value as there are simpler ways of answering the same question. Freund (1967) has claimed, however, that it is possible to detect 'faking good' or 'faking bad' should there be any likelihood of that occurring. In his case there was apparently a need to identify people who were simulating homosexuality in order to evade military service in Czechoslovakia. For this purpose he was relying on the detection of very small erectile responses to a large number of stimuli. The work of Laws and Rubin (1969) and Henson and Rubin (1971) suggested that as far as obvious erections are concerned it is certainly possible to inhibit their development by conscious control although less easy to produce them at will.

This measure has additional value as an indicator of more subtle sexual preferences. Erections to erotic fantasies can be measured as fantasies are gradually modified; in this way it is

† Technical aspects of penile plethysmography are discussed in the Appendix.

possible to identify the crucial components of an erotic fantasy which may not be apparent to the subject. An example of this use is reported by Bancroft (1971). Changes in erectile response have also been used as indicators of response to treatment (McConaghy 1969; Bancroft 1970*d*). The validity of this type of change will be discussed further below.

Various techniques of measuring genital response in the female have recently been described (Cohen and Shapiro 1971; Jovanovic 1971) but as yet no application of such measures to the assessment or treatment of sexual deviance has been reported.

SEXUAL GRATIFICATION

Although Thorne (1966*c*) described a questionnaire, distinct from his sex inventory, which was aimed at describing the quality of sexual experience, no report of its application was presented. No other measures specifically designed for this purpose have been reported.

SEXUAL AROUSABILITY

The only attempts to directly measure this have involved psychophysiological methods. In studies of drug effects on sexual response a variety of measures were used including the measurement of erections and self ratings of sexual arousal (on a 5-point scale) in response to a standard set of erotic stimuli consisting of fantasies, slides, and films (Tennent, *et al.* 1974; Bancroft, Tennent, Loucas, and Cass 1974).

The concept of sexual arousal has been discussed elsewhere (Bancroft and Mathews 1971; Bancroft 1971; Bancroft 1974), but it should be emphasized here that is is unlikely to be a unitary state, any more than general arousal is now considered to be. In other words, penile erection may or may not be accompanied by other forms of autonomic activity. Nevertheless in most situations penile erection is a physiological response to sexual stimulation and, more important, is likely to be interpreted as such by the subject. Bancroft (1971) reported the correlations between the degree of erectile response and self ratings of sexual arousal in a group of homosexual patients. Where the mean erectile response was greater than 0·4 mm increase in diameter, the correlations were almost all significant.

When the mean response was less than 0·4 mm the correlations were usually not significant. In the drug study already mentioned (Tennent *et al.* 1974), the correlation between erection and self ratings of sexual arousal was also examined in those testing sessions in which no drugs were involved. Rank order correlations were estimated for eleven subjects, each one based on 15 observations. Eight of the correlations were significant, four at the 1 per cent level and four at the 5 per cent level. The previously mentioned association between degree of correlation and mean erectile response was not observed in this situation. Other observations relating to methodology were also made in these two drug studies and reported separately (Bancroft and Staples 1974). The possibility of an order effect with a repeated presentation of erotic stimuli had obviously to be considered. Reifler, Howard, Lipton, Liptzin, and Widman (1971) reported a satiation effect with repeated exposure to pornography. This study, however, involved daily exposure over several weeks, whereas with the drug studies exposure was every 6 weeks. In neither of the drug studies was there any significant reduction of erectile response or self ratings with repeated testings using the same stimuli. In the first study there was a slight trend towards increased response to film; in the second study there was a slight trend towards decrease in response to slides. A number of factors may be relevant in this respect, including the duration between testing and the degree of inhibition in the laboratory situation which may decrease with repeated testing. For the moment, therefore, an order effect should be assumed and accounted for in the experimental design.

The relative strength of the three types of stimuli used in these drug studies was also assessed (Bancroft and Staples 1974). The fantasy and slide were not significantly different in either the erections or self ratings that they produced but film was more effective than either with both measures ($p<0{\cdot}001$). This is consistent with an earlier study (Corman 1968) in which film was shown to be more arousing than still pictures.

To summarize we can conclude that, with our present state of knowledge, sexual arousal in the male is a complex state which involves a number of physiological and autonomic responses of which penile erection is the most specific. The presence of erection should not be taken to indicate generalized arousal so that if sexual *arousal* is to be measured both erection and either subjective ratings or other autonomic responses (e.g. skin conductance or blood pressure) should be recorded. Sexual arousal in the female has not yet been sufficiently investigated to enable it to be used as a measure of change in treatment.

SEXUAL ACTIVITY

In assessing behaviour modification techniques the most relevant change to be measured is obviously change in the sexual behaviour being modified. This can be divided into overt acts and imagined acts and both are likely to be important. Although a number of measures have been suggested, little attention has been paid to the particular needs of treatment research in this respect.

Scaling of sexual experience

Podell and Perkins (1957) were the first to investigate the scaleability of sexual behaviour. Using a sample of 100 unmarried college students they constructed a scale of 15 heterosexual activities ranging from 'embrace' to 'oral contact with female genitalia'. They showed it to be highly predictable that an individual who had experienced any item in the scale would also have experienced all the items preceding it. Brady and Levitt (1965) carried out a further study of this kind on a smaller sample. Their conclusions, although basically agreeing with Podell and Perkins, rather surprisingly placed homosexual behaviour at the top of the continuum including heterosexual behaviour, thus implying that anyone who had experienced homosexual contact would also have experienced all the heterosexual behaviours. Bentler (1968 *a,b*) took this approach a stage further and using a procedure of multidimensional homogeneity scaling, a form of non-metric factor analysis, produced a male and a female scale both with a high degree of internal consistency and scaleability. In the male scale, the first item was 'one minute continuous lip kissing', the top item 'mutual oral manipulation of genitals to mutual orgasm'. The female scale was very similar with 2 items being in slightly different order. Bentler suggested that one of the applications of the scale would be to assess change resulting from treatment. It could certainly be used to indicate progression up the scale but it does not indicate frequency or quality of such behaviour and it is relatively insensitive to the early changes that would be required (e.g. changes in masturbation fantasy or 'dating' behaviour). Whereas the scaleability that it provides does have various research advantages, some other measure more appropriate for assessing treatment is still required.

Behavioural ratings

A number of workers have used changes in Kinsey ratings (Kinsey *et al.* 1948) as indicators of response to treatment (e.g. MacCulloch and Feldman 1967*a*; Birk *et al.* 1970). These ratings are on a 6-point scale briefly defined as follows:

0. Exclusively heterosexual with no homosexual reactions or experience.
1. Predominantly heterosexual, only incidentally homosexual.
2. Predominantly heterosexual, but more than incidentally homosexual.
3. Equally heterosexual and homosexual.
4. Predominantly homosexual, but more than incidentally heterosexual.
5. Predominantly homosexual, but incidentally homosexual.
6. Exclusively homosexual.

These definitions are expanded in the original text (Kinsey *et al.* 1948, p. 639).

As originally described these ratings were intended to refer to a defined period of time. They indicate little more than a simple assessment of the relative proportion of homosexual and heterosexual interest and behaviour. There is little scope for measuring change and for this reason they are of limited value for treatment research.

A variety of attempts to measure the frequency of sexual thoughts have been made. Barlow *et al.* (1969, 1973) used a 'notebook' method in which the subject recorded any incident of strong sexual urge, arousing thought, or act and these were then counted. Bancroft and Marks (1968) and Marks *et al.* (1970) used therapist's ratings based on detailed clinical interviews. They were separated into scores for frequency of sexual thoughts and fantasies and scores for overt acts. Bancroft (1969)

TABLE 8.2a (From Bancroft 1969)

HETEROSEXUALITY

(*a*) *Fantasies and interest*	
1. Fantasies (with or without masturbation)	
Occasional fantasies but less important or frequent than other types of fantasy	+1
or	
Not the exclusive type of fantasy but no obvious difference in importance or frequency from other types of fantasy	+2
or	
The most frequent or most important type of fantasy	+3
2. Finds some females that he sees sexually attractive:	max. +1
(*b*) *Relationships with females whom he finds sexually interesting*	
1. Takes them out for dates (or finds wife sexually interesting):	max. +1
2. Kissing and caressing but no genital contact	+1
or	
Genital contact, but no sexual intercourse	+3
or	
Sexual intercourse, but less frequent than other forms of orgasm as sexual outlet	+4
or	
Sexual intercourse, as most frequent and satisfying form of sexual outlet and orgasm	+5
3. Anxiety occasionally leading to impotence	−½
or	
Anxiety usually leading to impotence or avoidance of intercourse or no interest in initiating intercourse	−1
4. Reliance on deviant fantasies during intercourse:	
less than 50 per cent	−½
more than 50 per cent	−1

reported a comparable rating method which combined thoughts and behaviour giving a separate score for homosexuality and heterosexuality. Arbitrary weightings were given for different types of behaviour according to their assumed importance. This rating method is shown in Table 8.2 (a and b).

For each scale the maximum score possible for fantasies and interest (*a*) is 4, and for overt behaviour (*b*) 6, giving a combined maximum of 10 for each scale. When first reported, no assessment of the reliability of these ratings had been made.

TABLE 8.2b (From Bancroft 1969)

HOMOSEXUALITY

(*a*) *Fantasies and interest*	
1. Fantasy (with or without masturbation) (as for heterosexuality)	+1
	+2
	+3
2. Finds some males that he sees sexually attractive	max. +1
(*b*) *Relationships with males he finds sexually attractive*	
1. Keeps company with them because he finds them sexually attractive	+1
or	
Visits places where homosexual contacts may be made, for that purpose	+1
2. Occasional physical contact with males producing sexual arousal but no orgasm in either person	+1
or	
Sexual contact with male leading to orgasm in subject and/or partner:	
Less than once a month	+2
More than once a month but less frequent than heterosexual genital contact	+3
More than once a month and more frequent than heterosexual genital contact or more than once a week, but less frequent than heterosexual genital contact	+4
More than once a week, and the most frequent type of genital contact	+5
3. Experiences anxiety or revulsion during homosexual acts but does not prevent orgasm	$-\frac{1}{2}$
or	
Anxiety makes him impotent or avoid genital contact, or orgasm	−1
or	
Experiences no sexual arousal during homosexual act	−1

Recently they were used in the study carried out by James *et al.* (1973). In each of the fifty homosexuals treated two independent sets of behavioural ratings based on a 3-month period were made.† Heterosexual ratings were the same in

† I am indebted to Sheelah James and Keith Turner for providing me with their raw data and to Angela Skrimshire for calculating the reliability coefficient.

thirty-seven cases. The distribution of scores was highly skewed towards the zero end, however, and inter rater reliability was greater for the lower scores (See Fig. 8.3). Homosexual ratings were the same in thirty-five cases. Once again the distribution is skewed towards the 'deviant' end (high scores in this case), though less so than in the heterosexual scores. Again the reliability was greater for the more 'abnormal' scores. The reliability coefficients were surprisingly high for this kind of rating; heterosexual scores $r = 0{\cdot}96$ homosexual scores $r = 0{\cdot}93$. Further consideration should be given to using these scales in treatment research.

In the drug studies of sexual offenders (Tennent *et al.* 1974; Bancroft *et al.* 1974) a self rated Lickert scale for frequency of sexual thoughts was used. This scale is shown in Fig. 8.3.

Frequency of sexual thoughts

0	1	2	3	4	5
No sexual thoughts at all	Sexual thoughts very infrequent	Sexual thoughts some days but not every day	Sexual thoughts at least once or twice a day	Sexual thoughts frequent but only sometimes associated with sexual excitement	Sexual thoughts frequent and usually associated with feelings of sexual excitement

Please indicate how often you find yourself thinking sexy thoughts by marking the above line in the appropriate place. Mark between numbers if this seems indicated.

FIG. 8.3. Self-rating scale (Tennent *et al.* 1974).

This was the only measure to show significant differences between treatments in both studies. Test–retest reliability was checked by giving this scale at intervals of 1 week, asking the subject to rate for the previous week. The results are given for the pre-treatment period and for the 'active drug' period in Table 8.3. The reliability during the pre-treatment period is respectably high and indicates that this measure can also be used as a measure of change during treatment.

THE ASSOCIATION BETWEEN DIFFERENT MEASURES

It has been emphasized that there are different aspects of sexuality each of which can be separately measured. When a

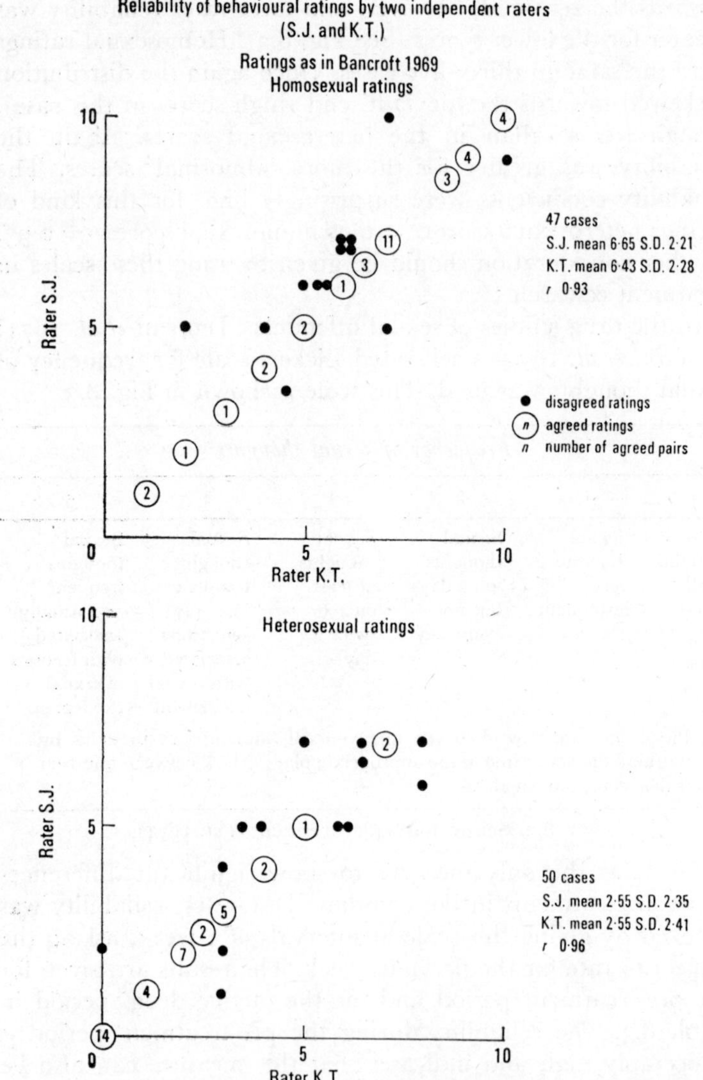

FIG. 8.4. The reliability of behaviour ratings by two independent raters using a rating scale reported by Bancroft (1969). The ratings which were in agreement are shown as circles, the number in the circle indicating the number of agreed ratings at that point. For further details, see text.

particular aspect of sexual behaviour is being modified it is obviously desirable to use measures which are most relevant to that aspect. Nevertheless it is of some practical importance to know what the association is between different measures. Measuring techniques are time-consuming and may confound treatment effects; clearly, it is better to use one measure if it

TABLE 8.3
Test–retest reliability for self rating of frequency of sexual thoughts (7 days interval)

	Pre-treatment period		*Drug treatment period*	
	1st testing	*2nd testing*	*1st testing*	*2nd testing*
Mean	3·13	3·13	1·59	1·75
Standard deviation	1·05	1·02	0·79	0·79
Reliability coefficient:	$r = 0{\cdot}766$ d.f. 24		$r = 0{\cdot}613$ d.f. 23	

gives as much relevant information as two or more. What, therefore, is the correlation between measures both in absolute terms and in terms of change?

Lee-Evans (1971) working with the Belfast group, used a non-parametric measure of erections, the Mann–Whitney U score. A U score of 100 means that all responses to heterosexual stimuli were greater than any response to homosexual stimuli; a score of 0 indicates the opposite. These scores were correlated with sexual orientation method homosexual and heterosexual scores (rank order correlation) in twenty homosexuals awaiting treatment. The correlations were as follows:

TABLE 8.4

Erectile response	*Sexual orientation method*		
	Homosexual score	*Heterosexual score*	*Homosexual score minus heterosexual score*
Increase in amplitude after 60s (U score)	−0·24	0·60†	−0·59†

† $p < 0{\cdot}001$

This work was continued by Harbison *et al.* (1973) who found that whereas the correlations with the SOM scores were significant, the correlations with semantic differential scores were not. The reason for this difference is not clear.

Bancroft (1970*c*) failed to find any significant correlations between pre-treatment erectile response, behavioural ratings, or attitude ratings (semantic differential). Of more importance to behaviour modification, however, were the correlations between change scores. In this same study when the two treatment groups (aversion and desensitization) were combined there was again a failure to find any significant correlations between change scores on any of these measures. When the treatment groups were looked at separately one correlation reached significance. This was between the heterosexual attitude change and change in erections to heterosexual stimuli in the desensitization group ($r = 0{\cdot}632$; $p < 0{\cdot}05$). However, as there were 49 correlations in this particular matrix this was no doubt a chance finding.

Marks *et al.* (1970) found a significant correlation between attitude change (semantic differential) and change in deviant behaviour scores in transvestites and fetishists being treated. Of particular interest was the high correlation between attitude change after only 3 days of treatment and final behaviour change as this raised the possibility of recognizing likely failures early in treatment.

However, in the drug studies of sexual offenders (Bancroft and Staples 1974) there was again low association between the measures used. These included a sexual interest score (see p. 201), sexual activity score (a frequency count of orgasms excluding nocturnal emissions), sexual attitude (semantic differential), and erectile response to three types of erotic stimuli (fantasy, slides, and film). Of the rank order correlations between pre-treatment scores only one reached significance; this was between erections to erotic slides and sexual activity score ($\rho = 0{\cdot}427$; $p < 0{\cdot}05$).

When the change scores were considered there were 3 significant correlations out of 15 computed. These were between change in attitude scores and change in sexual activity scores ($\rho = 0{\cdot}55$; $p < 0{\cdot}001$); change in erections to fantasy and change in sexual activity scores ($\rho = 0{\cdot}45$; $p < 0{\cdot}05$); and change in erections to slide and change in attitude score ($p = 0{\cdot}486$; $p < 0{\cdot}05$.) This particular selection of correlations is difficult to interpret.

When these various studies are considered together it becomes clear that there is an unpredictability of the association between most of these measures. It should therefore be concluded that with the measures currently available there is no justification for using a measurement of change in one area to indicate change in any other. Whenever possible a variety of measures should be used which cover the most important areas, or, when appropriate, one measure which clearly reflects the goals of treatment.

This issue is a fundamental one in behaviour modification research. There has been a tendency to develop objectivity in measuring devices at the expense of validity; it is crucial when considering measures of change to remember that each individual presenting for treatment presents a unique problem and a more or less unique set of goals. Most of the measures considered in this chapter may be reproducible and allow comparison between individuals but the extent to which they allow us to measure the efficacy of treatment is far from clear. The problem of developing measures which are both relevant to the individual patient's goals and suitable for the comparison of treatment between individuals and groups is one of the main areas requiring research in the behaviour modification field.

9 *Clinical Conclusions*

WHILST the conclusions about research in this area may seem to some to be unduly pessimistic, it is certainly not this writer's intention to discourage the treatment of individuals who seek to modify their deviant sexual behaviour. Although in many cases such treatment is extremely difficult or doomed to failure, in others there is a great deal that can be done to help. The author continues to treat such problems in a non-research setting in which he tries both to improve method and to teach it to others. For both purposes it is necessary to formulate as clearly as possible what is done in the treatment situation.

This chapter is therefore a detailed presentation of the programme of treatment that would be followed in tackling the clinical problem of sexual deviance. It is intended to be applicable to any of the types of sexual deviance discussed in this book, though it is probably most easily applied to homosexual problems in the male. At each stage the factors taken into consideration in making the decisions about management will be discussed. This is not intended to be a definitive form of treatment but rather an attempt to formulate what this particular author is doing at the time of writing. It is hoped that it may be of some value as a starting point for other therapists venturing into this field, or as a means of provoking discussion by those already experienced, or possibly as a source of testable ideas for research. Obviously as much as possible has been taken from research evidence already available but it will become quickly obvious that many of the decisions involved are based on clinical judgement.

OVER-ALL PLAN OF TREATMENT

The following stages in the assessment and treatment of the individual patient are suggested:

1. Initial contact with subject	(*a*) Define subject's goals. (*b*) Negotiate contract for treatment.
2. First part of course of treatment	(*a*) Complete initial identification of relevant attitudes and analysis of behaviour and plan behavioural goals in detail.
3. Remainder of treatment course	(*a*) Set graded behavioural goals (small steps). (*b*) Examine difficulties in attaining goals and hence clarify relevant attitudes. (*c*) Modify attitudes and related 'in-treatment' responses. (*d*) Stop treatment or change goals if no early signs of progress.

These different stages and procedures can now be looked at in more detail.

Define subject's goals

It is not an integral part of the traditional medical approach to establish at an early stage what it is that the patient is really seeking. It is more usual to establish first the nature of the problem or complaint, carry out any necessary examination and investigation and then advise the patient† what ought to be done. Whereas this might be justified in many instances in medicine when the patient, by presenting himself is asking for such advice, it is clearly not justified when the patient presents with a problem of sexually deviant behaviour. The first step after the opening discussion with the patient should therefore

† The term patient is used here in its proper sense to mean the physician's client. It is not intended to imply by its use that the client is necessarily ill. It is realized that the therapist may be non-medical (e.g. clinical psychologist or social worker). Nevertheless it is true in the United Kingdom that in most instances this type of help will be provided within a medical or para-medical setting.

be to establish what it is that the patient is hoping for. This simple step has a number of advantages. It establishes at the start the appropriate type of patient–therapist relationship—the therapist is acting as a professional agent 'employed' by the patient to carry out a certain job. This emphasizes the responsibility that lies with the patient. It counters any tendency of either party to consider the problem an 'illness' which should necessarily be 'treated' and underlines the degree of choice that the patient has. It also tends to expose ambivalence in the patient's attitudes which will need to be recognized and its causes identified.

The patient may reasonably ask what the chances of success are before committing himself, but before replying the therapist is entitled to establish what the patient would prefer the outcome of treatment to be, assuming it were possible.

The patient's preference can usually be placed in one of three categories:

(*a*) To be able to respond heterosexually and enjoy a heterosexual relationship. There may or may not be an accompanying wish to eliminate the deviant sexual interest when it is either an alternative (e.g. homosexuality), or a component of an otherwise heterosexual pattern (e.g. fetishism).

(*b*) To reduce or eliminate the deviant sexual behaviour and interest without altering heterosexual interest in any way. This may be because the existing heterosexual relationship is considered satisfactory or because the subject has no wish to engage in heterosexual behaviour and would prefer to be sexless.

(*c*) To reduce the problems involved in forming and maintaining a homosexual or other deviant relationship and improve a deviant adaptation.

Once the therapist has established the patient's preferences he is then in a position to make his own judgement as to the feasibility of achieving such goals. He has, of course, to consider the treatment resources that he has available.

In making this judgement several points are considered which are discussed below.

Previous and existing heterosexual interest and experience. The absence of any such interest at any stage should be taken as a poor prognostic sign for heterosexual improvement or re-orientation. If attempts at heterosexual contact have been made in the past, then their significance depends on the reaction at the time. If they were characterized by calm indifference, then this is of bad significance whereas if they were associated with anxiety this raises the possibility that the anxiety had masked or suppressed a potential heterosexual response. This is considered to be more hopeful.

Age. An age greater than 35 is a disadvantage unless there is already or has been a reasonably good heterosexual relationship established and the problem is mainly one of reducing deviant interest. In the presence of other good prognostic factors, however, age alone should not be considered a contra-indication.

Personality. Three particular aspects of personality should be considered:

1. Gender identity. In many cases, though not all, deviant behaviour becomes consistent with the individual's gender identity and vice versa (Bancroft 1972*a*). When this is so, and the gender identity is well-established and stable, the likelihood of changing the pattern of sexual behaviour is reduced. This is comparable to the chronic alcoholic who over the years establishes a way of life and a circle of friends which centres around alcohol and drinking places. The whole way of life and work role may have to change if the alcoholism is to be overcome. Similarly the homosexual may need to change his work situation, his circle of friends, his mannerisms, and many of his attitudes if he is to make a satisfactory heterosexual adjustment. The more that will need to change in this way, the less likely is it that treatment will succeed.

2. Social skills and assets. In those who hope to start or improve heterosexual relationships, various social skills will be required. An individual who is by nature very awkward, shy, or withdrawn, may have greater difficulty than one who is relatively capable in social situations. Similarly an attractive physical appearance and material assets will be an advantage.

On the other hand social awkwardness may be the main problem sufficient to prevent any heterosexual adjustment. When that is so prognosis will depend on the extent to which the social awkwardness can be improved.

Some individuals come to rely on their deviance as a justification for other failures or shortcomings in their life. When this is the case there may be a reluctance to part with the deviant role unless these shortcomings can be more adequately coped with. In addition some people use their deviant behaviour as a way of bolstering up their self-esteem (Rosen 1968; Bancroft 1970*a*). When this is the case the relative importance of this to the individual must be assessed. When great this may act as an obstacle to change.

3. 'Ego-syntonicity'. This concept from ego-psychology refers to the extent to which the individual can accept his deviant tendencies. Many people seeking treatment for sexual deviance find it extremely difficult to accept this part of themselves; it is regarded as an abhorrent appendage over which they have inadequate control. In such people, their deviance is 'ego-alien' or 'ego-dystonic'. These are the people who are most likely to seek treatment to reduce or eliminate deviant interest and are probably more likely to succeed than the person whose deviance is 'ego-syntonic'. He can accept the deviant part of his identity which seems to him quite natural though he may recognize its disadvantages and regret the stigma attached to it. It is in this latter group that consistent gender identity is likely to be an adverse prognostic factor.

External pressures. The question of motivation is complex (see p. 148). In many instances the only way to find out if a person genuinely wants to receive treatment is to see if he accepts it when offered to him. Then it is not always possible to be sure that he wants it to succeed. There are sometimes identifiable external pressures pushing the individual into treatment. The most obvious is from the court. The author's policy here is never to agree to a particular type or goal of treatment as a condition of a court order, e.g. probation order with psychiatric treatment. If it seems likely that the court will expect some intervention by a therapist, treatment can be agreed to without its precise nature being specified. In this way, once the court order has been made the therapist can more clearly establish what the patient himself wants. This is not a device to trick the court but rather to avoid wasting time as it is unlikely that treatment based on psychological mechanisms will be effective unless the patient wants it to be. Another common type of external pressure is from parents or spouse. A typical example is an 18-year-old homosexual male who leaves his diary lying around his room so that his homosexual feelings are discovered for the first time by his parents. There is a family crisis; the parents insist that he must get treatment and he agrees to consult a doctor. What he is probably hoping for is the advice that there is nothing that can be done to cure him of his homosexuality and that he (and his parents) should come to accept it. If such advice is given he has then made an effort and can feel less guilty about continuing with his homosexual role. It is of some interest in such a case why the diary is allowed to be discovered; it may reflect a need to bring matters with the parents to a head as a means of testing out their reaction and in the hope of ending pretence. In such a case it is futile to do other than tell the patient what he wants to hear, with the possible proviso that he may feel differently at a later stage. Similarly when pressure for treatment is from a spouse it is necessary for the therapist to establish, as best he can, how much the patient himself wants to change.

Mood. Although it is common for individuals to become depressed as part of a reaction to their sexual deviance, the association can also present differently, the wish to have treatment for the deviance reflecting a depressed mood. This sometimes happens after the break-up of a homosexual affair; the resulting sense of loss may lead to angry rejection of the homosexuality as the cause of all the current troubles. Even apparently endogenous depression may be associated with the rejection of the deviance which is reaccepted when the depression clears. If the therapist considers this to be the case then there is reason for postponing any decision about treatment until the depression has lifted, or if necessary has been successfully treated. In the author's experience behavioural techniques are unlikely to be successful in a patient who is depressed at the start of treatment, even if the mood is not directly related to the deviant behaviour. When it seems obvious that the depression is a reaction to the deviance it is still advisable to wait and try to improve the mood before embarking on treatment.

Depressive mood changes during aversion treatment are common (Bancroft 1969, 1970*c*; Marks *et al.* 1970; James *et al.* 1973; Mumford *et al.* 1973). In Bancroft's comparative study (1970*c*) such changes also occurred in the desensitization group although most of the individuals concerned had been prone to bouts of depression before treatment started. Depressive phases occurring in this way during treatment may be an inevitable part of the process of change and need not lead to cessation of treatment. Occasionally additional anti-depressant treatment may be needed before the behavioural approach can satisfactorily continue.

Negotiate contract for treatment

Having made the initial assessment, it should now be possible to negotiate a contract of treatment in which the subject and the therapist are agreed on what is an acceptable and feasible goal. This goal should fall into one of the three categories described above.

If it is goal c, the improvement of deviant adaptation, discussion of the appropriate help is beyond the scope of this book. Nevertheless, the main aims of such an approach should be mentioned to emphasize that they are real alternatives. They can be summarized as follows:

1. Improvement in the subject's ability to cope with the effects of stigmatization (including introduction to minority groups).

2. Help with interpersonal problems. These will be just as varied as the problems affecting heterosexual couples and in most respects the help needed will be similar. It is interesting how little has been written about the treatment of sexual inadequacy in homosexual relationships, but presumably one would approach this in the same way as one would heterosexual inadequacy (Masters and Johnson 1970; Bancroft 1972*b*).

3. In the case of transexualism, help in adjusting to a new gender role, and when appropriate, drug therapy and surgical

procedures (for a full review of treatment aspects of transexualism see Green and Money 1969).

If the aim of treatment is to produce an asexual state or a state in which the deviant interest can be sufficiently controlled to remain covert, without any accompanying heterosexual interest, one of the most important factors is the strength of sexual drive. If it is low, then it is relatively easy to help the patient develop appropriate self-regulation techniques. In those cases that involve high drive, however, there is no convincing evidence that techniques such as aversion therapy are successful in producing long-term suppression of deviant interest unless there is some accompanying increase in alternative sexual behaviour. It is occasionally possible for a subject after aversion to remain sexless for 1–2 years but to remain in that state for longer without some alternative pattern developing seems unusual

Another approach involves the use of libido-suppressing drugs. Oestrogens have been used for many years (Golla and Hodge 1949; Bierer and Van Someren 1950; Scott 1964), particularly for sexual offenders whose ability to control their deviant urges may be very poor. Oestrogen implants have been used recently to ensure that the compound is acting, as the ambivalent motivation of such subjects often leads to lapses of medication with oral preparations (Field and Williams 1970). There are other serious disadvantages with oestrogens; apart from side effects such as nausea and vomiting, gynaecomastia is often marked and may eventually lead to mammary carcinoma (Symmers 1968). Recently other drugs have been advocated, benperidol, progestogens and cyproterone acetate being the main examples. Only very recently have adequate attempts been made to evaluate these drugs and it is clear that we still know very little about their real effects on sexual behaviour (Tennent *et al.* 1974; Bancroft *et al.* 1974).

Apart from the group of sexual offenders who present formidable treatment problems for various reasons, there are other patients who benefit from this type of approach. The following case is an example. A 48-year-old schoolmaster had homosexual feelings since puberty and had never experienced any heterosexual interest. He was attracted to his pupils but had never been involved in any overt sexual act. He had a marked tendency to anxiety and would frequently find himself highly anxious in his work situation for fear he would reveal his homosexual inclination. A small dose of benperidol markedly reduced his homosexual interest and he ceased masturbating. Although he then felt relatively sexless he found life much less troublesome and had not lost anything that was previously rewarding. In his particular case it was considered at the outset that the chances of producing heterosexual responsiveness were minimal. In the author's experience, however, patients likely to benefit in this way do not often present themselves for treatment. In addition we remain ignorant of the consequences of long-term drug treatment of this kind.

If the goal of treatment is improvement in heterosexual adaptation certain aspects should be considered when negotiating the contract for such treatment. First, who is to carry out the treatment? It is the author's opinion that a warm, sexually non-threatening female therapist offers advantages in treating male patients, particularly when desensitization is to be used or where anxiety about heterosexual relationships is important. The desensitization technique with its relaxation and presentation of sexual imagery is inevitably a procedure which has sexual overtones. If the therapist is the same sex as the homosexual patient this can complicate treatment (see p. 138). If the therapist is of the opposite sex this effect can be exploited whilst still maintaining the necessary professional distance. This is a form of 'transference' of a special kind and although the therapist may not interpret it as such it can still have powerful desensitizing or anxiety-reducing effects. Sometimes a combination of male and female therapist can be particularly effective, the opposite sex therapist serving to reduce anxiety, the same sex therapist acting as a model and adviser on sexual approach behaviour and sexual technique. In addition the co-therapists present a model of a heterosexual relationship at least at the social level of interaction. The value of using co-therapists in this way is emphasized by Masters and Johnson (1970) in their treatment of sexual inadequacy.

The general principles of the treatment approach should be outlined and the frequency and duration of sessions as well as their likely number clarified, before finally agreeing on a 'contract' for treatment. In some cases, where a 'final goal' of normal heterosexual relationships is apparently too threatening for the patient, it may be advisable to agree on a more limited goal in the first instance. For example, whereas physical contact of any kind may be considered unacceptable, social contact may not be. The reduction of anxiety and development of appropriate behaviour in such situations could then be taken as the initial goal. When this stage is reached, further goals can be considered and the patient may by then be less threatened by the thought of overt sexual behaviour. A hierarchy of treatment goals is thus worked through, the patient only committing himself to one step at a time. In the majority of cases, however, the final goals can be agreed upon from the start.

The first part of treatment

Once the treatment 'contract' has been established the first task is to make a detailed analysis of the current sexual behaviour and attitudes in order to plan more precisely the treatment programme. This assessment will depend primarily on careful history taking. It can often be usefully augmented by psychophysiological assessment if the facilities are available. Some psychometric tests, particularly those assessing attitudes and anxiety traits, may sometimes be helpful particularly when therapist time is limited (see Chapter 8).

By means of careful and detailed questioning the following points should be clarified:

1. Level of sexual drive.
2. Nature of positive and negative sexual stimuli.
3. Details and consequences of sexual behavioural sequences.
4. Relevant attitudes.

These points will now be discussed in turn. The usefulness of much of this information will become clearer when the treatment procedure is described.

Level of sexual drive. This can be defined on the basis of frequency of overt sexual acts and masturbation, frequency of sexual thoughts, and the tendency to notice people as sexually attractive (e.g. when walking down a busy street).

A high frequency of nocturnal emissions associated with a low frequency of overt sexual acts or masturbation may indicate that a high level of psychological inhibition is operating.

The presence of high sexual drive will require that treatment aims at directing this appropriately at an early stage. If drive is low, on the other hand, more attention may be paid initially to social aspects of sexual behaviour.

Nature of positive and negative sexual stimuli. It is necessary to establish the characteristics of erotic stimuli that the patient finds particularly exciting as well as potential erotic stimuli that he finds aversive. What are the physical and emotional characteristics of an attractive partner and what are their relative importance? What range of stimuli does the subject respond to? Does he make use of photographs or literary material, and if so, how specific are such stimuli that he uses? What is the nature of his sexual fantasies, particularly those associated with masturbation? How fixed or specific are they? How important are they in producing a satisfactory response to either masturbation or sexual intercourse?

Details and consequences of sexual behavioural sequences. In a typical sexual incident, what is the precise sequence of events? What usually initiates the sequence and what, if any, are the key stages in the sequence? What are the usual consequences of the completed sequence (e.g. how does the subject feel after orgasm), or what happens if the sequence is interrupted or blocked at certain stages?

Particular attention should be paid to the subject's heterosexual interest and behaviour and reactions to different types of heterosexual partners or situations. The identification of anxiety in relation to heterosexual images or behaviour is of crucial importance.

Relevant attitudes. The importance of attitudes (or expectations) is that they may block behavioural change. Many such attitudes become clear as treatment proceeds and obstacles to behavioural change are revealed. Nevertheless it is desirable to recognize as many important attitudes at the start as possible, as they may influence one's over-all plan of treatment.

Important examples of attitudes include the belief that 'once a homosexual, always a homosexual' and the classification of women into two types, those like one's mother or sister that one may love, and those like tarts and prostitutes with whom one may enjoy sex. It is not uncommon for homosexuals to enjoy heterosexual relationships but only with the second category of woman. Another common account given by homosexuals is that in the early stages of their homosexual development they envied and wanted to be like other males who appeared to be masculine and, above all, attractive to women. This type of attraction usually becomes sexualized in adolescence so that its origins are concealed. It can be a useful starting point in treatment to give the interpretation to such a subject that his original attraction to males was based on an envy of their heterosexuality.

A careful account of parental attitudes to sex is often fruitful in identifying important influences which may still require correction. The history of pre-puberty or early adolescence may also reveal anxiety about the subject's gender identity which may have served to undermine his confidence in the heterosexual role (Bancroft 1970*a*). Pointing out contributory factors of this kind which counter the idea that the homosexual urge stems from an innate or immutable disposition may be valuable at the outset in correcting expectations of failure in treatment.

Psychophysiological assessment

If facilities are available for measuring erection (see Chapter 8) this will often add useful information at the assessment stage as well as increasing the range of possible therapeutic techniques.

The erectile response to erotic fantasies or other erotic stimuli will provide a measure of the sexual arousability of the subject. A failure to respond in such a test should not be taken as definite evidence of low arousability as some individuals find this type of testing inhibiting. On the other hand, the occurrence of strong responses does suggest high arousability and the awareness of erection in such individuals is likely to form an important erotic signal (Bancroft 1971).

When such arousability is present, the relative importance

of different types of fantasy is readily estimated. The patient is asked to imagine a specified fantasy for a period of time and his erectile response measured. This is done with a range of fantasies sometimes modifying the content only slightly. This not only validates the account already obtained but often provides insights which were not previously forthcoming. A dramatic effect on erectile response may result from apparently trivial alteration in the content of the fantasy thus revealing that the factor that was altered was of more importance than had hitherto been realized. An example of this is given on p. 45. This procedure also assesses the specificity of erotic fantasies, i.e. the extent to which fantasies used are always the same. Erectile responses to normal heterosexual fantasies can be checked and ratings of any anxiety accompanying them elicited. Measurements of this kind can provide baselines for treatment and part of the agreed goals of treatment may specify changes in these measures, particularly if treatment techniques directly affecting these measures are to be used. Defining goals of treatment in terms that are directly relevant to the technique in use is an important therapeutic principle.

Having completed the initial assessment it should then be possible to identify the main areas on which treatment is to be focused, and make a general plan as to what precise techniques will be used.

Treatment may be focused on four main areas:

(1) reduction of heterosexual anxiety;
(2) increase in heterosexual responsiveness;
(3) development of satisfactory heterosexual behaviour;
(4) reduction of deviant sexual interest.

This order to some extent reflects that involved in treatment. Thus if there is obvious heterosexual anxiety this should be reduced at an early stage. In such a case heterosexual responsiveness is more likely to increase when there has been such reduction of anxiety. It is not always necessary to attempt to reduce deviant interest directly as, if progress is made in the first three areas, this reduction may occur spontaneously. In establishing the contract of treatment it should usually be agreed that the continuation of some deviant interest is acceptable providing it does not interfere with the establishment of satisfactory heterosexual relationships. Although theoretically (and ethically) this is so, in practice there will usually need to be a fairly marked reduction if not elimination of deviant interest if treatment is to be successful. Nevertheless it is important that the patient should be able to enter treatment without the belief that deviant interest has to *disappear* in order to succeed. To many, at a time when success is all too uncertain, the prospect of losing something well known and in many respects rewarding for something uncertain and unknown is quite threatening. This is another example of the 'hierarchy of goals' principle mentioned earlier.

In some cases it may be necessary to directly reduce the deviant interest if in spite of heterosexual progress the deviant urges remain paramount and a serious distraction. Alternatively if no heterosexual progress has been made, then focusing treatment on the deviant interest may sometimes be more successful. There are also some patients who do not give any obvious scope for heterosexual improvement and in whom the fourth area should be tackled first. In such cases it is not unusual for heterosexual difficulties eventually to present themselves.

Whatever precise plan is adopted, one important principle always applies in this approach; the patient is given clearly defined behavioural goals from the start so that when he leaves the first treatment session he has something to do before the next session, however limited. Not only does this set the right level of active involvement but it also provides valuable information about obstacles to change which have to be recognized and dealt with. The ways in which the patient is involved will become clearer when the four focal areas of treatment are discussed in more detail.

Reduction of heterosexual anxiety

Heterosexual anxiety is of two main types; it either stems from some threat in the heterosexual situation itself (e.g. fear of genitalia, or disease, or injury, or punishment) or from the possibility that the subject may fail to perform adequately in the heterosexual situation (i.e. fear of failure). Homosexuals often claim that apart from being basically disinterested the only reason why they fear the heterosexual situation is that they will be shown up to be homosexual and a failure. Thus it would seem that their anxiety is secondary to the homosexuality and not the other way round, as has been suggested with the first type of anxiety (e.g. Rado 1940). In treatment it is indicated to the subject that in either case the anxiety is an obstacle to heterosexual progress which needs to be removed. In some cases disgust is better than anxiety as a description of the negative affect involved. Although it is not clear what differentiates these two affective states, it is therapeutically useful to take Lazarus' interpretation of disgust and present it to the patient (Lazarus 1966). (This describes disgust as an affective state characterized by a mixture of approach and avoidance valencies.) It is then treated in the same way as anxiety.

The treatment approach is comparable to that used for countering other types of situational anxiety or phobias. First an attempt is made to see if the anxiety stems from some false belief which might be susceptible to straightforward counsel and reassurance. Less straightforward but important is the possibility that the subject has always been exposed to influences from parental-type authority figures which have encouraged the anxiety. In such cases the contrary attitude of the therapist may achieve a great deal, provided that he has a positive relationship with the patient.

Failing this approach, one is left with anxiety which the subject accepts as irrational or excessive but which he cannot adequately control. If not too severe this may be tackled by advising a gradual approach to the real-life situation, starting with a very limited goal. Thus he may be asked simply to say 'Hello' to a girl he admires. Anxiety may be reduced not only by adopting small hierarchical steps in this way but also by giving precise instructions how to behave in such situations. Lack of confidence and uncertainty about appropriate behaviour is often an important factor.

If, however, the anxiety is sufficiently severe to prevent these early behavioural steps or is such that it affects situations which are not susceptible to this graduated approach, then systematic desensitization should be employed (for details, see p. 47). (An alternative and very different approach to non-sexual phobias is 'flooding' or 'implosion' (e.g. Stampfl and Levis 1967; Gelder *et al.* 1973). So far no one has reported using this technique with sexual anxieties.)

If treatment is limited to desensitization at the outset, it is still important to set behavioural goals outside treatment, such as practising relaxation and imagining hierarchy items.

Increase of heterosexual responsiveness

In most cases the fantasy or the reality of 'normal' heterosexual contact will be less erotically stimulating than the deviant counterpart, or not stimulating at all. It should be made clear to the patient that change in this respect will be gradual and the eventual pattern of responsiveness may be of a different quality to the deviant response, probably making up in general satisfaction what it may lack in intensity. Not infrequently there is an element of risk or 'wickedness' about the deviant act which endows it with a special intensity. In any case the road to a relaxed and optimal heterosexual relationship, even for many heterosexuals untroubled by deviant urges, is a long one and sudden changes should not be expected.

The first effort will probably be directed at modifying masturbation fantasies. The patient is asked to experiment during masturbation with different types of heterosexual fantasy in order to find one which is successful but slightly more heterosexual than his usual masturbation fantasies. Once he can masturbate to orgasm with this fantasy he should gradually modify it so that it becomes less and less deviant. For example, patients can often respond to 'voyeuristic' fantasies in which they are observing heterosexual behaviour performed by two other people. The aim in such a case is for the subject to find a way of gradually involving himself in the imaginary sexual behaviour—either by way of a 'ménage à trois' situation or by modifying the male's image to become increasingly like the subject. Progress in changing masturbation fantasies is often a good early sign and the subject should be reassured that it is not necessary at that stage for him to obtain as much pleasure from the heterosexual as from the usual deviant fantasies. (The practice of beginning with deviant fantasies and then substituting 'normal' fantasies immediately before orgasm has not proved to be helpful in this writer's experience.) Instruction about masturbation provides a simple behavioural goal that can usually be introduced early in treatment.

If facilities are available, and the subject in his initial physiological testing showed strong erectile responses either to visual stimuli or fantasies, then one of the fantasy 'shaping' or fading procedures can be employed (described on p. 45). Such procedures if successful will produce changes in responsiveness which can be reinforced during masturbation and thus provide a ready way of generalizing change outside treatment. Thus if fantasy 'shaping' is being used the patient should be encouraged to masturbate with the modified fantasy obtained at the last session in the same way as a patient undergoing systematic desensitization is asked to practise items already desensitized in the hierarchy.

Positive conditioning of erection either of classical or operant type provides a further alternative. Once again it is most likely to be successful if the subject is capable of producing moderately strong erections in the test situation. At the present time there is no clear indication for choosing 'fading' or fantasy 'shaping' rather than positive conditioning. Fantasy 'shaping' has the possible advantage of being most directly reinforced by masturbation. In Bancroft's comparative study (1970*c*) there was a negative correlation between increase in heterosexual erections during treatment and age. Thus it is possible that any technique which directly attempts to condition or increase erectile responses may be more successful in the younger age group. This could apply more to positive conditioning than to fantasy 'shaping' but as yet there is no evidence on this point.

Development of heterosexual behaviour

At some stage heterosexual approach behaviour must be attempted. In some cases the most trivial social approach will present difficulties, and these early stages sometimes represent the main obstacle; once overcome, later developments in the relationship may proceed more easily. In other cases any approach is regarded as a step on the road to heterosexual intercourse, which remains the threat. Not infrequently homosexuals will report that they have no problem relating socially to members of the opposite sex. Usually this means that they relate in a 'platonic' way which involves no sexual implications for either party. It should be made clear that they will need to approach even minimal heterosexual contact in a quite different way. They must regard the other person as a potential mate and give signals that will be interpreted in that way. Some discussion will usually be needed to clarify this point—to indicate that on the one hand a girl can be invited to the theatre in a manner indicating that sexual involvement is quite out of the question and on the other hand the invitation may contain a subtle suggestion that sexual contact could be a consequence. This 'sizing up each other as a potential mate' is very much taken for granted by the average heterosexual pair. Basic characteristics of this approach may need to be described to the homosexual contemplating such behaviour. It is often possible to illustrate the point by reference to the same type of rule-following behaviour that characterizes homosexual pairs, although the 'rules' may not be the same. Once this difference is grasped then it is unlikely that the homosexual will regard socio-sexual contact with the opposite sex with the same equanimity.

When it is felt that anxiety is not so severe as to prevent initial approach behaviour, limited behavioural goals however small should be set. Simply talking to a girl for a brief moment may be the first stage. At the next session any problems encountered should be discussed. This may reveal errors in technique for which advice can be given, alternatively relevant attitudes may be disclosed and require modification before any further progress can be made.

In the case of subjects who already have sexual partners, the behavioural goals should be the same as if the problem was one of heterosexual dysfunction employing the principles of Masters and Johnson (1970) (Bancroft 1972*b*). If possible, therefore, the partner should be involved in treatment at the appropriate stage.

Apart from the technique involved in overt sexual contact, sexually relevant behaviour in the social situation is of two main types, gender role behaviour, and interpersonal behaviour.

Gender role behaviour may need to be modified to improve the subject's self-confidence as well as acceptability and attractiveness to a potential partner (Barlow *et al.* 1973). Similarly the technique or social skill involved in relating to that person may need modification. Both areas are susceptible to the type of social skills training which has been advocated by Argyle, Trower, and Bryant (1973). This involves the use of visual and auditory feedback of the patient's social performance so that the behaviour requiring change can be clearly indicated. Modification then relies on modelling and role-playing. This approach not only requires equipment and 'stooges' (or other subjects requiring help) but is relatively expensive in therapist time. It is also in its early stages and many basic questions remain to be answered before its clinical usefulness can be properly evaluated. Nevertheless it is a technique which for some cases could be usefully incorporated into the behavioural approach.

Reduction of deviant interest

Hopefully, as a result of the first three approaches, the need to reduce deviant interest will have receded. Sometimes this will not be so, and, as mentioned earlier, there will be some cases where this fourth approach is the only one which gives any scope for change.

Aversion therapy is one obvious possibility. Of the various types of noxious stimuli that have been reported there is no reason at the present time to use other than electric shock for sexual deviance. However, the possibility that aversion therapy may be more effective if the noxious stimulus is chosen to be appropriate for the individual patient, deserves serious consideration. This point was discussed in more detail in Chapter 5. If deviant fantasies are an important part of the problem then simple punishment of fantasies (see p. 39) is the most appropriate technique. When the deviant behaviour can easily be involved in treatment (e.g. transvestism and fetishism), then simple punishment of the deviant behaviour should be used (see p. 38). If visual stimuli are important, e.g. pornographic material, then a simple classical conditioning procedure is probably most suitable. A combination of all three is useful. There seems to be no indication for employing the technically more complicated procedures such as anticipatory avoidance or aversion relief. At the present time punishment of erection is probably not the method of first choice, unless there remains a particular need to increase heterosexual responsiveness, in which case the paradoxical facilitation effect of this procedure may be exploited (see p. 39). It is probably contra-indicated in cases involving masochistic tendencies.

The indications for choosing covert sensitization rather than electrical aversion remain obscure. The presence of generalized anxiety is a point against aversion (see p. 155). The ability to produce vivid imagery of an aversive kind is a point in favour of covert sensitization. Until further evidence is available, the author does not use covert sensitization in subjects who are unable to produce vivid noxious imagery but prefers it to electric aversion in those who can.

Self-regulation (see p. 87) is most likely to be beneficial to those who experience fairly predictable sequences of behaviour leading to the deviant act and who are moderately orderly in their approach to life. Self-regulation may become more effective after a course of aversion or covert sensitization when the strength of the deviant urge has been reduced.

The duration of treatment

It should be clear to the reader by now that the behavioural approach to sexual deviance is a time-consuming business, even though it may involve substantially less time than orthodox psychoanalysis. An encouraging factor is that in most cases progress will show itself early if it is going to occur at all. Thus if there has been no change after, say, 10 weekly sessions it is reasonable to stop treatment or to revise the contract and strive for different goals.

When treatment is succeeding its duration will depend on the extent of change and help that is required. Treatment can be regarded as having two phases. The initial concentrated phase when sessions are once a week or more often, aims to initiate change which will then need to continue over a longer period. The first phase will usually require 15 to 20 sessions. The second phase should involve infrequent sessions (say once a month) over a period of approximately 1 year. In this way communication between subject and therapist is kept open and problems arising can be discussed and further advice given.

Conclusions

In modifying deviant sexual behaviour, the degree of difficulty clearly varies from case to case, but in general, it involves considerable commitment for both subject and therapist and should not be undertaken lightly by either.

The principles outlined in this chapter are applicable to most forms of deviant sexuality. As stressed at the beginning of the chapter, this formulation is based on an assessment of the currently available information and clinical experience. It should be progressively modified in the light of further experience and evidence. Two overriding principles have been involved: first, treatment is aimed primarily at improving heterosexual relationships—rather than reducing deviant interest; secondly, treatment proceeds by progressively setting limited behavioural goals and modifying attitudes that reveal themselves as obstacles to achieving those goals.

The therapist should not get his contribution, however successful, out of perspective. A course of treatment is one event in a lifetime of influences many of them working in contrary directions. It is not the focal point of the patient's life, as some therapists are inclined to imagine, but something that will recede into the past as time goes by. It may serve the patient and justify the therapist by promoting changes which become self-reinforcing. Nevertheless it is no more than a concentrated, selected, and carefully directed sample of life's experience.

Appendix: Technical Aspects of Penile Plethysmography

VARIOUS techniques used to measure change in the size of the penis have been reviewed by Jovanovic (1971). They fall into 4 categories:

1. Volumetric plethysmographs (Freund, Sedlacek, and Knob 1965).
2. Thermistors for measuring skin temperature change (Fisher, Gross, and Zuch 1965).
3. Mercury-in-rubber strain gauges (Fisher *et al.* 1965; Bancroft *et al.* 1966; Karacan 1969).
4. Metal ring strain gauges (Johnson and Kitching 1968; Barlow, Becker, Leitenberg, and Agras 1970).

It should not be assumed that the physiological changes measured by these various devices are the same. Volumetric plethysmography measures the increase of the total volume of the penis. The mercury-in-rubber strain gauges measure change in circumference of the shaft of the penis at one point only; the metal ring strain gauges cover a slightly wider section. Total volume change depends on lengthening of the penis as well as increase in its diameter. The thermistor, by measuring skin temperature, reflects changes in penile blood flow. The physiology of penile erection, although not adequately understood, is unlikely to depend solely on increased blood flow. The shunting of blood into sluice channels by closure of valves is probably also involved (Bancroft 1970*b*). If so temperature change will only reflect a proportion of the erectile change which could vary from individual to individual, and from occasion to occasion. The physiology of erection and the relationship between these various measures requires further research.

With this proviso, the choice of technique at the present time will depend on practical considerations. The two main applications of such measurements are the recording of erections during sleep, and in the waking state during exposure to erotic stimuli. During sleep recordings, any device must allow for the considerable body movement and change of position that may occur. During the waking state, body movement can be minimized. Sleep research has also been more concerned with timing the onset and duration of erection, than with quantifying it. For these two reasons relatively simple mercury-in-rubber strain gauges have been preferred in that field. Examining responses to erotic stimuli on the other hand requires more precise measurement and hence calibration, and in addition the device should be readily fitted and unobtrusive during use.

The writer's experience has been largely confined to mercury-in-rubber strain gauges although recently the metal ring type has been explored. The volumetric method of Freund has the disadvantage of being too cumbersome and possibly leading to more genital stimulation than other techniques (Fisher *et al.* 1965). The thermistor method is probably the simplest available but until its relation to erectile change is clarified, its calibration and interpretation will remain a problem. The metal ring strain gauge has certain advantages and disadvantages. The open ring is made of annealed spring metal covered with plastic to eliminate sharp edges. The ring opens sufficiently to fit round the penis. Solid state (semi-conductor) strain gauges are fixed with adhesive on to the outside of the ring opposite to the opening; strain as the ring opens is thus measured. As these strain gauges are temperature-sensitive, pairs of gauges matched to cancel out the effects of temperature change have to be used. The fixing of these gauges on to the metal is technically difficult but can usually be carried out by the manufacturers for a moderate charge. A satisfactory method of calibrating them has yet to be reported. They are also more prone to movement artefact. This type of strain gauge thus presents greater technical problems and expense in construction than the mercury-in-rubber type and in the writer's experience these problems have not yet been satisfactorily overcome. However, once working properly they are likely to have a longer life than the mercury-in-rubber gauges. The following technical details are largely based on the writer's experience with the latter type.

Construction of mercury-in-rubber strain gauges. The writer has used a more complex construction than most other workers in order that satisfactory calibration can be carried out. The strain gauge is shown in Plate 1. The purpose of the design is to permit the size of the rubber loop to be adjusted systematically. (See Fig. A.1.)

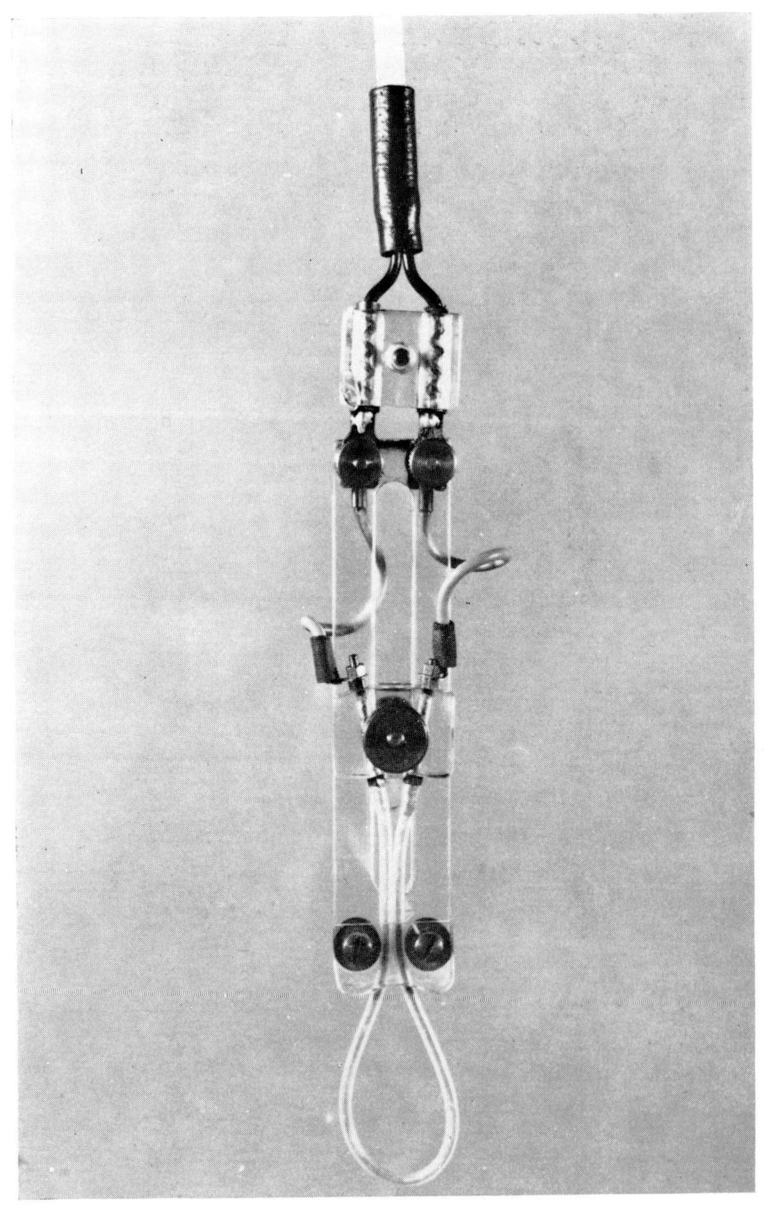

Plate I

The main disadvantage with mercury-in-rubber gauges is the temperamental nature of the electrode–mercury contact. Platinum is the best electrode metal, most other suitable metals leading to amalgamation with the mercury.† The writer has used threaded stainless steel which although it has a limited shelf life because of amalgamation, has the advantage of being inexpensive, self-fixing in the rubber tube and easy to replace.

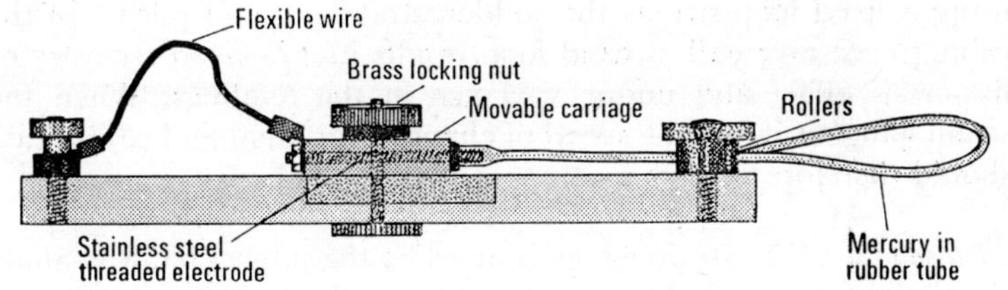

FIG. A.1. Side view of strain gauge (actual size).

Approximately 6 in. of clean silicone rubber tubing of internal diameter 0·025 in. is filled in the following way. Clean mercury is injected into the tube using a syringe and hypodermic needle. Care is taken to ensure that there are no breaks or air bubbles in the mercury column. The open end of the filled tube is then closed with one stainless steel electrode which is simply threaded into the tubing. The other end is then cut just below the hypodermic needle ensuring that the tube remains filled with mercury. The second electrode is then threaded into that end of the tube. The tube and electrodes can then be fitted into the perspex carriage and connected via the leads to the Wheatstone bridge circuit and amplifier (details of the complete circuit suitable for a portable apparatus are given in Bancroft *et al.* 1966); most polygraph DC amplifiers will contain a suitable bridge circuit). The strain gauge is highly sensitive to resistance change, hence electrical contacts must be sound and highly flexible leads should be used. The fracture of just a few strands in a multi-strand lead can cause intermittent contact and render the strain gauge useless.

Calibration. Two nylon discs are used. In the edge of each disc a groove is cut the width of the strain gauge tubing, with its base

† Jovanovic (1971) avoided this particular difficulty by using graphite instead of mercury. According to Karacan (1969), however, the graphite column has a tendency to separate and to be slow to recoalesce. He therefore preferred the mercury form.

providing a circle of known diameter. There is 1 mm difference in this diameter of the two discs. The strain gauge is marked with its adjustable carriage in a set position. The carriage is then moved forward to allow the tube to be fitted easily over the disc and then moved back gradually and locked in its original position. This is done for each disc in turn several times. The mean difference in pen deflection for the two discs then represents a difference of 1 mm in diameter. It is preferable to calibrate in this way rather than by using a fixed loop size as the sudden stretching and release of the tubing necessary with a fixed loop results in a delayed recovery or hysteresis effect and undue variance in the readings. When the strain gauge is in use the speed of change is gradual and calibration should therefore involve a comparable rate of change.

Method of use. The strain gauge is fitted by the subject halfway along the shaft of the penis. The loop should be sufficiently small to ensure slight tension around the flaccid penis. The strain gauge and perspex frame can then be placed comfortably inside the loosened trousers as the subject sits comfortably in a chair. The position of the strain gauge should be checked by the experimenter. The subject is asked to avoid any sudden marked movements during testing and sensitivity to movement artefact is checked by asking the subject to cough. If this produces more than a minimal deflection, the position of the strain gauge should be adjusted.

Baseline recording. Recording of a baseline for penile erection presents problems. The penis is a dynamic organ and its resting size depends on an interplay of positive and negative factors. In some situations negative stimulation results in marked retraction of the penis, a response that has been called 'hyperinvolution' by Masters and Johnson (1966). An example of this, recorded during aversion therapy, was reported by Bancroft and Mathews (1967). In this case the penis retracted to such an extent that it slipped out of the strain gauge.

It is thus impracticable to establish a baseline that can be applied across testing sessions and care should be taken in comparing the changes in different sessions. It is nevertheless desirable to establish a baseline for each testing session, particularly as the fitting of the strain gauge can be temporarily stimulating. The subject, after the gauge is fitted should be asked to relax and avoid sexual thoughts. Once the tracing becomes stable, the level can be taken as a baseline, to which the tracing should return between stimulus conditions. Detumescence can often be accelerated following stimulus presentation by giving the subject a mental arithmetic task. Occasionally the return to baseline proves impossible or takes a long time.

Measurement of change. Change can be measured in various ways. First when only the amplitude of response is being measured, the difference can be taken between the maximum level reached and either the level at the start of the trial (i.e. 'baseline') or the lowest level preceding the maximum. As there is frequently a slight reduction in penile size immediately following the presentation of a stimulus, the writer has chosen the second alternative (see Fig. A.2).

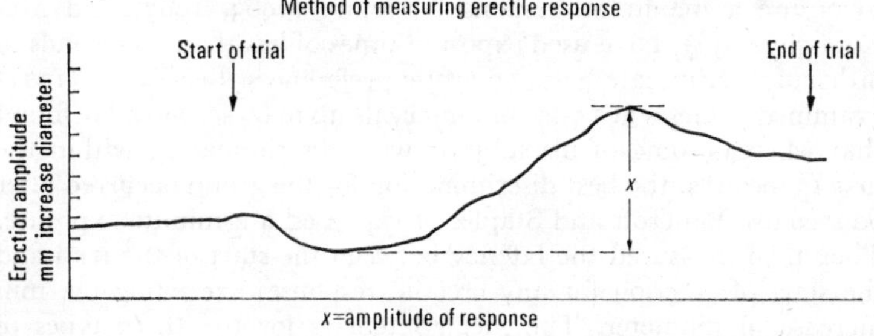

FIG. A.2. The method of measuring the amplitude of erectile response shown here uses the difference between the maximum level and the lowest level preceding it during that trial (x).

This is an arbitrary decision that should be stated in reporting the results. If the speed of change is being analysed or if erectile changes are being correlated with other physiological variables, then the recording can be divided into arbitrary time units and the mean level for each time unit taken. Change scores between consecutive means can then be analysed and correlated with other change scores. This procedure was used by Bancroft and Mathews (1971).

What is a valid erectile response? When establishing a 'resting level' of penile size, one quite often observes spontaneous fluctuations. Similarly fluctuations may occur when the subject is observing neutral stimuli. It is not possible to exclude internal erotic imagery as the cause of such fluctuations but it seems likely that the majority of them are not erotic responses. How large should an erectile response be, if it is to be regarded as a valid erotic response?

Bancroft and Staples (1974) measured erectile change to a series of neutral and erotic stimuli. The penile change whilst observing neutral stimuli (fantasies, slides, and film) ranged from 0 to 2 mm increase in diameter. The distribution was skewed with a mean of 0·37 mm, 80 per cent being under 0·4 mm and 93 per cent under 0·6 mm ($n = 108$). The distribution of responses to erotic stimuli was bimodal with a small peak at 0·2 mm. This suggested that a proportion of the responses during 'erotic' trials were non-erotic responses, showing a distribution similar to those occurring during neutral trials. For erotic stimuli, 73 per cent of responses were greater than 0·6 mm. An arbitrary cut-off point between erotic and non-erotic response could therefore be between 0·4 and 0·6 mm.

Latency of response. How long should a stimulus be presented in order to ensure a maximum response? Freund (1963, 1967) and McConaghy (1967) have used exposure times of less than 20 seconds in order to discriminate between erotic preferences. Lee-Evans (1971) examined changes at 15-second intervals up to 60 seconds. He found that whereas some of his subjects were discriminating within the first 15 seconds, the best discrimination for the group occurred after 60 seconds. Bancroft and Staples (1974) used a 2-minute exposure. They then measured the latency between the start of the trial and the start of erection for any erectile responses exceeding 0·5 mm increase in diameter. The mean latencies for the three types of stimuli are shown in Table A.1.

TABLE A.1

	n	*Mean latency/s*	*S.D.*
Fantasy	17	46·8	51·1
Slide	13	20·6	20·34
Film	21	20·71	25·39

Although there was no significant difference between the stimuli in this respect, the responses to fantasy tended to have longer latencies. The time from the start of a response to its maximum varied from 6 to 120+ seconds, depending on its degree and rapidity. In order to record the maximum change in the majority of cases, therefore, an exposure time of no less than 2 minutes should be allowed.

Patterns of erectile response. The pattern or 'shape' of an erectile response varies considerably from subject to subject and to a lesser extent within the same individual. Some individuals characteristically produce a rapid rise response in which the maximum or near maximum is reached within 15–20 seconds. Others typically show a more gradual and varied rise. An interesting pattern that occurs in some individuals shows rhythmic oscillations as the erection develops. Usually the subject is aware of these but is not deliberately producing them. They are probably related to rhythmic contractions of the ischiocavernosus and bulbospongiosus muscles. Examples of these various patterns are shown in Fig. A.3. A further frequently observed phenomenon is the 'rebound' effect discussed on p. 128.

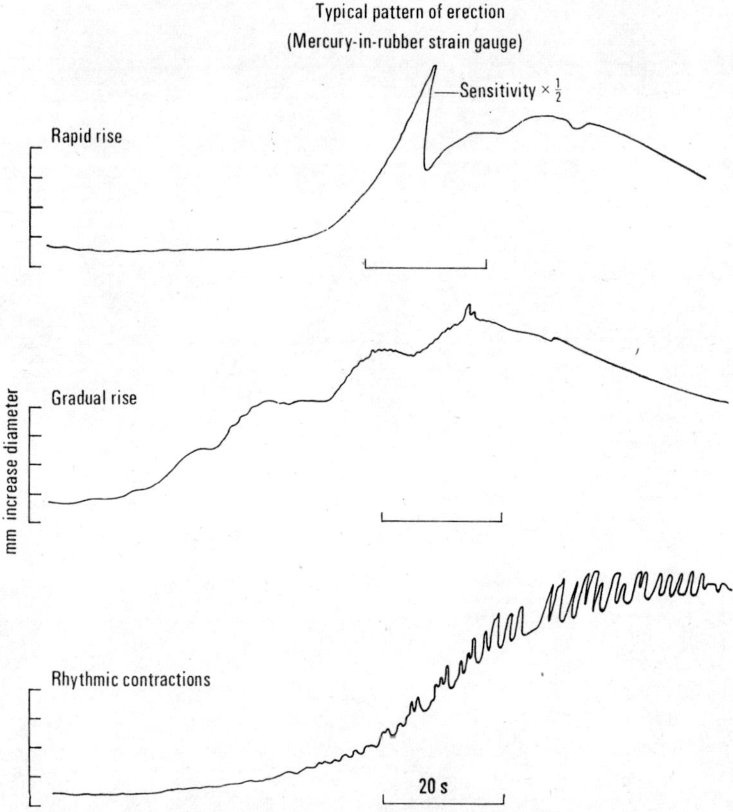

Fig. A.3. Three typical patterns of erection are shown. In the top tracing there is a steady and rapid increase to a maximum requiring a re-setting of the record by halving the sensitivity. The middle tracing shows a more gradual and intermittent increase. The lower tracing shows a rhythmic tracing which is characteristic of some individuals and probably reflects involuntary rhythmic contractions of the ischiocavernosus and bulbospongiosus muscles.

Bibliography and Author Index

Pages on which work is cited appear in square brackets after each reference.

Abel, G. G., Levis, D. J., and Clancy, J. (1970). Aversion therapy applied to taped sequences of deviant behaviour in exhibitionism and other sexual deviations: a preliminary report. *J. behav. ther. exp. Psychiat.* **1**, 59–66. [37, 119, 161]

Abelson, R. P. and Rosenberg, M. G. (1958). Symbolic psychologic: a model of attitudinal cognition. *Behav. Sci.* **3**, 1–13. [170]

Albany Trust (1965). *Some questions and answers about homosexuality.* Pamphlet published by Albany Trust, London. [19]

Alexander, F. G. and Selesnick, S. T. (1967). *The history of psychiatry.* G. Allen and Unwin, London. p. 141. [10]

Allen, R. M. and Haupt, T. D. (1966). The sex inventory: test–retest reliabilities of scale scores and items. *J. clin. Psychol.* **22**, 375–7. [189]

Allyon, T. and Michael, J. (1959). The psychiatric nurse as a behavioural engineer. *J. exp. Anal. Behav.* **2**, 323–34. [167]

Amsel, A. (1972). Behavioural habituation, counter conditioning and a general theory of persistence. In *Classical conditioning II* (ed. A. H. Black and W. F. Prokasy) Appleton–Century–Crofts, New York. [121]

Argyle, M. (1969). *Social interaction.* Methuen, London. [188]

——, Trower, P. and Bryant, B. (1974). Explorations in the treatment of personality disorder and neurosis by social skills training. *Br. J. med. psychol.* In the press. [223]

Aronfreed, J. and Reber, A. (1965). Internalized behaviour suppression and the timing of social punishment. *J. Personality soc. Psychol.* **1**, 3–16. [106]

Azrin, N. H. and Holz, W. C. (1966). Punishment in *Operant behaviour; areas of research and application.* (ed. W. K. Honig). Appleton–Century–Crofts, New York. [91, 106, 109, 127]

Baer, D. M., Wolf, M. M., and Risley, T. R. (1968). Some current dimensions of applied behavior analysis. *J. appl. Behav. Anal.* **1**, 91–7. [168]

BANCROFT, J. H. J. (1966). *Aversion therapy.* Unpublished dissertation for the D.P.M., University of London. [27, 44, 91]

—— (1969) Aversion therapy of homosexuality. *Br. J. Psychiat.* **115**, 1417–31. [32, 39, 42, 44, 85, 98, 105, 106, 108, 109, 110, 147, 153, 154, 199, 202, 212]

—— (1970*a*) Homosexuality in the male. *Br. J. Hosp. Med.* Feb., p. 168. [133, 210, 217]

—— (1970*b*) Disorders of sexual potency. In *Modern trends in psychosomatic medicine.* (ed. O. W. Hill). Butterworths, London. [126, 139, 227]

—— (1970*c*) A comparative study of two forms of behaviour therapy in the modification of homosexual interest. Unpublished thesis for Doctorate of Medicine, University of Cambridge. [47, 62, 66, 100, 103, 105, 110, 114, 123, 150, 151, 153, 154, 155, 174, 187, 204, 212, 222]

—— (1970*d*) A comparative study of aversion and desensitization in the treatment of homosexuality. *Behaviour Therapy in the 1970s.* (ed. L. E. Burns and J. L. Worsley). Wright, Bristol. [30, 40, 42, 47, 66, 86, 89, 101, 109, 120, 129, 134, 141, 145, 146, 147, 153, 160, 174, 178, 191, 195]

—— (1971). The application of psychophysiological measures to the assessment and modification of sexual behaviour. *Behav. Res. Ther.*, **9**, 119–30. [39, 45, 47, 49, 50, 129, 131, 139, 141, 161, 162, 194, 195, 217]

—— (1972*a*). The relationship between gender identity and sexual behaviour: some clinical aspects. In *Gender differences: their ontogeny and significance.* (ed. C. Ounsted and D. C. Taylor). Churchill–Livingstone, Edinburgh. [15, 151, 158, 184, 185, 209]

—— (1972*b*). The Masters and Johnson approach to marital sexual problems used in a N.H.S. setting. Paper read at second annual conference of European Behaviour Therapy Association. Wexford, Ireland, September 1972. [212, 223]

—— (1974). Psychological and physiological responses to sexual stimuli in men and women. In *Society, Stress, and Disease.* III. The productive and reproductive age. (ed. L. Levi). Oxford University Press. In the press. [126, 194, 195]

——, GWYNNE JONES, H., and PULLAN, B. R. (1966). A simple device for measuring penile erection. Some comments on its use in the treatment of sexual disorders. *Behav. Res. Ther.* **4**, 239–41. [39, 69, 156, 227, 229]

—— and MARKS, I. (1968). Electric aversion therapy of sexual deviations. *Proc. R. Soc. Med.* **61**, 796–9. [13, 112, 145, 146, 156, 199]

—— and MATHEWS, A. M. (1967) Penis plethysmography; its physiological basis and clinical application. Proceedings of the seventh European conference in psychosomatic research. Rome. *Acta med. Psychosomat.* 475. [230]

—— (1971). Autonomic correlates of penile erection. *J. psychosomat. Res.* **15**, 159. [49, 195, 231]

—— and STAPLES, D. (1974). Measuring change in sexual behaviour: some further methodological considerations. In preparation. [39, 51, 196, 204, 231, 232]

——, TENNENT, T. G., LOUCAS, K., and CASS, J. (1974). The control of deviant sexual behaviour by drugs. I. Behavioural changes following oestrogens and anti-androgens. *Br. J. Psychiat.* In the press [195, 201, 213]

BANDURA, A. (1969). *Principles of behaviour modification.* Holt, Rinehart, and Winston, London. [18, 90, 91, 93, 168, 170, 171, 172, 173]

BANNISTER, D. and MAIR, J. M. M. (1968). *The evaluation of personal constructs.* Academic Press, London. [186]

BARKER, J. C. (1965). Behaviour therapy for transvestism: a comparison of pharmacological and electrical aversion techniques. *Br. J. Psychiat.* **111**, 268–76. [35, 40, 54]

BARLOW, D. H. (1973). Increasing heterosexual responsiveness in the treatment of sexual deviation: A review of the clinical and experimental evidence. *Behav. Ther.* **4**, 655–71. [31]

—— and AGRAS, W. S. (1971). An experimental analysis of 'fading' to increase heterosexual responsiveness in homosexuality. Paper presented at South Eastern Psychological Association meeting, Miami Beach, Florida. April, 1971. [45, 50, 87, 139]

——, REYNOLDS, E. J., and AGRAS, W. S. (1973). Gender identity change in a transexual. *Archs Gen. Psychiat.* **28**, 569–76 [159, 223]

——, BECKER, R., LEITENBERG, H., and AGRAS, W. S. (1970). A mechanical strain gauge for recording penile circumference change. *J. appl. Behav. Anal.* **3**, 72. [227]

——, LEITENBERG, H., and AGRAS, W. S. (1969). The experimental control of sexual deviation through manipulation of the noxious scene in covert sensitization. *J. abnorm. Psychol.* **74**, 596–601. [83, 85, 198]

——, LEITENBERG, H., AGRAS, W. S., CALLAHAN, E. J., and MOORE, R. C. (1974). The contribution of therapeutic instructions to covert sensitization. *Behav. Res. Ther.* In the press. [83, 84, 198]

BARR, R. F. and MCCONAGHY, N. (1971). Penile volume responses to appetitive and aversive stimuli in relation to sexual orientation and conditioning performance. *Br. J. Psychiat.* **119**, 377–83. [140]

BAUM M. (1970). Extinction of avoidance responding through response prevention (flooding). *Psychol. Bull.* **74**, 276–84. [118, 122]

BEECH, H. R. (1960). The symptomatic treatment of Writer's Cramp. In *Behaviour therapy and the neuroses.* (ed. H. J. Eysenck). Pergamon, Oxford. [104]

——, WATTS, F., and POOLE, A. D. (1971). Classical conditioning of sexual deviation: a preliminary note. *Behav. Ther.*, **2**, 400–2. [50]

BEKHTEREV, V. M. (1923). Die Krankheiten der Persönlienkert vom standpunkt der reflexologie. *Z. Ges. neurol. Psychiat.*, **80**, 265–309. [26].

BENTLER, P. M. (1968*a*). Heterosexual behaviour assessment. I. Males. *Behav. Res. Ther.* **6**, 21–5. [197]

—— (1968*b*). Heterosexual behaviour assessment. II. Females. *Behav. Res. Ther.* **6**, 27–30. [197]

BEUMONT, P. J. V., BANCROFT, J. H. J., BEARDWOOD, C. J., and RUSSELL, G. F. M. (1972). Behavioural changes following treatment with testosterone: a case report. *Psychol. Med.* **2**, 70–72. [141]

BIEBER, I. (1967). Reply to MacCulloch and Feldman's article. *Br. med. J.* **111**, 372. [148]

——, DAIN, H. J., DINCE, P. R., DRELLICH, M. G., GRAND, H. G., GUNDLACH, R. H., KREMER, M. W., RIFKIN, A. H., WILBUR, C. B., and BIEBER, T. B. (1962). *Homosexuality: a psychoanalytic study.* Basic Books, New York. [13, 18, 47, 148, 152, 153, 154]

BIERER, J. and VAN SOMEREN, G. A. (1950). Stilboestrol in outpatient treatment of sexual offenders. *Br. med. J.* i, 935. [213]

BIRNBRAUER, J. S. (1968). Generalization of punishment effects—a case study. *J. Appl. Behav. Anal.* **1**, 201–11. [107]

BIRK, L., HUDDLESTON, W., MILLER, E., and COHLER, B. (1971). Avoidance conditioning for homosexuality. *Archs Gen. Psychiat.* **25**, 314–23. [63, 145, 146, 147, 198]

BLAKEMORE, C. B., THORPE, J. G., BARKER, J. C., CONWAY, C. G., and LAVIN, N. I. (1963). Application of faradic aversion conditioning in a case of transvestism. *Behav. Res. Ther.* **1**, 26–35. [30, 38, 41]

B.M.A. (1955). Memorandum on homosexuality and prostitution drawn up by a special committee of the British Medical Association, London. [16]

BOND, I. K. and HUTCHINSON, H. E. (1960). Application of reciprocal inhibition therapy to exhibitionism. *Can. med. Assoc. J.* **83**, 23–5. [161]

BRADY, J. P. and LEVITT, E. E. (1965). The scalability of sexual experiences. *Psychol. Rec.* **15**, 275–9. [197]

BREMER, J. (1959). *Asexualization, a follow-up study of 244 cases.* Macmillan, New York. [2].

BROWN, J. A. C. (1963). *Techniques of persuasion.* Penguin Books, London. [29]

CALLAHAN, E. J. and LEITENBERG, H. (1973). Aversion therapy for sexual deviation: contingent shock and covert sensitization. *J. abnorm. Psychol.* **81**, 60–73. [85, 108, 110]

CAMPBELL, B. A. and MASTERSON, F. A. (1969). Psychophysics of punishment. In *Punishment and aversive behaviour.* (eds. B. A. Campbell and R. M. Church). Appleton–Century–Crofts, New York. [40]

CAMPBELL, D., SANDERSON. R. E., and LAVERTY, S. G. (1964). Characteristics of a conditioned response in human subjects during extinction trials following a single traumatic conditioning trial. *J. abnorm. soc. Psychol.* **68**, 627–39. [97]

CAMPBELL, D. T. and STANLEY, J. C. (1963). Experimental and quasi-experimental designs for research on teaching. In *Handbook of research on teaching.* (ed. N. L. Gage). Rand McNally. [178]

CAPALDI, E. J. (1966). Partial reinforcement: a hypothesis of sequential effects. *Psychol. Rev.* **73**, 459–77. [121]

CAUTELA, J. R. (1966). Treatment of compulsive behaviour by covert sensitization. *Psychol. Rec.* **16**, 33–41. [30]

—— (1967). Covert sensitization. *Psychol. Rep.* **20**, 459–68. [43, 44, 85]

CHAPANIS, N. P. and CHAPANIS, A. (1964). Cognitive dissonance: five years later. *Psychol. Bull.* **61**, 1–22. [170, 171]

CHARCOT, J. M. and MAGNAN, V. (1882). Inversion du sens genital. *Archs neurol.* **3**, 53–60; **4**, 296–322. [25]

CHURCH, R. M. (1963). The varied effects of punishment on behaviour. *Psychol. Rev.* **70**, 369–402. [91]

CLARKE, R. V. G. (1965). The Slater selective vocabulary test and male homosexuality. *Br. J. med. Psychol.* **38**, 339–40. [186]

COHEN, H. D. and SHAPIRO, A. (1971). A method for measuring sexual arousal in the female. *Psychophysiology* **8**, 251–2. [195]

COOPER, A. J. (1963). A case of fetishism and impotence treated by behaviour therapy. *Br. J. Psychiat.* **109**, 649–53. [27, 35]

COPPEN, A. J. (1959). Body build of male homosexuals. *Br. med. J. ii*, 1443–5. [14]

CORMAN, C. (1968). Physiological response to a sexual stimulus. B.Sc. (Med.) Thesis, Univ. Manitoba—cited in Zuckerman (1971). [196]

DAHLSTROM, W. G., WELSH, G. S., and DAHLSTROM, L. E. (1972). MPI *Handbook, Vol. 1, Clinical Interpretation*, Minneapolis University Press. [185]

D'AMATO, M. R. (1970). *Experimental psychology; methodology, psychophysics and learning*. McGraw–Hill, New York. [93, 96, 117, 122, 165, 166]

DAVIS, K. (1938). Mental hygiene and the class structure. *Psychiatry* Feb., 55–65. [16]

DAVISON, G. C. (1968). Elimination of a sadistic fantasy by a client-controlled counter-conditioning technique: A case study. *J. abnorm. Psychol.* **73**, 84–90. [44, 161]

DAVISON, K., BRIERLEY, H., and SMITH, C. (1971). A male monozygotic twinship discordant for homosexuality. A repertory grid study. *Br. J. Psychiat.* **118**, 675–82. [188]

DEANE, G. E. (1961). Human heart rate responses during experimentally induced anxiety. *J. exp. Psychol.* **61**, 489–93. [123]

DIAMOND, M. (1965). A critical evaluation of the ontogeny of human sexual behaviour. *Q. Rev. Biol.* **40**, 147–75. [15]

ELLENBERGER, H. F. (1970). *The discovery of the unconscious. The history and evolution of dynamic psychiatry*. Allen Lane, London. [9, 11, 15]

ELLIOTT, R. (1966). Effects of uncertainty about the nature and advent of a noxious stimulus (shock) upon heart rate. *J. Personality Soc. Psychol.* **3**, 353–6. [123]

ELLIS, A. (1956). The effectiveness of psychotherapy with individuals who have severe homosexual problems. *J. cons. Psychol.* **20**, 191–5. [13, 18, 148, 152, 154, 155]

ELLIS, HAVELOCK (1915). *Studies in the psychology of sex. Vol. 2. Sexual inversion*. F. A. Davis and Co., Philadelphia, [7, 11, 12, 15, 25]

ERIKSEN, C. W. and KUETHE, J. L. (1956). Avoidance conditioning of verbal behaviour without awareness: a paradigm of repression. *J. Abnorm. soc. Psychol.* **53**, 203–9. [115]

ESTES, W. K. (1969). Outline of a theory of punishment. In *Punishment and aversive behaviour* (eds. B. A. Campbell and R. M. Church). Appleton–Century–Crofts, New York. [90]

EVANS, D. R. (1968). Masturbatory fantasy and sexual deviation. *Behav. Res. Ther.* **6**, 17–19. [23, 159]

—— (1970). Subjective variables and treatment effects in aversion therapy. *Behav. Res. Ther.* **8**, 147–52. [159, 161]

EYSENCK, H. J. (1969). *Behaviour therapy and the neuroses*, p. 277. Pergamon Press, Oxford. [90]

—— (1964). *Experiments in behaviour therapy*, p. 1. Pergamon Press, Oxford. [21, 29]

—— and RACHMAN, S. (1965). *The causes and cures of neurosis*. Routledge and Kegan Paul, London. [27, 104]

FELDMAN, M. P. (1971). Abnormal sexual behaviour in males. In *Handbook of abnormal psychology*. (ed. H. J. Eysenck). Pitman, London. [185]

—— MACCULLOCH, M. J. (1965). The application of anticipatory avoidance learning to the treatment of homosexuality: I. Theory, technique and preliminary results. *Behav. Res. Ther.* **2**, 165–83. [63, 118, 122, 126, 145]

—— —— (1971). *Homosexual behaviour: therapy and assessment*. Pergamon Press, Oxford. [15, 36, 38, 42, 57, 67, 146, 150, 151, 153, 154, 192]

—— MACCULLOCH, M. C. (1968). The aversion treatment of a heterogeneous group of five cases of sexual deviation. *Acta Psychiat. Scand.* **44**, 113–24. [193]

——, MELLOR, V. and PINSCHOF, J. M. (1966). The application of anticipatory avoidance learning to the treatment of homosexuality III; the sexual orientation method. *Behav. Res. Ther.* **4**, 289–99. [49, 58, 191]

FELDMAN, S. (1966). *Cognitive consistency*. Academic Press, New York. [170]

FESTINGER, L. (1957). *A theory of cognitive dissonance*. Stanford University Press, Stanford. [170]

FIELD, L. H. and WILLIAMS, M. (1970). The hormonal treatment of sex offenders. *Med. Sci. Law* **10**, 27. [213]

FISHBEIN, M. (1966). The relationships between beliefs, attitudes, and behaviour. *In Cognitive consistency*. (ed. S. Feldman). Academic Press, New York. [172]

FISHER, C., GROSS, J., and ZUCH, J. (1965). Cycle of penile erections synchronous with dreaming (REM) sleep. *Archs Gen. Psychiat.* **12**, 29–45. [227, 228]

FISHER, S. H. (1965). A note on male homosexuality and the role of women in Ancient Greece. In *Sexual Inversion* (ed. J. Marmor). Basic Books, New York. [8]

FOOKES, B. H. (1969). Some experiences in the use of aversion therapy in male homosexuality, exhibitionism and fetishism–transvestism. *Br. J. Psychiat.* **115**, 339–41. [146, 147, 157, 160]

FORD, C. S. and BEACH, F. A. (1952). *Patterns of sexual behaviour*. Eyre and Spottiswoode, London. [7]

FRANK, J. D. (1961). *Persuasion and healing*. Johns Hopkins Press, Baltimore. [2, 155, 172, 173]

FRANKS, C. M. (1963). Behaviour therapy, the principles of conditioning and the treatment of the alcoholic. *Quart. J. Stud. Alc.* **24**, 511. [27]

—— (1969). *Behaviour Therapy: appraisal and status.* McGraw-Hill, New York. [31]

FREUD, S. (1920). The psychogenesis of a case of homosexuality in a woman. In *Collected papers, Vol. II* (1953). Hogarth Press, London. [12]

FREUND, K. (1960). Problems in the treatment of homosexuality. In *Behaviour therapy and the neuroses.* (ed. H. J. Eysenck). Pergamon Press, Oxford. [13, 27, 32, 42, 145, 146, 149]

—— (1963). A laboratory method for diagnosing predominance of homo- or hetero-erotic interest in the male. *Behav. Res. Ther.* **1**, 85–93. [54, 194, 232]

—— (1967). Diagnosing homo- or hetero-sexuality and erotic age preference by means of a psychophysiological test. *Behav. Res. Ther.* **5**, 209–28. [194, 232]

——, SEDLACEK, F. and KNOB, K. (1965). A simple transducer for mechanical plethysmography of the male genital. *J. exp. Anal. Behav.* **8**, 169–70. [227]

GAGNON, J. H. and SIMON, W. (1967). *Sexual deviance.* Harper and Row, New York. [5, 6]

GARCIA, J. and KOELLING, R. A. (1966). Relation of cue to consequence in avoidance learning. *Psychon. Sci.* **4**, 123–4. [97]

GELDER, M. G., BANCROFT, J. H. J., GATH, D. H., JOHNSTON, D. W., MATHEWS, A. M., and SHAW, P. M. (1973). Specific and non-specific factors in behaviour therapy. *Br. J. Psychiat.* **123**, 445–62. [167, 177, 179, 180, 220]

——, MARKS, I. M., and WOLFF, H. H. (1967). Desensitization and psychotherapy in the treatment of phobic states: a controlled study. *Br. J. Psychiat.* **113**, 53–73. [177]

GLYNN, J. D. and HARPER, P. (1961). Behaviour therapy in transvestism. *Lancet* i, 619. [27]

GOLD, S. and NEUFELD, I. L. (1965). A learning approach to the treatment of homosexuality. *Behav. Res. Ther.* **3**, 201–4. [46]

GOLDIAMOND, I. (1965). Self-control procedures in personal behaviour problems. *Psychol. Rep.* **17**, 851–68. [168]

GOLDSTEIN, A. P. and SIMONSON, N. R. (1971). Social psychological approaches to psychotherapy research. In *Handbook of psychotherapy and behaviour change.* (eds. A. E. Bergin and S. L. Garfield). Wiley, New York. [170, 172, 175]

——, HELLER, K., and SECHREST, L. B. (1966). *Psychotherapy and the psychology of behaviour change.* Wiley, New York. [170, 178]

GOLLA, F. L. and HODGE, S. R. (1949). Hormone treatment of the sex offender. *Lancet* i, 1006. [2, 213]

GOODMAN, L. S. and GILMAN, A. (1970). *The pharmacological basis of therapeutics* (4th edn). Macmillan, London. [34, 35]

GOY, R. N. (1968). Organizing effects of androgens on the behaviour of rhesus monkeys. In *Endocrinology and behaviour.* Oxford University Press, Oxford, [14]

GRAHAM, L. A., COHEN, S. I., and SHMAVONIAN, B. M. (1964). Physiological discrimination and behavioural relationships in human instrumental conditioning. *Psychosom. Med.* **26**, 336. [117, 118]

GRAHAM, P. J., HARBISON, J. J. M., QUINN, J. T., and MCALLISTER, H. (1971). A new measure of sexual interest. Paper presented at third annual conference in behavioural modification, Wexford, Ireland. (Sept. 1971). [193]

GREEN, R. and MONEY, J. (1969). *Transexualism and sex reassignment.* Johns Hopkins Press, Baltimore. [213]

GREEN, R. T. (1962). The absolute threshold of electric shock. *Br. J. Psychol.* **53**, 107–16. [40]

GREENBLATT, D. H. and TURSKY, B. (1969). Local vascular and impedance changes induced by electric shock. *Am. J. Physiol.* **216**, 712–18. [40]

GRYGIER, T. G. (1970). *The dynamic personality inventory.* Windsor, N.F.E.R. [186]

HALLAM, R. S. (1971). Unpublished dissertation for Ph.D., University of London. [94, 101]

——, RACHMAN, S., and FALKOWSKI, W. (1972). Subjective attitudinal and physiological effects of electrical aversion therapy. *Behav. Res. Ther.* **10**, 1–13. [95, 97]

HAMMERSLEY, D. W. (1957). Conditioned reflex treatment. In *Hospital treatment of alcoholism.* (ed. R. S. Wallerstein). Basic Books, New York. [96]

HAMPSON, J. L. and HAMPSON, J. G. (1961). The ontogenesis of sexual behaviour in man. In *Sex and internal secretions.* (ed. W. C. Young). (3rd edn). Williams and Wilkins, Baltimore. [15]

HARBISON, J. J. M., GRAHAM, P. J., MCALLISTER, H., and QUINN, J. T. (1973). Assessment and treatment of sexual dysfunction. Paper read at annual conference, British Association for Behavioural Psychotherapy. University of Leicester (April 1973). [193, 204]

HARRÉ, R. and SECORD, P. F. (1972). *The explanation of social behaviour.* Blackwell, Oxford. [163, 171]

HARRIS, G. W. and LEVINE, S. (1965). Sexual differentiation of the brain and its experimental control. *J. Physiol.* **181**, 379–90. [14]

HASLAM, D. R. (1966). The effect of threatened shock upon pain threshold. *Psychon. Sci.* **6**, 309–10. [41]

HEIDER, F. (1946). Attitudes and cognitive organization. *J. Psychol.* **21**, 107–12. [170]

HELLER, C. G. and MADDOCKS, W. O. (1947). The clinical uses of testosterone in the male. *Vitamins Hormones* **5**, 393–423. [14]

HENSON, D. E. and RUBIN, H. B. (1971). Voluntary control of eroticism. *J. appl. Behav. Anal.* **4**, 37–44. [140, 194]

HERMAN, S. H., BARLOW, D. H. and AGRAS, W. S. (1971). Exposure to heterosexual stimuli: an effective variable in treating homosexuality? Paper read at American Psychological Association meeting, Washington D.C., Sept. 1971. [50, 87, 140]

—— —— —— (1973). An experimental analysis of classical conditioning as a method of increasing heterosexual arousal in homosexuals. *Behav. Ther.* In the press. [50]

Heston, L. L. and Shields, J. (1968). Homosexuality in twins. *Archs Gen. Psychiat.* **18**, 149–60. [14]

Hinkle, L. E. and Wolff, H. G. (1956). Communist interrogation and indoctrination of 'enemies of the state'. *Archs neurol. Psychiat.* **76**, 115. [29]

Hirschfeld, M. (1958). The homosexual as an intersex. In *Homosexuality.* (eds. C. Berg and A. M. Krich). Allen and Unwin, London. [12, 13]

Hoehn-Saric, R., Frank, J. D., and Gurland, B. J. (1968). Focused attitude change in neurotic patients. *J. nerv. ment. Dis.* **147**, 124–33. [174]

—— ——, Imber, S. D., Nash, E. H., Stone, A. R., and Battle, C. C. (1964). Systematic preparation of patients for psychotherapy. I. Effects on therapy behaviour and outcome. *J. psychiat. Res.* **2**, 267–81. [172]

Hoffman, H. S. and Fleshler, M. (1964). Stimulus aspects of aversive controls: stimulus generalization of conditioned suppression following discrimination training. *J. exp. Anal. Behav.* **7**, 233–9. [120]

Hoffman, M. (1968). *The gay world.* Basic Books, New York. [19]

Homosexual Law Reform Society. (1966). Report, 1963–66. [17]

Hooker, E. (1965). An empirical study of some relations between sexual patterns and gender identity in male homosexuals. In *Sex research: new developments.* (ed. J. Money). Holt, Rinehart, and Winston, New York. [6, 185]

Hovland, C. I. and Janis, I. L. (1959). *Personality and persuasibility.* Yale University Press, New Haven. [171]

—— ——, and Kelley, H. H. (1953). *Communication and persuasion.* Yale University Press, New Haven. [171]

Hunter, R. and MacAlpine, I. (1963). *Three hundred years of psychiatry.* Oxford University Press, London. [10]

Imber, S. D., Pande, S. K., Frank, J. D., Hoehn-Saric, R., Stone, A. R., and Wargo, D. G. (1970). Time-focused role induction. *J. nerv. ment. Dis.* **150**, 27–36. [172]

Jackson, B. (1969). A case of voyeurism treated by counter-conditioning. *Behav. Res. Ther.* **7**, 133–4. [44]

Jacobson, E. (1964). *Anxiety and tension control.* Lippincott, Philadelphia. [87]

James, B. (1962). A case of homosexuality treated by aversion therapy. *Br. med. J.* **i**, 768–70. [27]

James, S., Orwin, A., and Turner, R. K. (1973). Personal Communication. [145, 146, 147, 200, 212]

Janis, I. L. and Mann, L. (1965). Effectiveness of emotional role-playing in modifying smoking habits and attitudes. *J. exp. Res. Personality* **1**, 84–90. [175]

Johnson, A. M. and Robinson, D. B. (1957). The sexual deviant (sexual pyschopath): causes, treatment and prevention. *J. Am. Med. Ass.* **164**, 1559–65. [16]

Johnson, J. and Kitching, G. R. (1968). A mechanical transducer for phallography. *Biomed. Eng.* Sept. 416–18. [227]

Johnston, J. M. (1972). Punishment of human behaviour. *Am. Psychol.* Nov., 1033–54. [107]

Jones, A., Bentley, P. M., and Petry, G. (1966). The reduction of uncertainty concerning future pain. *J. abnorm. Psychol.* **71**, 87–94. [123]

Jovanovic, U. J. (1971). The recording of physiological evidence of genital arousal in human males and females. *Archs Sex. Behav.* 309–20. [195, 227, 229]

Kalcev, B. (1967). Aversion therapy of homosexuals. Letter. *Br. med. J.* **ii**, 436. [19]

Kallmann, F. J. (1952). A comparative twin study on the genetic aspects of male homosexuality. *J. nerv. ment. Dis.* **115**, 283–98. [14]

Kantorovich, N. V. (1930). An attempt at associate reflex therapy in alcoholism. *Psychol. Abstracts* 4282. [26]

Katkin, E. S. and Murray, E. N. (1968). Instrumental conditioning of autonomically mediated behaviour: theoretical and methodological issues. *Psychol. Bull.*, **70**, 52–68. [140]

Karacan, I. (1969). A simple and inexpensive transducer for quantitative measurements of penile erection during sleep. *Behav. Res. Meth. Instrum.* **1**, 251–2. [227, 229]

Kelly, G. A. (1955). *The psychology of personal constructs*, Vols I and II. Norton, New York. [186]

Kiesler, D. H. (1971). Experimental design in psychotherapy research. In *Handbook of psychotherapy and behaviour change.* (eds. A. E. Bergin and S. L. Garfield). Wiley, New York. [178, 182]

Kimble, G. A. (1961). *Conditioning and learning.* Hilgard and Marquis, Methuen, London. [139]

Kinsey, A. C., Pomeroy, W. B., and Martin, C. E. (1948). *Sexual behaviour in the human male.* Saunders, Philadelphia. [153, 198]

Kline, P. (1968). The validity of the dynamic personality inventory. *Br. J. med. Psychol.* **41**, 307–13. [186]

Kohlberg, L. (1967). A cognitive-developmental analysis of children's sex role concepts and attitudes. In *The development of sex differences.* (ed. E. E. Maccoby). Tavistock, London. [185]

Kolodny, R. C., Masters, W. H., Hendryx, J., and Toro, G. (1971). Plasma testosterone and semen analysis in male homosexuals. *New Eng. J. Med.* **285**, 1170–4. [14]

Kolvin, I. (1967). Aversion imagery treatment in adolescents. *Behav. Res. Ther.* **5**, 245–8. [43]

Kostyleff, N. (1927). L'inversion sexuelle expliquée par la reflexologie. *Psychol. Vie* **1**, 8–12. [26]

Kraft, T. (1967). A case of homosexuality treated by systematic desensitization. *Am. J. Psychother.* **21**, 815–21. [30, 47]

Krasner, L. (1971). The operant approach in behaviour therapy. In *Handbook of psychotherapy and behaviour change.* (eds. A. E. Bergin and S. L. Garfield). Wiley, New York. [31, 168]

KROUT, M. H. and TABIN, J. K. (1954). Measuring personality in developmental terms. *Genet. Psychol. Monogr.* **50**, 289–335. [186]

LADER, M. H. (1967). Palmar conductance measures in anxiety and phobic states. *J. Psychosom. Res.* **11**, 271–81. [132]

—— and MATHEWS, A. M. (1968). A physiological model of phobic anxiety and desensitization. *Behav. Res. Ther.* **6**, 411–21. [132]

LANG, T. (1940). Studies in the genetic determination of homosexuality. *J. nerv. ment. Dis.* **92**, 55–64. [13]

LAVIN, N. I., THORPE, J. G., BARKER, J. C., BLAKEMORE, C. B., and CONWAY, C. G. (1961). Behaviour therapy in a case of transvestism. *J. nerv. ment. Dis.* **133**, 346–53. [27]

LAWS, D. R. and RUBIN, H. B. (1969). Instructional control of an autonomic sexual response. *J. appl. Behav. Anal.*, **2**, 93–9. [140, 194]

LAZARUS, R. S. (1966). *Psychological stress and the coping process.* McGraw-Hill. New York. [220]

LEE-EVANS, M. (1971). Penile plethysmographic assessment of sexual orientation. Paper read at third annual conference on behaviour modification. Wexford, Ireland, Sept. 1971. [194, 203, 232]

LEITENBERG, H., AGRAS, S., THOMSON, L. E., and WRIGHT, D. E. (1968). Feedback in behavior modification: an experimental analysis in two phobic cases. *J. appl. Behav. Anal.* **1**, 131–7. [142]

LEMERE, F. and VOEGTLIN, W. L. (1950). An evaluation of the aversion treatment of alcoholism. *Quart. J. Stud. Alc.* **2**, 199–204. [26]

LEWIS, A. (1967). *The state of psychiatry.* Routledge and Kegan Paul. London. [10]

LEWIS, D. J. (1960). Partial reinforcement: a selective review of the literature since 1950. *Psychol. Bull.* **57**, 1–28. [121]

LICHT, H. (1932). *Sexual life in ancient Greece.* Routledge and Kegan Paul, London. [8]

LIFTON, R. J. (1961). *Thought reform: a psychiatric study of brainwashing in China.* Gollancz, London. [29]

LORAINE, J. A., ISMAIL, A. A., ADAMOPOULOS, D. A., and DOVE, G. A. (1970). Endocrine functions in male and female homosexuals. *Br. Med. J.* **4**, 406. [14]

LOVAAS, O. I. (1966). A program for the establishment of speech in psychotic children. In *Early childhood autism.* (ed. J. K. Wing). Pergamon Press, London. [167]

—— and SIMMONS, J. Q. (1969). Manipulation of self destruction in three retarded children. *J. Appl. Behav. Anal.* **2**, 143–57. [107]

LOVIBOND, S. H. (1969). The aversiveness of uncertainty: an analysis in terms of activation and information theory. *Aust. J. Psychol.* **20**, 85–96 [123]

MCCONAGHY, N. (1967). Penile volume change to moving pictures of male and female nudes in heterosexual and homosexual males. *Behav. Res. Ther.* **5**, 43–8. [194, 232]

—— (1969). Subjective and penile plethysmograph responses following aversion–relief and apomorphine aversion therapy for homosexual impulses. *Br. J. Psychiat.* **115**, 723–30. [33, 52, 54, 126, 145, 146, 195]

—— (1970*a*). Subjective and penile plethysmograph responses to aversion therapy for homosexuality: a follow-up study. *Br. J. Psychiat.* **117**, 555–60. [55]

—— (1970*b*). Penile response conditioning and its relationship to aversion therapy in homosexuals. *Behav. Ther.* **1**, 213–21. [140]

MacCulloch, M. J. and Feldman, M. P. (1967*a*). Aversion therapy in the management of 43 homosexuals. *Br. med. J.* **2**, 594–7. [13, 32, 57, 65, 119, 145, 147, 149, 153, 156, 198]

—— —— (1967*b*). Personalities and the treatment of homosexuality. *Acta psychiat. scand.* **43**, 300–17. [154]

—— ——, Pinshoff, J. M. (1966). The application of anticipatory avoidance learning to the treatment of homosexuality. II. Avoidance response latencies and pulse rate changes. *Behav. Res Ther.* **3**, 21–43. [98, 119]

McGuire, R. J. and Vallance, M. (1964). Aversion therapy by electric shock: a simple technique. *Br. med. J.* **2**, 594–7. [40, 110]

——, Carlisle, J. M., and Young, B. G. (1965). Sexual deviations as conditioned behaviour: a hypothesis. *Behav. Res. Ther.* **3**, 185–90. [23, 43, 160]

McGuire, W. J. (1964). Inducing resistance to persuasion: some contemporary approaches. In *Advances in experimental social psychology*, Vol. 1, pp. 191–229. Academic Press, New York. [173]

—— (1966). The current status of cognitive consistency theories. In *Cognitive consistency*. (ed. S. Feldman). Academic Press, New York. [170]

Magee, B. (1968). *One in twenty*. Corgi Books, London. [19]

Magnan, V. (1913). Inversion sexuelle et pathologie mentale. *Bull. de l'Acad. Med.* **70**, 226–9. [25]

Mandell, K. H. (1970). Preliminary report on a new aversion therapy for male homoxexuals. *Behav. Res. Ther.* **8**, 93–5. [33, 36]

Mantegazza, P. (1935). *The sexual relations of mankind* (Trans. S. Putnam). Eugenics Publishing Co., New York. [10]

Marks, I. M., Boulougouris, J., and Marset, P. (1971). Flooding versus desensitization in the treatment of phobic patients: a cross over study. *Br. J. Psychiat.* **119**, 353–75. [177]

Marks, I. M. and Gelder, M. G. (1965). A controlled retrospective study of behaviour therapy in phobic patients. *Br. J. Psychiat.* **111**, 561–73. [133]

—— —— (1967). Transvestism and fetishism: clinical and psychological changes during faradic aversion. *Br. J. Psychiat.* **113**, 711–30. [39, 41, 97, 114, 121, 169, 191]

—— —— (1968). Controlled trials in behaviour therapy. In *The role of learning in psychotherapy* (ed. R. Porter). Ciba Foundation symposium. Churchill, London. [129]

—— —— (1969). Aversion treatment in transvestism and transexualism. In *Transexualism and sex reassignment* (ed. R. Green and J. Money). Johns Hopkins Press, Baltimore. [110]

Marks, I. M., Gelder, M. G., and Bancroft, J. H. J. (1970). Sexual deviants two years after electric aversion therapy. *Br. J. Psychiat.* **117**, 173–85. [32, 39, 40, 41, 42, 105, 110, 112, 114, 120, 129, 155, 157, 159, 160, 161, 174, 191, 199, 204, 212]

——, ——, and EDWARDS, G. (1968). Hypnosis and desensitization for phobias: a controlled prospective trial. *Br. J. Psychiat.* **114**, 1263–74. [177]

——, RACHMAN, S., and GELDER, M. G. (1965). Methods for assessment of aversion treatment in fetishism with masochism. *Behav. Res. Ther.* **3**, 253–8. [161]

——, and SARTORIUS, N. H. (1968). A contribution to the measurement of sexual attitude. *J. nerv. ment. Dis.* **145**, 441–51. [68, 88, 189]

——, GELDER, M. G., and EDWARDS, G. (1968). Hypnosis and desensitization for phobias: a controlled prospective study. *Br. J. Psychiat.* **114**, 1263–74. [177]

MASTERS, W. H. and JOHNSON, V. E. (1966). *Human sexual response.* Churchill, London. [230]

—— —— (1970). *Human sexual inadequacy.* Churchill, London. [24, 173, 212, 214, 223]

MAYERSON, P. and LIEF, H. I. (1965). Psychotherapy of homosexuals: follow-up study of nineteen cases. In *Sexual inversion* (ed. J. Marmor). Basic Books, New York. [13, 148, 152, 153, 154, 155]

MAX, L. (1935). Breaking a homosexual fixation by the conditioned reflex technique. *Psychol. Bull.* **32**, 734. [26]

MAXWELL, A. E. (1958). *Experimental design in psychology and the medical sciences.* Methuen, London. [179]

MEERLOO, J. A. M. (1961). *The rape of the mind; the psychology of thought control, menticide and brainwashing.* Grosset. [29]

MEHRABIAN, A. (1972). *Nonverbal Communication.* Atane Atherton, Chicago. [188]

MELLOR, V. P. (1972). *The treatment of sexual offenders using an automated conditioning apparatus.* Paper read at the Northwest Behaviour Modification Study Group, Sept 1972. [145, 146, 149, 156]

MILLER, N. E. (1969). Learning of visceral and glandular responses. *Science* **163**, 434–45. [49, 139]

MISCHEL, W. (1967). A social–learning view of sex differences in behaviour. In *The development of sex differences* (ed. E. E. Maccoby). Tavistock, London. [185]

MOLL, A. (1911). Die Behandlung sexueller Perversioner mït Vesonderer Berüchsichtigung der Assoziationstherapie. *Z. Psychother.* **3**, [25]

MORENO, J. L. (1946). *Psychodrama.* Beacon, New York. [175]

MORGENSTERN, F. S., PEARCE, J. P., and LINFORD REES, W. (1965). Predicting the outcome of behaviour therapy by psychological tests. *Behav. Res. Ther.* **3**, 253–8. [155, 157]

MUMFORD, S. J., LODGE PATCH, I. C., and ANDREWS, N. (1973). Personal communication. [145, 146, 147, 152, 212]

NORMAN, C. (1892). Sexual perversion. In Hack Tuke's *Dictionary of psychological medicine.* Churchill, London. [11, 23]

Osgood, C. E., Suci, G. J., and Tannenbaum, P. H. (1957). *The measurement of meaning.* University of Illinois Press, Urbana. [189, 191]

—— and Tannenbaum, P. H. (1955). The principle of congruity in the prediction of attitude change. *Psychol. Rev.* **62**, 42–55. [170]

Oswald, I. (1962). Induction of illusory and hallucinatory voices with consideration of behaviour therapy. *J. ment. Sci.* **108**, 196–212. [27, 28]

Pare, C. M. B. (1956). Homosexuality and chromosomal sex. *J. psychosom. Res.* **1**, 247–51. [13]

—— (1965). Etiology of homosexuality: genetic and chromosomal aspects. In *Sexual inversion.* (ed. J. Marmor). Basic Books, New York. [14]

Paul G. L. (1969). Behaviour modification research: design and tactics. In *Behavior Therapy: Appraisal and Status* (Ed. C. M. Franks). McGraw-Hill, New York. [83, 129, 178, 179]

Pavlov, I. P. (1927). *Conditioned reflexes.* (trans. G. V. Anrep). Oxford University Press, London. [127]

Pavlov, I. P. (1928). *Lectures on conditioned reflexes,* Vol. 1. (Trans. W. H. Gantt). International Publishers, New York. [28]

Pearce, J. F. (1963). Aspects of transvestism. Unpublished M.D. thesis, University of London. [34, 41, 96, 157]

Perloff, W. H. (1965). Hormones and homosexuality. In *Sexual inversion.* (ed. J. Marmor). Basic Books, New York. [14]

Peters, R. S. (1960). *The concept of motivation* (2nd edn). Routledge and Kegan Paul, London. [171]

Pfeiffer, C. A. (1936). Sexual differences of the hypophyses and their determination by the gonads. *Am. J. Anat.* **58**, 195–222. [14]

Phillips, J. P. N. (1968). A note on the scoring of the sexual orientation method. *Behav. Res. Ther.* **6**, 121–3. [192]

Podell, L. and Perkins, J. C. (1957). A Guttman scale for sexual experience —a methodological note. *J. abnorm. soc. Psychol.* **54**, 420–2. [197]

Powell, J. and Azrin, N. (1968). The effects of shock as a punisher for cigarette smoking. *J. appl. Behav. Anal.* **1**, 63–71. [106]

Pringle, P. (1971). *Sunday Times,* 9th May, 1971, p. 8. [19, 29]

Quinn, J. T., Harbison, J. J. M., and McAllister, H. (1970). An attempt to shape human penile responses. *Behav. Res. Ther.* **8**, 213–16. [31, 49, 139, 140, 168]

——, McAllister, H., Graham, P. J., and Harbison, J. J. M. (1973). An approach to the treatment of homosexuality in *Behaviour therapy—verhaltenstherapie; praktische und theoretische aspekte* (eds. J. C. Brengelmann and W. Tunner). Urban and Schwarzenberg, München. [49, 127]

Rachman, S. (1961). Aversion therapy: chemical or electrical? *Behav. Res. Ther.* **2**, 289–99. [40, 54, 140]

—— (1966). Sexual fetishism: an experimental analogue. *Psychol. Rec.* **16**, 293–6. [140]

—— (1967). Systematic desensitization. *Psychol. Bull.* **67**, 93–100. [129, 166]

—— and Hodgson, R. (1968). Experimentally induced 'sexual fetishism': replication and development. *Psychol. Rec.* **18**, 25–7. [140]

—— and Teasdale, J. (1969). *Aversion therapy and behaviour disorders: an analysis*. Routledge and Kegan Paul, London. [33, 91, 93]

Rado, S. (1940). A critical examination of the concept of bisexuality. *Psychosom. Med.* **2**, 459–67. [13, 15, 47, 220]

Ramsey, G. V. (1943). The sexual development of boys. *Am. J. Psychol.* **56**, 217. [143]

Raymond, M. (1956). Case of fetishism treated by aversion therapy. *Br. med. J.* **2**, 854–6. [27]

Reifler, C. B., Howard, J., Lipton, M. A., Liptzin, M. B., and Widmann, D. E. (1971). Pornography: an experimental study of effects. *Am. J. Psychiat.* **128**, 575–82. [196]

Rescorla, R. A. and Solomon, R. L. (1967). Two process learning theory: relationships between pavlovian conditioning and instrumental learning. *Psychol. Rev.*, **74**, 151–82. [96, 117]

Reynolds, G. S. (1961). Behavioral contrast. *J. exp. anal. Behav.* **4**, 57–71. [127]

Robbins, D. (1971). Partial reinforcement: a selective review of the alleyway literature since 1960. *Psychol. Bull.*, **76**, 415–31. [121]

Rooth, G. and Marks, I. M. (1974). Aversion, self-regulation and relaxation in the treatment of exhibitionism. *Archs sex. Behav.* In the press. [87, 159, 160]

Rosen, I. (1968). The basis of psychotherapeutic treatment of sexual deviation. *Proc. R. Soc. Med.* **61**, 793–6. [13, 18, 210]

Rosnow, R. L. and Robinson, W. J. (1967). *Experiments in persuasion.* Academic Press, New York. [171]

Rubinstein, L. H. (1958). Psychotherapeutic aspects of male homosexuality. *Br. J. med. Psychol.* **31**, 14–18. [47]

Sargant, W. (1957). *Battle for the mind.* Heinemann, London. [28]

Schmidt, E., Castell D., and Brown, P. (1965). A retrospective study of 42 cases of behaviour therapy. *Behav. Res. Ther.* **3**, 9–19. [105, 146, 147, 153, 154, 155]

Schneider, K. (1958). *Psychopathic personalities.* Cassell, London. [154]

Schofield, M. (1965). *Sociological aspects of homosexuality.* Longmans, London. [19]

Schrenck-Notzing, A. von (1895). *The use of hypnosis in psychopathia sexualis with special reference to contrary sexual instinct* (translated by C. G. Chaddock) (1956). The Institute of Research in Hypnosis Publication Society and the Julian Press, New York. [7, 9, 11, 23, 43]

Schultz, J. H. and Luthe, W. (1959). *Autogenic training.* Grune and Stratton, New York. [87]

Scott, P. D. (1958). Psychiatric aspects of the Wolfenden Report. *Br. J. Delinq.* **9**, 20–32. [17]

—— (1964). Definition, classification, prognosis, and treatment. In *The Pathology and treatment of sexual deviation.* (ed. I. Rosen). Oxford University Press, London. [213]

Seligman, M. E. P. and Hager, J. L. (1972). *Biological boundaries of learning*, pp. 1–6. Appleton–Century–Crofts, New York. [97]

Shapiro, M. B. (1961). *Manual of the personal questionnaire.* Institute of Psychiatry, London. [191]

Sherrington, C. (1947). *The integrative action of the nervous system.* University of Cambridge Press, Cambridge. [128, 132]

Siegel, S. (1956). *Non-parametric statistics for the behavioural sciences.* McGraw-Hill, New York. [54]

Slater, E. and Slater, P. (1947). A study in the assessment of homosexual traits. *Br. J. med. Psychol.* **21**, 61–74. [185]

Slater, P. (1944). *Selective vocabulary test handbook.* Harrap, London. [185]

—— (1964). *The principal components of a repertory grid.* Andrews, London. [186]

—— (1965). The use of the repertory grid technique in the individual case. *Br. J. Psychiat.* **111**, 965–75. [186]

Solomon, R. L. (1964). Punishment. *Am. Psychol.* **19**, 239–53. [91]

—— and Brush, E. S. (1956). Experimentally derived conceptions of anxiety and aversion. In *Nebraska symposium on motivation.* (ed. M. R. Jones) University of Nebraska Press. [117]

—— and Wynne, L. C. (1953). Traumatic avoidance learning. The principles of anxiety conservation and partial irreversibility. *Psychol. Rev.* **61**, 353–85. [117, 119]

Solyom, L. and Miller, S. (1965). A differential conditioning procedure as the initial phase of behaviour therapy of homosexuality. *Behav. Res. Ther.* **3**, 147. [32, 105, 145, 146, 155]

Spenger, J. and Institoris, H. (1928). *Malleus malleficarum.* Rooker. [9]

Stampfl, T. G. and Levis, D. H. (1967). Essentials of implosive therapy: a learning theory based psychodynamic behavioural therapy. *J. abnorm. Psychol.* **72**, 496–503. [220]

Stoller, R. J. (1969). *Sex and gender.* Hogarth, London. [158, 184]

Stringer, P. (1970). A note on the factorial structure of the dynamic personality inventory. *Br. J. med. Psychol.* **43**, 95–103. [186]

Symmers, W. St. C. (1968). Carcinoma of breast in trans-sexual individuals after surgical and hormonal interference with the primary and secondary sex characteristics. *Br. med. J.* **2**, 83–5. [213]

Szasz, T. S. (1965). Legal and moral aspects of homosexuality. In *Sexual inversion* (ed. J. Marmor). Basic Books, New York. [7]

Taylor, G. R. (1954). *Sex in history.* Ballantine, New York. [7, 8]

Tennent, G., Bancroft, J. H. J., and Cass, J. (1974). The control of deviant sexual behaviour by drugs: a double-blind controlled study of benperidol, chlorpromazine and placebo. *Archs sex. Behav.* **3**, 261–271. [2, 195, 196, 201]

Terman, L. M. and Miles, C. C. (1936). *Sex and personality.* McGraw-Hill, New York. [185]

Thorne, F. C. (1966*a*). The sex inventory. *J. clin. psychol.* **22**, 367–74. [189]

—— (1966*b*). A factorial study of sexuality in adult males. *J. clin. Psychol.* **22**, 378–86. [189]

—— (1966*c*). Scales for rating sexual experience. *J. clin. Psychol.* **22**, 404–7. [195]

THORPE, J. G., SCHMIDT, E., BROWN, P., and CASTELL, D. (1964). Aversion–relief therapy: a new method for general application. *Behav. Res. Ther.* **2**, 71–82. [37, 54, 125]

—— ——, and CASTELL, D. (1964). A comparison of positive and negative (aversive) conditioning in the treatment of homosexuality. *Behav. Res. Ther.* **1**, 357–62. [43]

TURNER, L. H. and SOLOMON, R. L. (1962). Human traumatic avoidance learning. *Psychol. Monogr.* **76**, 40 (no. 559). [117]

TURNER, R. K., JAMES, S. R. N., and ORWIN, A. (1973). A note on the internal consistency of the sexual orientation method. *Behav. Res. Ther.* In the press. [193]

TURSKY, B. and WATSON, P. D. (1964). Controlled physical and subjective intensities of electric shock. *Psychophysiology* **1**, 151–62. [40]

—— ——, and O'CONNELL, D. N. (1965). A concentric shock electrode for pain stimulation. *Psychophysiology* **1**, 296–8. [40]

ULLMAN, L. P. and KRASNER, L. (1965). *Case studies in behaviour modification.* Holt, Rinehart, and Winston, New York. [18, 21]

VALINS, S. (1966). Cognitive effects of false heart rate feedback. *J. Personality soc. Psychol.* **4**, 400–8. [174

—— 1967. Emotionality and information concerning internal reactions. *J. Personality soc. Psychol.* **6**, 458–63. [174]

VOEGTLIN, W. L. and LEMERE, F. (1942). Treatment of alcohol addiction. *Quart. J. Stud. Alc.* **2**, 717–803. [27]

—— ——, BROZ., W. R. (1940). Conditioned reflex therapy of alcohol addiction. III. An evaluation of present results in the light of previous experiences with this method. *Quart. J. Stud. Alc.* **1**, 501–6. [35]

WALTERS, R. H. and DEMKOW, L. (1963). Timing of punishment as a determinant of response inhibition. *Child Develop.* **34**, 207–14. [106]

WATSON, J. P. (1970). A repertory grid method of studying groups. *Br. J. Psychiat.* **117**, 309–18. [186]

WEST, D. J. (1960). *Homosexuality* (2nd edn). Pelican Books, Harmondsworth. [14]

WHALEN, R. E. (1966). Sexual motivation. *Psychol. Rev.* **73**, 151–63. [184]

WHITLOCK, F. A. (1964). Letter. *Br. med. J.* **1**, 437. [19]

WIEDEMAN, G. H. (1962). Survey of psychoanalytic literature on overt male homosexuality. *J. Am. psychoanal. Ass.* **10**, 386–409. [12]

WILSON, G. T. and DAVISON, G. C. (1968). Aversion techniques in behaviour therapy: some theoretical and metatheoretical issues. *J. consult. clin. Psychol.* **33**, 327–9. [97]

WOLFENDEN, (1957). *Report of the committee on homosexual offences and prostitution.* Cmnd. 247. London. [17]

WOLPE, J. (1958). *Psychotherapy by reciprocal inhibition.* Stanford University Press. [43, 47, 129, 132]

WOODWARD, M. (1958). The diagnosis and treatment of homosexual offenders. *Br. J. Delinq.* **9**, 44–59. [148, 149, 152, 153, 154]

Woodward, R., McAllister, H., Harbison, J. J. M., Quinn, J. T., and Graham, P. J. (1973). A comparison of two scoring systems for the sexual orientation method. *Br. J. soc. clin. Psychol.* **12**, 411–14. [193]

Wootton, B. (1966). *Social science and social pathology.* Allen and Unwin, London. [17]

Yates, A. J. (1970). *Behaviour therapy.* Wiley, New York. [3, 18, 21, 27, 52, 121, 167, 168, 169]

Zuckerman, M. (1971). Physiological measures of sexual arousal in the human. *Psychol. Bull.* **75**, 297–329. [194]

Subject Index